What People Ar(
Gay Men and The New Way Forward

"Thoughtful and clearly written, Raymond Rigoglioso's wondrous book holds wisdom for gay men of each generation. Historical in its sweeping vision yet practical on a daily level, a copy of *The New Way Forward* should be given to every gay man on planet earth. Because in healing ourselves with the profound insights offered here, we have the capacity to heal the world itself."

—Mark Thompson, author of the *Gay Spirit, Gay Soul,*
Gay Body trilogy

"Gay Men and The New Way Forward is a miracle of a book. Raymond Rigoglioso goes to the social, psychological, ethical, and mythical roots of what it means to be a gay man in the world today. Urging a journey from shame into a world of self-love and acknowledgment of the social and moral gifts that gay men can offer the world, this book is visionary in the best sense of the word. It is grounded in material reality, and yet understands the past and can see a potential future that is loving, healthy, and radiant not only for gay men, but the entire world."

—Michael Bronski, author of *A Queer History of the United*
States and *The Pleasure Principle: Sex, Backlash and the*
Struggle for Gay Freedom and Professor of the Practice in
Activism and Media in the Studies of Women, Gender and
Sexuality at Harvard University

"At the outset of the modern LGBT movement, Harry Hay posed three existential questions: 'Who are we? Where did we come from? What are we for?' In the great awakening of LGBT people that has swept the world in the decades that followed, answering these questions has been the road less taken. Now comes Raymond Rigoglioso's *Gay Men and The New Way Forward*, taking up the quest, opening new byways, and revealing the vistas that await us when we embrace our queer difference and seek its meaning...and in doing so, make our gift to the world."

—Will Roscoe, editor of *Radically Gay: Gay Liberation in the Words of Its Founder,* and author of *Changing Ones: Third and Fourth Genders in Native North America* and *Jesus and the Shamanic Tradition of Same-Sex Love*

"In each generation, gay men have asked, 'What is our meaning?' In these pages, Raymond Rigoglioso offers his answers, his hopes of lighting the winding road to gay self-creation. He recasts on the waters gay tribal truths for a new generation of readers."

—David Nimmons, author of *The Soul Beneath the Skin: The Unseen Hearts and Habits of Gay Men*

"Raymond Rigoglioso has issued a powerful call to gay men everywhere to see our gayness as a gift and to become more skillful at using this gift for ourselves, our communities, and humanity. He has effectively synthesized many ideas regarding gay spirituality and perennial wisdom. His work is clear, provocative, and inspiring. His bold invitation and challenge to take our gay gifts seriously and to transform ourselves to be gifts for the world will have a powerful impact on this generation of queer seekers. Bravo, Ray!"

—John Stasio, founder of Easton Mountain

"*Gay Men and The New Way Forward* is an urgently important book for our time, and I recommend it highly. It illumines the painful and beautiful secrets gay men wrestle with in the privacy of our hearts, and then gives us—and the world at large—a new way to understand our unique mission as a people. This lucid, wise, and inspiring work is a handbook for a new world."

—Ken Page, author of *Deeper Dating*

Gay Men
and
The
New
Way
Forward

Raymond L. Rigoglioso

Foreword by Toby Johnson

Mond Press
White Plains NY

www.gaymenofwisdom.com
Published by Mond Press, March 2, 2015

Editors: Toby Johnson and Will Fellows
Cover Design and Interior Illustrations: Allen Siewert
Interior Design: Toby Johnson

ISBN-13: 978-0-9862633-0-9
ISBN-10: 0-9862633-0-3

Library of Congress Control Number: 2014920590

To Keith, for being my rock and my cheerleader.
Your love and support have helped me fulfill my dreams.
To all the boys and men who have been born into our tribe,
to all those who have yet to join us,
and to the ancestors who have gone before us.

Table of Contents

Acknowledgements

When I began writing this book, I envisioned it would be a solo endeavor: me sitting at the computer for hours on end churning out a manuscript that I could proudly call my own. While much of that vision stood the test of time, this project became, much to my pleasant surprise, a truly collaborative endeavor. *Gay Men and The New Way Forward* simply would not exist if it weren't for the support of many caring people who selflessly supported me.

My partner, Keith D. Pettey, gets the top prize. He has stood by me at every step along the way—from the inception of the Gay Men of Wisdom project, to my declaration that I would need to devote much of a year to writing a book, through the editorial and production processes. He encouraged me to take the long solo writing retreats he knew I needed, and he listened to the heartaches of my search for a publisher. Without his moral, practical, intellectual, and financial support, these ideas would not have made it to print. He is the silent partner in this project (we joke that he is "Mrs. Gay Men of Wisdom") and deserves due acknowledgement. To Keith: you have my enduring love and gratitude.

Will Fellows inspired me three times: with his book *A Passion to Preserve: Gay Men as Keepers of Culture*, which launched me on the quest that became Gay Men of Wisdom, and with his completely unexpected and incredibly generous offer of a grant. He and his partner, Bronze Quinton, through their business, Bronze Optical in Milwaukee, Wisconsin, made a financial gift that helped me leave my consulting work and focus on writing this book. Will encouraged me to launch a fundraising campaign for the book, to which more than 40 people contributed. His offer to serve as co-editor sealed my trifecta of gratitude. I cannot possibly thank him enough or repay him.

Though Toby Johnson and I had known each other less than a year and had only met via videoconference as of this book's publication, Toby offered to co-edit the book and share his years of wisdom and experience in gay spirituality with me. His careful eye, encyclopedic knowledge of the field, and sheer generosity of spirit have enriched this project and left me indebted. He contributed to my fundraising campaign, and he produced this book for print and electronic formats, donating significant amounts of time and relieving me of the stress of having to learn mystifying technical processes. Toby has served as a true elder. With Toby and Will, I found my dream editorial team.

Special thanks go to the people who supported my fundraising campaign at the highest levels—Craig Bodoh, Richard Gange, Bernie Kettle, and Joe Stalzer—and to the men and women who contributed at every level. To the dozens of people who have shared their words of support—by email, postal mail, phone, and in person—I send a heartfelt "thank you." Their words always seemed to arrive just when I needed them most.

Many gay men have nurtured me throughout this project. Harry Faddis, program director at Easton Mountain, helped me launch Gay Men of Wisdom by inviting me to present my work there. John Stasio, Easton's founder, helped me keep the faith in the project when I almost lost it. The men who lead the Gay Coaches Alliance—Harry Faddis, Michael Cohen, Dave Allen, and Allen Siewert—created a container that helped this project grow. Allen's beautiful designs have graced the website and my printed materials, including this book.

Michael Bronski believed in this book from the moment he read my proposal. Over months, he advocated for me and patiently served as my guide to the publishing industry. Terry Hildebrandt gave me wise counsel and moral support early on in the writing process, for which I am most grateful. Friends Robert Malmgren and Julie R. graciously offered their homes on Cape Cod to me, which gave me uninterrupted stretches of time to write in truly serene settings. My cousin Charles gave me invaluable guidance that helped me embrace and navigate the new world of self-publishing.

The men who have attended Gay Men of Wisdom programs unwittingly and graciously served as collaborators in this book. Their wisdom, enthusiasm, and love have made this project a joy and an honor to lead. Their willingness to experiment and consider my many probing questions helped validate the ideas and framework presented here.

And finally, to the many wise men whose insights have moved me, and from whom I have learned and borrowed, I extend my deepest gratitude and honor.

Foreword

It is an heroic thing to bring truth where there is misunderstanding, light where there is darkness, hope where there is sadness and despair; to end ignorance and fear, to transform straw into gold and shame into pride; to show the way forward.

In Joseph Campbell's famous formulation, the cycle of the Hero's Journey begins when the hero—he or she—is confronted with a problem or task. This hero in myth, religion, and fairytale, as well as in novel and movie and TV plot, always symbolizes the self in each human being. Every person's life manifests the pattern of the Hero's Journey.

Because heroes are different in some way from everybody else, with their own traits and talents, desires and predilections, they are called out of their everyday existence to venture forth through the unknown. There, beyond mere ego and social persona, they solve their problem, perform the task and achieve a decisive victory. The heroes then come back from this mysterious adventure with the power to bestow boons on their fellow human beings and to transform the everyday existence they had left behind.

This book is the boon of such a Hero's Journey, a book written for gay men about the qualities and traits of gay men based on the testimony of gay men. It offers guidance —from boon companions and fellow travelers—on how to pursue the path of the modern gay man to our own kind of herohood. It shows the way for us to transform the world. And this begins with changing how we understand ourselves, for false stereotypes have clouded the truth and called us such negative things. The first task in any gay hero's journey is vanquishing the stereotypes.

At least since the Middle Ages in the West, homosexuality and love between men has been shrouded in ignorance, opprobrium, and silence, blamed for the plague, called the worst of sins, been burdened with the sexual shadow of the human race—"the love that dare not speak its name."

Raymond Rigoglioso dares to speak that name as "men of wisdom"—that is, saints and exemplars, societal participants and contributors, attractive people, appealing characters, sweet fellows, good guys beloved by most they meet, heroes. We are not at all the shadowy characters the negative stereotypes portray.

There are some among us who fall victim to these negative stereotypes and act them out. There are some who learn to loathe themselves so badly out of these negative messages that their lives are ruined and their contributions lost. It is precisely for these reasons that we need to change the way gay people's lives, lifestyles, and personal behavior are perceived both by the so-called general public and, perhaps especially, by us gay people ourselves.

On the road of trials, the archetypal heroes are faced with tests and challenges and along the way meet various characters who help or hinder them as they ascend to the heights or plunge to the depths of their personal problem-task—and of their own souls.

One of the characters the hero might meet along the road of trials is called the "wise old man"; he gives advice and shows the way. Another such character is the guide and traveling companion. I was quite fortunate in my life as a young gay man, living in San Francisco in the 1970s, to have been part of the crew that organized Joseph Campbell's appearances in the Bay Area, so that Joseph Campbell himself became, for me, my wise old man. And for a guide and companion, I had Harvard-trained researcher and gay scholar Toby Marotta—my guardian angel, I used to call him in whimsy.

I met Toby Marotta in the late 1970s, when he was doing a study of social services in the Tenderloin District of San Francisco for an agency called Hospitality House. I was a psychiatric counselor in a community mental health clinic in that downtown district. Though mandated to serve the local neighborhood, the clinic had a special program to see gay men and lesbians from throughout the city. This program had evolved indirectly from a volunteer gay peer-counseling hotline that I'd helped establish several years before as my first gay activism. Toby came into the Tenderloin Clinic for his research visit on a day I happened to be doing intake at the front desk.

Because Toby was a handsome gay hippie, like I wanted to think of myself, and because we shared this odd, but cute and boyish, nickname, Toby and I hit it off from the start. He was then living in the East Bay with his long-term lover who'd been a popular professor at Harvard; he was working for Hospitality House and finishing up his dissertation at Harvard's Kennedy School on "The Politics of Homosexuality." As our friendship developed, I proofread Toby's dissertation and then joined up with him as an editor and literary assistant in rewriting the academic text into a readable book for publication.

Toby had interviewed most of the principals in what he identified as the "three waves of gay community organizing" in New York City up to the late 1970s. *The Politics of Homosexuality* was a survey of political and cultural themes in the thinking and activism of the Homophile Movement, Gay Liberation, and Lesbian-Feminism. From working on this project, I learned the rich and complex history of the homosexual rights struggle and modern gay/lesbian culture.

One of Marotta's findings—and in a way the main message of the book—was that gay liberation represented a major flower of the 1960s/1970s counterculture and its values of peace and love, non-conformity, authenticity, self-actualization. Toby argued that we gay people demonstrated the success of the counterculture's "New Age" faith that the way to change the world—and that's what the hippies and youth culture were all about—was "Revolution through Consciousness Change." Homosexuals changed how they thought about themselves and the reality of what it meant to be homosexual changed. Repealing laws and electing politicians, organizing demonstrations and mounting protests were all part of it, but the important dynamic was that we changed our self-image.

One Saturday afternoon, Toby and I were standing on the corner of Castro and 18th in the heart of the thriving gay ghetto. We were waiting for a bus. It was a warm day for San Francisco and many of the men had taken this as an excuse to discard clothing. Guys wearing cut-off jeans, some with skimpy T-shirts or tanktops, some bare-chested, were walking by or leaning suggestively against lampposts or buildings. The whole scene was sexually charged.

Over lunch, we'd been talking about our working together as cultural activists, producing books that would educate and inform the world about the reality of gay life. Toby Marotta was remarkably positive and upbeat, a very happy and bright-eyed guy who might have been called a Pollyanna by some old grump, but who could explain with statistics and footnotes how gay people's lives had been improved by community organizing and transforming our self-identity.

Working in mental health, I listened to clients all day who reported being lonely, depressed, fearful, neurotic, guilty, self-loathing, etc., etc. Many of them were gay men who'd come to Gay Mecca and still found themselves unfulfilled and unhappy. As I looked at the stream of men passing by, I thought about my clients. Maybe I projected my own fears and insecurities in such a sexually charged environment. I saw the men avoiding eye contact as they passed one another. I saw them glancing furtively, looking away quickly when someone appeared to look back. They seemed almost afraid of being caught in the act of cruising. I recalled reports I had heard from clients of how they'd felt rejected and put down as they cruised Castro Street. I recalled their stories of the futile hunt for "Mr. Right," the fantasy lover. I recalled their acknowledgment of how such fantasies, based on particular kinds of sexual attractiveness or physical appearance, seemed to keep them imprisoned in only the most superficial assessments of people.

Continuing the lunch conversation, I remarked to Toby that it would be great if we could do something to alleviate the pain of the poor suffering homosexuals there walking by us on Castro Street.

Toby looked at me quizzically: "What suffering homosexuals?"

I shared with Toby my perceptions of the surging crowd. He said he didn't perceive things that way at all. What he saw were liberated gay men, enjoying the sunny day, reveling in their sexuality, delighting in the beauty of their own and others' bodies, showing off to one another, sharing their delight, and exulting in their liberation.

"But what about all the sexual rejection and internalized self-hate?" I objected.

"That's the whole point," Toby replied. "These men are free from fear and self-loathing. They're not suffering queens and oppressed faggots. They're being natural and open in the styles the subculture has developed. They're behaving just like everybody else walking on a public street, acknowledging friends and acquaintances, noticing an attractive face now and then, but being pretty oblivious to the passing stream. They aren't feeling sexual rejection because they're not hunting sex. They're on their way to the supermarket or the drugstore.

"Of course, most of them are aware of the sexual energy in the air; they enjoy it; that's partly why they're out here today. Some of them are cruising for sex, especially the ones in the bars," he allowed. "But even then they're doing that because they enjoy the game; it's a sport, a way to spend a lazy Saturday afternoon. It's not all that serious."

Suddenly I felt in myself an odd change of consciousness. Just as switching the lights on a stage from a dim and cold blue to a bright and sunny amber can abruptly change the mood in a theater play, so in my mind a filter switched. I saw what Toby was seeing and everything was different. Instead of a repressed demimonde, full of desperate, suffering, compulsively sexual homosexuals, I felt surrounded by gay community, full of natural, happy, liberated gay men. I was astonished by how differently I experienced the world around me and how differently I experienced myself standing on that street corner.

"Why do you think they're desperate?" Toby asked, breaking into my astonishment. I started to explain, but stopped myself, not wanting to spoil my vision. "Well, I don't know; your explanation of it all is much more appealing than mine."

That minor experience on the street corner that day changed me. It is one of the things for which I remain most grateful to Toby Marotta. In a moment, I understood "Revolution through Consciousness Change." The point was made. Both visions of what was going on were right. There were people who were unhappy and psychologically disturbed; there were also happy liberated men enjoying their day and feeling charged and powerful. I could determine how I saw it, and that would change my experience and, indeed, it changed my own life. Over the course of working with my cock-eyed optimist friend, learning the rich history of the gay movement and understanding the human and political dynamics that drove gay liberation, I transformed how I understood homosexuality—my own and that of those with whom I worked to achieve a positive vision.

It was from working with Marotta that I got my own start in publishing and the gay literary business. Creating and promoting books about positive gay culture, being a writer, being an editor, being a gay bookstore operator—these were ways to change how people experienced their lives, ways to change the lights on their stage from blue to amber. This was a kind of "cultural radical" activism, to use one of Toby's categories for the various themes in gay politics, the process of offering social, psychological, and intellectual services to other gay people to change gay culture for the better, rather than fighting for changes in laws that straight people wrote and enforced in our regard. The faith, of course, was that by changing ourselves, we'd change the world in which such laws could be written at all.

That was some forty years ago. The original collaboration lasted five or six years and resulted in two books for each of us (and for me, later, a few more) and an incredible adventure together in a federally funded study of teenage prostitution. And through those forty years both Tobys have been working away at bringing on positive change; that was the essence of the countercultural thought that inspired both of us.

Of course, there were going to be more changes in consciousness in the Castro as the years passed. That joyful liberated sexuality turned out to have unexpected consequences. And there were more layers of that consciousness change to go through. Consciousness change truly involves a Hero's Journey and heroism demands confronting death and dying—and the gay community was going to have to become heroic as we changed hearts and minds about what homosexuality means.

This idea of changing how you see the world is not new. Jesus said, "The Kingdom of Heaven is spread out upon the earth, and men do not see it." This idea underlies ancient Greek Gnosticism, Hermeticism, and Medieval Kabbalah. It shows up in pop culture, sometimes in silly ways, sometimes in profound ways, as The Power of Positive Thinking, Creative Visualization, and The Law of Attraction.

The dynamic by which negative messages manifest themselves in bad behavior and positive messages manifest themselves in good behavior is, in great part, so-called self-fulfilling prophecy. What you expect to happen is likely to happen because by expecting it you set it up to happen. If you say "I'm no good and nobody loves me," you're liable to act like somebody nobody will love. If you say, "I'm kind, generous, well-meaning, and doing my best," you're liable to attract other kind, generous, well-meaning people who'll love you and affirm you as one of them. We become what we expect by intention, conscious or unconscious, and by what we pay attention to. What we look for is what we see.

I was quite pleased to discover that Raymond Rigoglioso is doing similar work of consciousness change. He has investigated the idea that there's a special wisdom gay men possess. He has asked a current generation about this positive and incredibly lucky and wonderful side of gay life that so often remains unspoken of. He is doing the current era's version of revolution through consciousness change by asking gay men to report on the skills and talents and the goodness and virtue they manifest in their daily lives. Getting groups of gay men together, in person and by phone and Internet, to talk about their positive experience of being gay—and then sharing the discoveries—implements the dynamic of self-fulfilling prophecy. Equipped with these positive qualities, we can potentially be guides for a new way forward for the planet.

And, of course, I was quite pleased to be able to offer my experience with publishing (and my software and capability with layout and book design) to assist when he told me he had decided to self-publish.

What Ray reports about gay men is not true of all gay men, of course, but that doesn't make it any less so about many gay men. And it would be true of even more if more of us understood and acknowledged our homosexuality as a source for goodness and virtue.

The Movement has had amazing success. That same-sex marriage has swept the nation and the great majority of Americans now want to see gay men and lesbians living happy and fulfilling lives is evidence. There is still more progress to be made, more transformation of our own consciousness as we assist in transforming that of the planet. Within the new vision that is emerging in our times—of mind and consciousness, of myth and religion and the "supernatural" and forces beyond—gay people are world-saviors. Everybody is, of course. But each and every body has his or her own contribution to make to this new world. Gay people need to comprehend and honor our own special role in this transformation.

That's what this book is about. That's what we're doing.

Toby Johnson
Austin TX
Winter Solstice 2014

Part I
Toward a New Identity
for Gay Men

Introduction

We are living in profoundly dynamic times. Today, humanity's gravest threats are of our own making: In the very near future, we could push the planet's ecosystem so far out of balance that it could cease to support our life. In this country and elsewhere, we see a rise in fundamentalism, which poisons hearts and minds with rigid, harsh dogmas that seek to control, subjugate, and destroy. The specter of full-scale war, with the firepower to decimate life on the planet, remains ever-present. The legacies of the colonial era still pockmark the African continent, hampering economic development and stability for many of its countries. The colonial era lives on for African-Americans and Native Americans, who continue to experience the lingering effects of slavery and decimation, respectively, through socio-economic marginalization and the heavy psychological toll of being devalued minorities. In these and countless other ways, humanity is facing the predictable results of patriarchy.

In this patriarchal system, the masculine shadow maintains a stranglehold on power, which results in diminishing the feminine in all its manifestations. The system rests on hierarchy, with those on top controlling and subjugating those further down the pyramid. This translates into economic slavery, male domination over women, dominion of religious hierarchies over followers, concentration of wealth and political power in a few hands at the expense of the many, state-sponsored violence that can be justified on the flimsiest of grounds, the epidemic of men murdering women, and so on. Patriarchy, which governs our social, political, and legal systems and most of our religions, is so ingrained in our ways of thinking that we cannot always recognize it. It appears in our most subconscious thoughts, where we instantly size up a person's value based on external appearances and culturally determined criteria. It takes the emergence of gay people, who carry a fundamentally different consciousness, to bring into stark relief the insanity of this way of being.

At the same time, we are also witnessing unprecedented awakening in global consciousness, accelerated by interconnectedness that has shrunk the distance between nations and individuals. We have created electronic communication tools that can promote greater understanding and cooperation—and even launch revolutions. Our economic systems have become so interdependent that we need each other now more than ever. Along with the potential for tremendous peril, humanity faces the real potential to wake up to love—love for oneself, love for others, and love for the planet that sustains all life. We are on the precipice.

Humanity needs a New Way Forward—a way that restores balance between the masculine and feminine, individual freedom and the collective good, human activity and nature. A way that integrates multiple and even competing perspectives into a new global outlook. A way that collapses hierarchies, consigns shame to the history books, and honors the inalienable right to live according to our deepest longings. An Internet search for the term "new way forward" reveals multiple applications of the phrase, most pointing toward a better, more harmonious future. Humanity longs for this imagined future, and is searching for how to create it. Gay men possess the innate gifts to lead all people through this New Way Forward.

By coming out on such a massive scale, gay men have already shifted human consciousness. As a man in a discussion group that I ran put it, "Coming out is a revolutionary act. It sets off millions of transformations. It causes people to look at things differently." Indeed, our coming out has already opened minds, expanded hearts, and inspired untold numbers to live freely and authentically. But we have much more work to do. I hope that this book serves as a clarion call to gay men everywhere to awaken to their gifts and realize their full potential. We contain within ourselves nothing short of the solution to humanity's crisis. We are what the world has been waiting for.

In 2012, we heard a lot about the end of the Mayan calendar, accompanied by well-worn doomsday proclamations. Spiritual thinkers interpreted the end of the calendar more metaphorically—as the end of one era and the beginning of another. Most everyone I knew agreed that 2012 held an energy that accelerated change. We could feel something afoot. That year proved pivotal for me, and it sowed the seeds for this book.

On a visit to Provincetown, Massachusetts, in February 2012, I met a friend who introduced me to a book that would change my way of seeing gay men. This book, *A Passion to Preserve: Gay Men as Keepers of Culture*, by Will Fellows, proposed that gay men play important social roles in the human family, and that gay men's distinct traits emerge well before puberty. This electrified me. That weekend, at a gathering in town, I had another electrifying experience—an almost indescribable sense of brotherhood with other gay men. I felt like I had stepped into a realm that was both of the moment yet ancient, taking place in Provincetown yet connected to something global. I had heard gay men use the term "tribe" before, but it had sounded contrived. Now I understood how gay men could be connected in a way that transcends both time and place.

Subsequently, I decided to attend the first International Gay Coaches Alliance Conference, which was held at Easton Mountain that May. I had become certified as a life coach several years earlier, which for me represented a natural outgrowth of my career as a writer in the nonprofit sector. I had spent years reflecting organizations' achievements in writing, and I discovered that I had an equal gift for helping individuals to recognize their own talents and capacities. Coaching gave me a formal tool kit through which to apply this skill. I had never visited Easton Mountain, and I didn't know what I expected from the coaches' conference. I just knew I *had to* attend. Days before the event, while I was in the shower, words came to me: "gay men of wisdom." Confused by these words, but exhilarated by their energy, I simply made a mental note of them.

Clarity came to me during the conference. At a session about how to use workshops to market one's coaching practice, I decided I would create a project called Gay Men of Wisdom. Through this project, I would offer workshops to help gay men discover how their distinct ways of being benefit the people around them. Between conference sessions I purchased the website domain name. Before I left Easton I had arranged to give two workshops at a camp there during the summer.

Spurred on by Will Fellows' book, I developed a deepening curiosity about gay men's purpose and function. *"Just who are we?"* I wanted to understand. *"What unique contributions do we make to the human family?"* *"Why does the world need us?"* I began to read everything I could find about gay men in history, the early gay rights movement in the United States, and the roles gay men play in the world today. I discovered a treasure trove of scholarship—some books more academic in bent, others more inspirational. I learned that gay men have been asking questions about who we are since at least the mid-nineteenth century, beginning with Karl Heinrich Ulrichs and Edward Carpenter. In the 1950s, Harry Hay launched the Mattachine Society—one of the first organized groups in the early gay rights movement, and the most influential of its era—with three questions: "Who are we?" "Where do we come from?" "What are we for?" In fact, Hay spent years considering these questions and searching for a theory about what makes gay men different.

As I pored through these books, I discovered an incredible irony: With all the brilliant ideas in print, gay men still lack a cohesive, shared understanding of our place in the world. We have no collective narrative that says, "This is why we are here." For as far as we have come politically, legally, and socially, we still don't know ourselves.

Compelled by this awareness, I decided to expand the scope of the project. From September 2012 to July 2013, I ran a discussion group at New York City's LGBT Community Center. I brought this group to the Triangle Community Center in Norwalk, Connecticut, for several months during this time as well. From September 2013 to April 2014, I ran an online version of this group using videoconference technology, which gathered men from around the U.S. and Canada. I created a Weekend Intensive, which I conducted at Easton Mountain several times, and I presented workshops throughout the northeastern United States. Through these programs, I sought to address the disconnect between the brilliant ideas of the great gay thinkers, which I was immersed in, and the lack of a shared narrative among gay men about our function and purpose. I hoped that the explorations I led would translate these ideas into lived experiences for the men in the groups. If Gay Men of Wisdom were successful, I held, every man who participated would know in his bones how he serves and benefits humanity.

And yet, despite the dawning—and sometimes breathtaking—realizations I observed in the men who attended these programs, I still sensed that, for the men involved, and even for me as the leader, something remained incomplete. I realized that I could not provide a framework that captures the totality of gay men's distinct gifts. It was not for lack of insights in the gay literature. In fact, gay thinkers have proposed so many ideas about gay men's gifted nature that it can bewilder the reader. I was confused, in fact: Whose theories should I draw from, and which parts of those theories? How could I reconcile seemingly disparate and overlapping narratives among the thinkers? What implications do the historical roles that men-who-loved-men played in indigenous cultures have for today's gay men? Where could I simply find a definitive list of gay men's distinct gifts?

With *Gay Men and The New Way Forward*, I aim to present an updated, organized, and usable framework that describes the unique gifts that gay men give to humanity. This framework synthesizes ideas from many of the great gay thinkers. I could not include every thinker, of course, but I believe I have chosen a representative sample. To this mix, I have added my own ideas and observations. Importantly, I discuss the implications of gay men's gifts at this moment in history. I hope that gay men will use this book to consider the extent to which the ideas presented within it manifest in them. Toward this end, I have included a self-assessment in the last chapter. Ultimately, I hope that this book will help gay men create the narrative that explains our functions in the human family.

My training as a life coach deeply informs the Gay Men of Wisdom work and this book. From this work's inception, I have employed what I consider to be coaching's most important and powerful tools: curiosity and powerful questions. By structuring most of this exploration around questions, without fully realizing it at the time, I had created a laboratory in which men in my groups tested, refined, and expanded upon the ideas of the great gay thinkers. Our collective inquiry prompted men to introduce ideas of their own, which became refined and expanded upon by their peers. Inspired by this exchange, I added my own ideas to this mix, which went through a similar "vetting" process. Ultimately, men who participated in Gay Men of Wisdom have assisted in the research and development of this book. In fact, I have included many of their ideas throughout these chapters.

Throughout this journey, I have experienced the best of gay men. In the groups I have run, I have seen what happens when gay men pull together, support each other, share their gifts generously, and encourage each other to shine. The experience of tribe, which seemed like a fluke in Provincetown, happens whenever gay men gather with intention and open hearts. I have observed how this experience transforms gay men's lives, and how it ripples out into the larger world. This journey ignited what has become my passionate belief in gay men's potential. When we come to value and love ourselves, when we recognize our gifted nature, and when we discover how much humanity needs our distinct contributions, we will fully express our gifts. And the world desperately needs them.

To Harry Hay's original questions—"Who are we? Where do we come from? What are we for?"—I add, "Who can we become?"

A Deliberate and Respectful Focus

In the LGBT (and some also add "QIA" to include "queer," "intersex," and "asexual" or "ally") umbrella, our genuine and commendable desire to seek inclusion and commonality often means that we tend to diminish or forget the fundamentally different lived experiences that these letters reflect. I believe that this work—creating a shared narrative that explores the gifts and distinct contributions of a given group—needs to take place among and arise from within that group. Claiming to represent others seems disingenuous and disrespectful to me.

I cannot speak about the lived lesbian experience. I am not a woman who loves women, nor have I been socialized as a woman. As a gay man who is decidedly not bisexual, I cannot claim to represent the perspective of someone who is sexually and emotionally attracted to both men and women. I cannot speak about what life is like when one feels that one's presenting gender differs from one's internal gender.

For these reasons, I focus my work, and this book, exclusively on men-who-love-men. There is something distinct about being born into a male body—and feeling comfortable with that gender identity—and being sexually and emotionally attracted to other males. It creates life-long patterns and longings, and has specific implications for humanity. As I explore throughout this book, much of gay men's distinct challenges arise from being a *man* who loves men, and much of our influence and potential reside in our ability to relate to other men *because we are men*. Gay men's distinct patterns of sexuality play a tremendous part in our experience and place in the world. Whereas racial and cultural differences can affect and modify the gay male experience, I observe enough striking commonalities among gay men of different races and cultures—and I have met enough gay men from different parts of the world with whom I have felt an immediate sense of tribe—to feel confident that, if I cannot account for every difference, at least I make my argument from a place that seems grounded in a common experience.

This focus does not intend to imply that lesbians, bisexuals, and transgender people do not possess distinct gifts of their own. Nor does it suggest that some of the gifts outlined here do not also apply to lesbians, bisexuals, and transgender people. Rather, I respectfully leave it to members of those groups to ask those questions and discover the answers for themselves. In fact, I sincerely hope that this model inspires others within our umbrella to create shared narratives of their own. I believe that this approach holds tremendous potential to help disenfranchised groups of *all* types to discover their intrinsic value, and to better understand the contributions they make to the human family.

A Word about Terminology

I deliberately choose and affirm the term "gay." In its pre-1950s popular meaning, denoting "joy," "happiness," or "being carefree," "gay" captures an essence about us—our vitality, the eroticism we bring into all aspects of our lives, our impact on others, and the model we set for the human family. Personally, I find the term "queer" to be confrontational and rooted in negativity, not unlike "faggot" or the "N" word. I arrive at this decision from experience: I adopted "queer" during the years of my involvement with ACT UP and Queer Nation, but I grew tired of seeing allies wince when I used it. As Toby Johnson reminded me, our allies cannot use the term "queer." The president of the United States cannot address us as such, for he would be roundly condemned for being disrespectful. My parents and family would never risk calling me "queer," as it carries too many years of hatred and baggage attached to it. The general public uses "gay" out of respect.

I understand that younger generations—and even men of my generation—have different perspectives on terminology. I hope that men-who-love-men of all ages, regardless of the term they claim for their identity, find meaning, insights, and applicability within these pages. And maybe—just maybe—this argument might persuade the doubtful about the inherent "gayness" of men-who-love-men.

Words Need to Come Alive

The written word holds tremendous power. Ideas start revolutions. But left on the page, ideas wither. Words come alive because people think about them, talk about them, adopt them, and live differently as a result. Through this book and Gay Men of Wisdom, my goal is nothing short of the complete transformation of how we as gay men see ourselves—and how the world views us.

I hope this book will inspire you to view yourself in a new light. I also know that the words here represent just part of the work to be done: gay men must create processes to bring this understanding alive so each gay man knows and owns it in his bones. Part III, "A Call to Action," includes suggested ways to help bring about this understanding.

The Use of "We"

I purposely use the pronoun "we" throughout this book. This breaks most editorial conventions, which require authors to maintain third-person distance from their subjects. I choose to break this rule to emphasize gay men's commonalities, even as we embrace the variations that exist among gay men. I also do so because I count myself as part of the subject being discussed—namely, that I am a gay man speaking primarily to other gay men—though I hope other audiences will find this subject compelling enough to inspire them to read this book. Maintaining the distance of a disinterested third party seems insincere to me. With this said, I do not intend to suggest that every "we" indicates that a given statement applies to me as the author; nor do I suggest that every use of the word applies to every reader.

Chapter 1
The Coming Out Continuum and the Gay Hero's Journey

"Don't we lead mythical lives? Even the most
unassuming of us can tell amazing stories of victory
against overwhelming odds, self-respect forged out of
mind-boggling hate, invention and wit mothered by
inescapable necessity. When Joseph Campbell spoke
of the hero's journey he should have used us as his
example—although he never did."
—Will Roscoe[1]

In my Gay Men of Wisdom groups, I have asked participants to consider the impact they have on others simply by being their full selves as gay men. Men's responses have revealed an intriguing phenomenon: those who are more out, and who have been out longer, tend to report having a greater impact on the people around them than those who are more closeted or who have more recently come out. This would stand to reason: the more secure a gay man feels, the more likely he would express more of who he is. The more closeted, the more likely he would hide any traits that could give him away as gay—from his actual sexuality to personality characteristics that he might think are associated with being gay.

This phenomenon suggests the existence of a Coming Out Continuum: the more out a gay man is, the greater the impact he has on the world around him. It might look like this:

Coming Out Continuum

(Least impact from distinct gay male gifts)   **(Most impact** from distinct gay male gifts)

This Continuum neatly captures our current shared narrative—the Gay Hero's Journey. The journey begins with a man or boy who is painfully repressed, due to society's conditioning that tells him his deepest longings are wrong. Courageously, he awakens to his sexuality and against all odds, comes out. Eventually, he fully integrates his sexual identity, becoming a proud, out gay man—the ultimate goal. If he is lucky, his family and friends embrace him. This journey, and its successful completion, has inspired entire genres of movies and literature, and has increasingly found its way into popular understanding of the gay experience.

But what happens to our Gay Hero once he successfully comes out? Currently, our narrative and journey end there. We assume that, when we have met this goal—which once seemed unattainable on such a broad scale—happiness and fulfillment await us.

This story's ending, however, leaves us feeling lost, unmoored, and purposeless. This is the place so many gay men have found themselves. On some level, gay men are beginning to question, *"Is that all there is?"* The problem is that we lack a cogent and relevant narrative to lead us forward.

Toward that end, I propose an expanded Gay Hero's Journey. I base it on the Gay Men of Wisdom vision:

> *Gay men serve an evolutionary purpose on the planet. Our attributes and ways of being are gifts we give to humanity and some of the most important contributions we make. We envision a time in which the role of the gay man is honored in every culture on the globe.*

In this second phase of the journey, the Gay Hero discovers his purpose and role on the planet. He understands intrinsically how he helps the people he encounters in his life to grow and evolve. He commits to personal growth so that he can step into his full power as a gay man. He takes full responsibility for his own experience, works to heal from the wounds inflicted by a harsh world, and owns and manages his shadow. He grows in self-love to the point where he has banished shame and serves as an example for all people about how to love oneself. He consciously uses his gifts to benefit the world. He endeavors to live as an evolutionary leader, understanding that this goal is not so much an end point, but a state of being which he continually strives to attain.

This model might seem to imply that men in the closet do not have much of an impact on humanity. That is not intended. Closeted men can indeed have a beneficial impact. For instance, they can make wonderful, sensitive, loving fathers. Closeted teachers can demonstrate many of the gifts of sensitivity to their students that are the hallmark of gay men, though they may be more guarded and less available to their students out of fear of reprisal. Some men in the closet drive themselves to such an extent—to compensate for their homosexuality—that they become great leaders. Far too many closeted gay men, unfortunately, remain tentative and disempowered in their lives because of homophobia's wounding. They can diminish themselves due to fear and lack of confidence. When a gay man hides the traits that make him different, he deprives the world of energies and talents that it desperately needs.

The next half of the Gay Hero's Journey will be more subtle but also more profound. Gay men will discover that the gifts with which we are innately imbued are tools that help transform global consciousness. By understanding this potential, we can more powerfully use these gifts to contribute to good and healing—in our own lives, and for the human family. In the first half of our journey, we reclaimed our sexuality. In the second half, we discover and assert our true roles as stewards for humanity's evolution. If there were ever a time when the world needed the tribe of loving, sensitive men, that time would be now.

Viewed graphically, the New Gay Hero's Journey looks like this:

The New Gay Hero's Journey

Stage of Awareness	Deep denial of sexuality	Awakening to sexuality	Coming out to others
Impact on Humanity	Distinct gay male gifts are least expressed and have least impact on humanity	Wrestles with sense of being different; little noticeable external impact	Models honesty and courage; inspires others
Self-Love	Least self-love	Begins to accept desire for sex with men; may seek affirmation through sexual contact	Self-love grows, trumping negative societal messages
Inner Work	Much work to be done	Begins to question and confront societal messages	Learns to take risks

Fully integrating sexuality (current end point in our narrative)	Awakening to one's roles and purpose	Embracing and expanding one's roles as a gay man	Evolutionary leader for humanity. Gay man fully realizes and expresses his distinct gifts and potential. Fully embraces being part of the evolution of consciousness.
Lives authentically in all areas of life; models this	Growing understanding lays groundwork for greater impact	Power of distinct gifts begins to emerge	Gay man has the greatest impact on humanity. He is conscious of his impact and committed to his form(s) of service to humanity.
Overcomes shame, self-doubt, and self-loathing over sexuality	Begins to question the downplaying of differences and distinct gifts	Loves oneself for being gay and having special gifts	Greatest self-love and joy. Here the gay man fully accepts and embraces all aspects of himself. Shame released from the erotic, enabling deep appreciation for its power and gifts. Shame of all types released.
Sexuality becomes just one facet of life	Negotiates the paradox of having special gifts and being equal to others	Accepts gifts with humility. Motivated to grow personally and make a difference.	Much inner work done; ongoing maintenance. Here, the gay man has greatest level of self-awareness and takes full responsibility for his life experience.

Chapter 2
The Limitations of Our Current Identity

"We don't waste people the way white society does.
Every person has their gift."
—Crow, Native American tribal elder

Human beings are much more alike than they are different. People across the planet share the same basic needs. We have similar wants, desires, hopes, and fears. All people experience and express love, know sadness and grief. Parents give birth to children, who then follow predictable life stages. All people ask similar questions about the mysteries of life—even if we come to different conclusions. If we had to hazard a guess, we could propose that all people are about 90 percent alike. (Genetically, of course, humans are much closer. On average, any two people are about 99.9 percent identical in terms of their DNA sequences.)[2]

Within that 10 percent variance lies people's and groups' distinct contributions to the human family. If we peered into the stew of human diversity, we could imagine that differences in worldview, religion, culture, temperament, language, cuisine, values, likes and dislikes, and special gifts reside there. When peace activists claim that people are all the same, they are right. When mayors wax eloquent about the rainbow of diversity that enriches their cities, they too are right.

To the extent that all people are alike, gay men and lesbians are just like everyone else. We share far more in common with heterosexuals and bisexuals than we do differences. Yet, to the extent that people vary, we embody essential variations. An honest assessment of who we are must acknowledge those distinctions.

We Are Different

Gays are called "queer" for a reason: we are different. Homophobes know it. Supportive allies know it. Parents know on some level when their boys are gay—usually long before puberty—because they will often exhibit typically gay (gender variant) characteristics. How often have we looked back at family photos of ourselves when we were younger and found ourselves startled by the now clear evidence of our gayness? (A wonderful book, *Born This Way*, reclaims and celebrates those gay childhood photos.)[3]

The perceptive schoolyard bully knew it. Without having the language or conscious understanding, he intuitively understood that we were *other*—that our energy was fundamentally different from that of other boys. He honed in on what he perceived as a weakness, and trounced.

We know we are different, yet we deny it to make ourselves feel like we belong. Our established narrative holds that we are just like everyone else except for our sexual orientation. The leaders of our political organizations diligently adhere to this party line. Our gay media provide no alternate vision here either—they focus on political victories and upsets, entertainment, fashion, and coming out stories. When we read the gay media, we hear the story of political struggle with a subtext that suggests that when we achieve equality, all will be well with the world. There's nothing terrible about this subtext, but it does not give us the full picture of who we are.

Among ourselves, we may laugh at the clueless straight person who can't pick up on the obvious signs that someone is gay, but we won't discuss what those obvious signs are. We might joke about our differences, but we don't allow this to rise to the level of serious dialogue. We enforce silence—even among our allies—around truths that are so obvious that we prevent ourselves from knowing and honoring who we truly are.

This "minority dissonance" is not unique to gay men. It affects the public conversations about nearly every minority group in the United States. Who, for instance, has permission to name African-Americans' clear cultural differences from whites? As someone who has been with an African-American man for a long time, I can attest that even I lack this permission. I can point out the difference in my partner's accent, intonations, and choice of words he uses after he has had a conversation with someone in his family, but I can't acknowledge to other members of his family that he is "talking black." (I've made that mistake—they weren't amused.) He knows I find the differences fascinating and even funny at times—such as the ways that only black folk can be frank—but to say this to his family or publicly implies bigotry. In our culture, to point out any difference—no matter how obvious or innocent—implies derogation, devaluing, dishonoring.

This dissonance is a hallmark of patriarchy. In this way of thinking, if any two things are different, one must be better and the other worse, one dominant and the other subordinate. In their quest to achieve equal treatment, few minority groups in the United States have challenged this precept. To my knowledge, no group has ever protested under the banner, "Different but equal." In many ways, this reflects a shrewd po-litical calculus, and it can be viewed as an adaptive response of minority groups, under a patriarchal system, to obtaining basic rights. It comes at great cost, however: to gain a place at the table, most minority groups have publicly denied or minimized their differences and enforced si-lence about what makes them unique—with stiff penalties for anyone who dares break the taboo. I know the pain this has caused gay people. I can only imagine the impact this has had on African-Americans or others striving for equal treatment.

For gay men, this dissonance leaves us split—within ourselves, and from each other. This dissonance resides in our collective and individual consciousness, because it is not just a story we tell others—we tell it to ourselves, and we believe it.

Consider how this dynamic plays out for our Gay Hero: We grow up feeling isolated and alienated in our own families—the place where we should ostensibly feel the safest. We discover from a very young age that we are different, and that that difference places us in danger. We develop all manner of coping mechanisms to reduce this danger: hiding, lying, subverting, suppressing, denying, pretending, being the best little boy in the world, being as "masculine" as we can, becoming invisible, and so on. At some point, we come out. We find others who are like us, who have shared the same struggle, and who have accepted their sexuality. We have triumphed.

Many of us then join social circles where gay men pretend that these differences don't exist, or which purport that survival means hiding those differences. Others find friendships in groups where we can be as gay as possible. But even among these "gayer" groups, we learn that while we can flaunt who we are, we can't talk about it. We discover that those parts of ourselves that are different remain just as threatening to gay men as to our families of origin. No one suggests that these differences might actually be gifts.

Our interactions with each other thus create dissonance. On the one hand, we come together believing that what we share in common is a sexual orientation. On the other, we know we share something deeper, but we have not allowed ourselves to discuss and discover that deeper truth. We thus fail to see the full picture of who we truly are, and this prevents us from making meaningful connections with each other. We re-experience the alienation and isolation we felt in our families of origin, only this time it's worse—because we know it doesn't have to be this way.

Our Gay Hero doesn't realize that the disconnect begins within. When he discovers those parts of himself—those gifts—that were previously considered taboo, he opens himself to wholeness. And when he creates wholeness within himself, he invites authentic and meaningful connections with other gay men.

Differences matter. They may be politically inconvenient, but they form the basis for what gay men have in common and how we benefit the world. But we need not allow those feelings to limit us. We can *honor* our differences. We can value them. We can discover what it is about a variation that presents a gift to the world. We can explore how our differences make the world a better place to live in. When we heal the disconnect within ourselves, we will offer a model for how other minority groups—beginning with our lesbian, bisexual, and transgender brothers and sisters—can embrace their contributions to the human family. When we own and honor our differences, we own and honor those elements of all human beings that patriarchy attempts to suppress.

A Focus on Sexuality Alone No Longer Serves Us

Gay men and lesbians have created an identity based on the concept of being a sexual minority that deserves the rights that the sexual majority takes for granted. The LGBT movement has been terrifically successful in advancing this notion, and the pace of change has been dizzying. We see evidence of this success everywhere—in political and legislative arenas as well as in shifting societal perceptions of gay and lesbian people. When we look back at this period in history, we will recognize how gay men and lesbians have, despite all odds, led humanity to choose love over hatred.

And yet, in some ways, we have become victims of our own success. The experience of some younger gay men illustrates this point: I have heard many tell me they feel excluded from the gay world—especially the one inhabited by older gay men—because they never experienced the sense of struggle, which they observe has created camaraderie and closeness among the older generations. And while they may partly romanticize the AIDS epidemic and the earlier stages of the movement, their observation poses keen and timely questions: Without the struggle, who are we? When our sexuality becomes recognized as a normal variation, what will cement us together? If we no longer have to fight for basic rights, what is our purpose? Our current identity and Gay Hero's Journey tell us we have arrived—that we have completed our work.

For most older gay men, the positive developments in basic rights have come at a pace far faster than expected. Most men of a certain age never expected to see gay marriage in their lifetimes, let alone such changes in societal attitudes. We can be forgiven if our identity has not kept pace with changes that we have fought hard to advance.

Now that we are on the cusp of achieving equal status as human beings, at least in much of the Western world, the original questions that Harry Hay posed to the Mattachine Society seem particularly contemporary: "Who are we?" "Where do we come from?" "What are we for?" Hay always viewed these questions as integral to our movement, but in the face of intense adversity and the need to establish basic rights, the political side of the movement gained much greater prominence. Gay men have been exploring Hay's questions for years, but their ideas have rarely garnered headlines. Recent political and social developments provide good reason to consider these thinkers' collective wisdom.

We can view the LGBT movement through many lenses. Let's consider two: Maslow's hierarchy of needs, and the stages of human development. Each gives us insight into where we have been and where we find ourselves now.

Maslow's Hierarchy of Needs

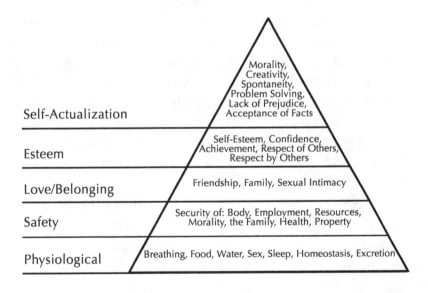

When viewed through the lens of Maslow's hierarchy of needs, we would consider the LGBT movement up to this point as engaged in meeting what Maslow termed "deficiency needs." These needs occupy the lower three layers of the pyramid (Physiological, Safety, and Love and Belonging).[4]

For instance, our efforts to meet our Physiological and Safety needs would include:

- Securing protection from police entrapment and brutality, and safety from violence at the hands of gay bashers

- Advocating for equal treatment in housing, employment, in hospitals, and in other public accommodations

- Changing sodomy laws so we are not jailed for having sex

Our efforts to meet our Love and Belonging needs would include:

- Activism to shift public norms so that we can live freely and without public condemnation

- Our push to establish laws protecting our relationships, including domestic partner and marriage initiatives

Now that we are moving closer to meeting these deficiency needs, gay men can move up the hierarchy to meet our higher-level needs of Esteem and Self-Actualization. This will necessitate an updated identity and an expanded Gay Hero's Journey. Continuing to equate our identity with sexual orientation alone and a struggle against an oppressor will prevent us from knowing ourselves and realizing our full potential.

Viewed another way, our movement could be seen in terms of human development—where we have successfully completed childhood, adolescence, and early adulthood, and we are now ready to enter middle adulthood. Our efforts could be organized historically as such:

Childhood, 1950 to 1969:

Homophile movement begins: Harry Hay launches the Mattachine Society in Los Angeles, laying the groundwork for massive change. Donald Webster Cory publishes *The Homosexual in America,* the first book that advances the idea of gays being a distinct minority deserving of equal treatment. Franklin Kameny, leader of the Washington, DC, chapter of the Mattachine Society, brings the first gay rights case to the

Supreme Court; he coins the slogan "Gay Is Good." Stonewall Riots in 1969 mark the close of childhood and the explosive push into adolescence (puberty).

Adolescence, 1969 to 1981:

Stonewall Riots give public attention to the gay side of the sexual revolution. Gay men sharply individuate and distinguish ourselves from our parents (the larger world). We make space for ourselves in opposition to what we had come from. Out of anger for having been victimized, we create a world that allows us to express our individuality. We flock to major cities, establish gay neighborhoods, and create bars, restaurants, and other businesses that provide services and capitalize on sexual freedom. We build new political organizations that challenge the status quo. We begin to see results—and backlash.

First Crisis of Young Adulthood, 1981 to 1996:

An unknown virus begins to decimate gay men. With the spread of AIDS, we take care of the sick and dying and create entirely new systems of care. We refocus our politics toward preventing AIDS discrimination and moving the government to speed development of new treatments. This crisis eventually forces the general public to recognize gay men as an identifiable minority, and homosexuality as not a choice. Introduction of anti-retroviral drugs ends immediate crisis, turning AIDS into a chronic condition.

Finding Our Way as Young Adults, 1997 to 2012:

Rebelliousness gives way to a desire to be recognized as full-fledged adults. Political side of the movement refocuses its efforts on gays in the military and same-sex marriage. Message shifts toward accepting gays as "normal" and no different from others.

Middle Adulthood, 2013 on:

The Defense of Marriage Act falls, opening the door to the real possibility of gay marriage across all 50 states. This signal moment marks the LGBT movement's entry into middle adulthood. As mature adults, the task for gay men becomes twofold: 1) to identify who we are, not in opposition to the majority, but *as integral to the human family*; and 2) to discover how we wish to contribute to the human family.

Our current identity as a sexual minority keeps us stuck in adolescence and young adulthood and—due to the struggle embedded within this identity—victimhood. Just as teenagers and young adults shed beliefs and ways of being that no longer serve them as they mature, so too must gay men release old, limiting concepts if we are to embrace our full adult selves. The identity we have created, which has served us well through our tumultuous early years, must expand so that we can grow.

With this said, not every gay man will want or be ready to take these next steps. Some may choose to live perfectly content, "equal and nearly same" lives, blending into the dominant cultural landscape and not rocking the boat. Doing so will exact a price, however. It means entering another closet—this one more subtle. For accepting this as the endpoint of our current Gay Hero's Journey requires disowning or at least disregarding those parts of oneself that are fundamentally different from other men.

For some, the tradeoff of considering oneself "normal" might be worth the price that this belief exacts. Full realization of these differences can take time, as well. An "equal but nearly the same" identity may serve an important step along the path to full acceptance. As the men in my groups have taught me, gaining awareness of how we are truly different—beyond our sexual orientation—helps us begin to see how much we have been living in another closet. Once we become aware of our special gifts, we can choose to remain in this closet or burst open the doors.

Part II
Gay Men's Distinct Gifts

Chapter 3
An Invitation to Explore

"The most important thing we can tell each other as
gay men is that we are here for a reason and all of us
know what the reason is. We know when we sit with
ourselves and notice who we are, what we do, and
what we bring to the world. There's a line from a Na-
tive American medicine chant that I really love: 'You
bring to all of life your special touch.' We gay men
know what our special touch is."
—Andrew Ramer[5]

We have been victims for so long, we have not noticed that we have become teachers. Gay men lead by example. Without even consciously understanding our impact, our authenticity and courage inspire those around us to live more authentically and courageously. In this current unconscious state, we already serve an important evolutionary function—but we realize only part of our potential. It is time for the gay male tribe to awaken to its true magnificence.

There is a qualitative and palpable difference between the gay man who is unaware of his impact and the gay man who knows and claims it. When gay men stand tall in their gifts, they project a different energy and confidence. This creates a magnetic response in others—among gay and straight people alike. And it serves the gay man well. Self-knowledge opens new doors to creativity, possibility, and opportunity in all areas of one's life. When we gain this knowledge, we claim our place of honor in the human family. And the world takes note.

About This Section

Part II brings together the 14 Distinct Gay Male Gifts, providing a framework to see ourselves and to consider the implications that our gifts have for the human family. These gifts are divided into three categories: Serving and Healing, Reinventing Manhood, and Freeing and Enriching the Human Spirit. The visual model, presented below, includes three overlapping circles, indicating that, while the gifts remain distinct, they share commonalities. These commonalities appear throughout the chapters that follow, reflecting the challenge of describing gay men's gifts within a structured framework.

Masculine-feminine integration forms the basis for many of the 14 Distinct Gay Male Gifts, as explored in the next chapter, and as such appears as the foundation for this model. A full picture of who gay men are would not be complete without acknowledging the darker, shadow sides of ourselves individually and collectively. This exploration appears in Part III, Chapter 19.

I purposefully discuss gay men's distinct gifts and our shadow elements in different sections of this book. Among gay men, we so often follow any positive assessment of ourselves with criticism, we have become oblivious to what is good about us. We can easily describe gay men's faults, but we rarely consider what is right about gay men. At the same time, in this book I give greater weight to the positive—a permission we rarely afford ourselves—so we can see and truly appreciate our magnificence. Critique is too comfortable. Self-love is the hard part.

Some may balk at this structure and deliberate emphasis, choosing instead to highlight gay men's faults. To this I would respond, "We see what we expect to see." Our beliefs color and create our reality. If we choose a pessimistic view, we will search for and find evidence that supports it, and we will create experiences that reflect it. We can always conjure examples of gay men behaving badly, but that does not negate the overwhelming evidence of our gifts.

Discussion of these gifts reflects the intersection of gay men's distinct traits, the LGBT movement, and the current state of human affairs. Some of these gifts will remain timeless, while others may morph with changing times and trends in the larger culture. These gifts may evolve as gay men across the globe fully embrace their role as evolutionary leaders. As the Coming Out Continuum suggests, gay men's distinct gifts have a greater impact when we have the courage to live authentically.

Throughout this section and Chapter 19, I make generalizations about gay men. Generalizations provide helpful tools to describe the many observable traits that exist among the large and diverse group that constitutes gay men. This approach also carries risk: generalizations seldom apply to every member of a given group.

I do not intend to suggest that every gift or observation applies to every gay man. Rather, I hope—by making reasoned arguments based on evidence and the existing vision about our roles and purpose, along with my own insights and observations—that I capture the spectrum of distinct, observable traits among gay men. If I have done my work well, you the reader will see yourself more often than not, and you will come to better appreciate gay men who manifest a different constellation of gifts than yourself.

I thus present the 14 Distinct Gay Male Gifts as an *invitation* to consider the extent to which the traits that appear within our group apply to *you*. To avoid redundancy with every argument I advance, I acknowledge this approach here and intend for it to apply throughout this book. I occasionally repeat it where it seems most necessary.

A Gaze into the Mirror

This exploration will give you insights into different parts of yourself. Allow for the possibility that you may manifest certain gifts at different times in your life. You may enthusiastically embrace some gifts now while not relating to others; at other times, you may find yourself embracing what you once eschewed. If you re-read this book five years from now, you may see these gifts—and yourself—differently.

The traits and attributes discussed here may provoke reactions or resistance among some readers. When you come across a concept that you feel does not apply to you, take a moment to gauge your inner reaction. Do you feel judgment or resentment? Do you reject it out of hand? Do you feel anger or shame around it? If you have any of these responses, chances are there is information for you in it. Society has done a remarkable job of shaming and minimizing gay men; undoing this damage is a lifelong process.

Consider this process as an extended gaze into the mirror. Can you recognize yourself? Can you love what you see? Can you fall in love with the tribe that is gay men? I hope the answer will be "Yes." And I hope that you will use this book to help you find healing, and to step into human leadership with love.

Gay Men's 14 Distinct Gifts to Humanity

Serving and Healing

- A Gentle, Collaborative Social Orientation
- An Orientation toward Service
- Religious Reformers and Spiritual Leaders
- Teachers of Compassion, Generosity, and the Authentic Masculine
- Models of Forgiveness

Reinventing Manhood

- Friends, "Soul Mates," and Co-Revolutionaries with Straight Women
- Esthetic Outsiders and Gender Tricksters: The Art of Camp and Drag
- Modeling Sustainable Manhood

Freeing and Enriching the Human Spirit

- Sexual Leadership
- Fine Attunement to Beauty, Creators and Keepers of Culture
- A "Gay" Spirit
- Models of Authenticity and Courage, Cleansers of Shame
- Outsiders Driving Evolutionary Advancement

The Foundational Gift: Masculine-Feminine Intelligence

These three circles, and the gifts they contain, overlap, reflecting the interrelated nature of gay men's distinct contributions to humanity. Masculine-feminine intelligence appears in nearly every distinct gift, making it foundational.

Chapter 4
Masculine-Feminine Intelligence: The Foundational Gift

"As we transition out of this patriarchal era and collectively find our way into a more balanced state of homeostasis, a good question for men and women to ask is how to balance the inner male and inner female. Who more appropriate than queer people to undertake this exploration and teach others how to do it?"
—Christian de la Huerta[6]

Up to this point, and for better or worse, our shared narrative has advanced the notion that gay men's defining characteristic is that of homosexuality. We took a term that once pathologized us and turned it into gay pride. We created an entire culture and movement centered around this notion. And we are discovering that, while this idea may have once fit us, it has become as constricting as a pair of shoes that our teenage selves have outgrown.

To succeed in the tasks that our mature adult identity presents, and to meet our needs of Self-Esteem and Self-Actualization, we must ask ourselves, "Who are we beyond our sexuality?" The clues lie in plain sight, of course, hidden in what we most fervently deny.

Of all the ways that gay men differ, we come pre-wired with one core competency, which serves as the basis for and manifests within most of the other distinct gay male gifts—masculine-feminine intelligence. This refers to:

1. The balance of masculine and feminine that we innately possess

2. The seamless ability to invoke each as the need arises

Many gay thinkers have recognized this foundational gift. Harry Hay proposed that gay people, "May be a combination of both hetero masculine and hetero feminine, but mostly we are *a combination of neither*." He termed this "spiritual neitherness."[7] Andrew Harvey proposed that, "In a sacred world...gay men and women would be clearly seen for what they are from birth...as people who point to an inner fusion of male and female, a holy androgyny, that all beings could aspire to."[8] Contemporary Native Americans' two-spirit identity, which modernizes and reclaims the special roles played by gender-variant men and women prior to and during white conquest, honors the integration of the masculine and feminine. While masculine-feminine intelligence is an innate gift, once we become aware of it, we can consciousness employ it for greater human benefit.

The notion of a specific type of intelligence is not without precedent. Psychologist Howard Gardner proposed a Theory of Multiple Intelligences, in which he suggests there is not one single type of intelligence, as measured by IQ, but eight: spatial, bodily-kinesthetic, musical, linguistic, logical-mathematical, interpersonal, intrapersonal, and naturalistic.[9] Gardner describes intelligence as "the ability to solve problems or fashion products that are of consequence in a particular cultural setting or community."[10] As we will explore throughout this book, masculine-feminine intelligence gives gay men the innate ability to solve some of humanity's most pressing problems and create "products" that are of very substantial consequence.

Masculine-feminine intelligence usually appears at a young age. People notice it first as a tendency for gay boys to gravitate to activities more closely associated with girls. On a deeper level, however, people are responding to the more feminine energy that gay boys and men, on the whole, tend to have. Parents notice this energy, and so does the schoolyard bully. What most people don't discern—gay men included—is that we masterfully embody *both* masculine and feminine traits. Because males in our culture are supposed to be only masculine, the presence of any feminine sets off all kinds of alarms, obfuscating deeper truths about us. No one notices the inherent *balance* we possess.

To gain greater insight into this natural intelligence, let's establish definitions for "masculine" and "feminine." When we think about a person's masculinity or femininity, we tend to imagine a person falling somewhere on a single scale of masculine to feminine. A closer look, however, reveals three dimensions to each: 1) personality traits; 2) external traits, such as body language, mannerisms, and vocal inflection—where effeminacy and "butchness" are instantly sized up; and 3) personal energy. Masculine-feminine intelligence relates to these three dimensions, and the interplay among them.

Masculine and Feminine Personality Traits

Psychologist Sandra Bem captured the generally accepted understanding of what constitutes feminine and masculine personality characteristics in her Bem Sex Role Inventory (BSRI), published in 1974. This self-assessment helps individuals determine the extent to which they are psychologically masculine, feminine, or "androgynous." It contains a listing of 60 traits—20 masculine, 20 feminine, and 20 neutral. Respondents rate the extent to which each applies to them. While debate exists in the scholarly world about its continued reliability, studies as late as 1998 and 2004 found that the BSRI is still, for the most part, a valid measure.[11] The following chart includes the masculine and feminine traits in the BSRI.

Of all three dimensions of the masculine and feminine, personality traits are the most malleable. While people tend to gravitate toward certain traits as defaults, external circumstances can often prompt responses that fall outside of one's default behaviors. A man who rarely shows emotions might be moved to comfort a child who skinned her knee, for instance. Someone who is normally not aggressive might display this trait when attacked. This suggests that some masculine and feminine traits can be learned.

Masculine and Feminine Personality Characteristics Identified in the Bem Sex Role Inventory

Masculine	Feminine
Acts as leader	Affectionate
Aggressive	Cheerful
Ambitious	Childlike
Analytical	Compassionate
Assertive	Does not use harsh language
Athletic	Eager to soothe hurt feelings
Competitive	Feminine
Defends own beliefs	Flatterable
Dominant	Gentle
Forceful	Gullible
Has leadership abilities	Loves children
Independent	Loyal
Individualistic	Sensitive to needs of others
Makes decisions easily	Shy
Masculine	Soft spoken
Self-reliant	Sympathetic
Self-sufficient	Tender
Strong personality	Understanding
Willing to take a stand	Warm
Willing to take risks	Yielding

For the most part, Sandra Bem's assessment assumes that the masculine and feminine exist in the realm of personality traits only. It does not account for the lived experience that gay men know all too well: the feminine and masculine manifest in decidedly external ways.

External Masculine and Feminine Traits

More often than not, visible and audible masculine and feminine traits communicate much more succinctly and immediately than personality traits. In an instant, a person's voice, body movements, posture, and style of dress tell us the extent to which a man is "masculine" or "effeminate."[12]

When I ran my first Gay Men of Wisdom Weekend Intensive, I led the participants through an exercise to develop a working definition of these visible and audible masculine and feminine traits. The table below captures what the men came up with. I have added a few traits to this list.

External Masculine and Feminine Traits

Voice/Speech		Body Movements/Posture		Style of Dress	
Masculine	Feminine	Masculine	Feminine	Masculine	Feminine
Deep	Higher pitch	Hands firmly at one's sides	Hand on hip	Few colors, more muted tones	Multi – colored, colorful
Dominant	Gentler	Legs crossed: ankle over knee	Legs crossed: knee over knee	Looser fit	Fitted
Less talkative / fewer words	More talkative / more words	Straight wrist	Bent wrist	Fewer choices	More choices
Fewer adjectives	More adjectives / flowery language	Sitting: Legs open	Sitting: Legs closed	Showing little skin	Showing skin
Limited emotional vocabulary	Greater range of vocabulary	Stride	Sashay	Long shorts	Short shorts
Less expressive	More expressive	Closed arms	Open arms / body posture	Loose, haphazard style	A more planned, considered style.
Clear and strong diction	Lisp	Hold one's body rigidly, solidly	More flowing. Greater range of movements. "Femme."		

That weekend, we were gifted with the presence of a blind man in the group. This made exploration of the visible manifestations of masculine and feminine at once challenging and revealing. We learned that he had no idea about the visual cues that most gay men take for granted.

And through explaining to him the body movements and postures that characterize effeminacy, we learned how potent these visual cues really are.

Some external masculine and feminine traits tend to be more fixed: we are born with or mature into our natural voice/speech and body movements and postures. For many more-effeminate gay boys, these traits can provoke intense scorn and shaming from our families, peers, and communities, which can lead boys to try to hide or change these traits. In the context of cultural scorn, these external traits can be viewed as malleable, but only to the extent that a culture demands strict conformity to gender expectations for boys. Style of dress is the most malleable of the three types of external traits: while it usually expresses one's inner preferences, it can be more readily changed.

As with all three dimensions, heterosexual and gay men embody variations when it comes to external masculine and feminine traits. As a group, however, it is safe to say that heterosexual men tend to present more masculine external traits in this dimension, while gay men as a group present a wider spectrum. Some gay men have a decidedly masculine appearance, while many gay men have a preponderance of effeminate traits. That said, of course, some heterosexual men are more effeminate in appearance than some gay men.

Masculine and Feminine Energies

Personality traits and external manifestations of the masculine and feminine come from deep within an individual. They express a person's energy. Whereas situations can prompt an intensifying or softening of that energy, in our resting state we typically have a default energy that is essentially fixed. Energy is something that is both immeasurable and palpable. We know it when we feel it. Parents can even sense it in their newborns.

One's energy affects how one manifests personality and external masculine and feminine traits. It is why a heterosexual man and a gay man can express the same trait but do so in qualitatively different ways. To illustrate this, let's consider the personality trait of assertiveness. Imagine two separate scenarios: a typical heterosexual man and a typical gay man have just arrived at their cars to find a parking enforcement officer issuing them a ticket. Their parking meters had expired just one minute earlier. Feeling aggrieved, each man confronts the officer. How might each man respond?

The hypothetical, typical heterosexual man might forcefully contest the ticket by raising his voice, trying to intimidate the officer, or perhaps becoming demanding, aggressive, or threatening. The gay man might, rather, negotiate his way out of the ticket by being reasonable, trying to ingratiate himself or flatter the officer, or becoming obsequious or coy. When I posed this scenario to men in my weekend intensive, they gave a range of responses, from assertive confrontation to ingratiation to negotiation. None veered into aggressiveness. As this scenario suggests—and as gay men seem to universally acknowledge—gay men embody a fundamentally different energy. And that energy is decidedly more feminine.

The Three Dimensional Masculine-Feminine Model

With these three dimensions, we can construct what I term the Three Dimensional Masculine-Feminine Model (see below). We can use this model as an informal self-reporting tool to create a richer sense of our masculine and feminine traits. To measure the personality traits dimension, a respondent would identify those masculine and feminine traits that are typical of his personality—ways he usually behaves by default. He would add up the total number of masculine and feminine traits he selected, then place himself on a scale of 1 to 9, where 1 represents completely masculine and 9 represents completely feminine. If he possesses an equal number of masculine and feminine traits, he would rank himself at 5, indicating an equal balance. If he possesses more masculine than feminine traits, his score would move correspondingly closer to 1. If he has more feminine than masculine traits, his score would move correspondingly closer to 9.

For external traits, a respondent would identify those traits in the Voice/Speech, Body Movements/Posture, and Style of Dress columns that apply to him. He would add up the totals for each column. Using those totals and his gut as a guide, he would place himself on a scale of 1 to 9 on this dimension. If masculine and feminine are fairly in balance, he would assign himself a 5. If more masculine external traits tend to manifest in him, he would place himself on the masculine side of this scale. If feminine external traits are more pronounced, he would place himself on the feminine side of the scale.

Self-assessment for energy involves a gut check and even a conversation with others: How would the people around this man describe his energy? Does he tend toward the dominant, passive, or collaborative? Would people describe him as aggressive, gentle, or somewhere in between? Is his energy sharper or softer? He would assign himself a number from 1 to 9.

Graphically, the model appears as follows:

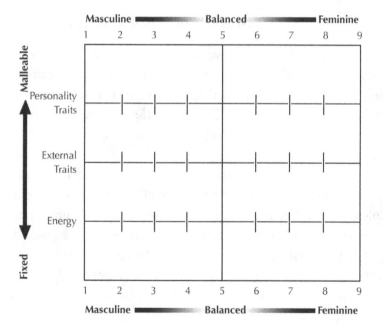

The Three-Dimensional Masculine-Feminine Model

A typical heterosexual man's Three Dimensional profile might look like this:

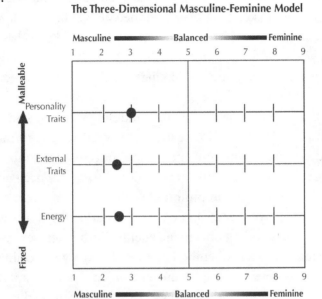

A typical gay man's profile might look like this:

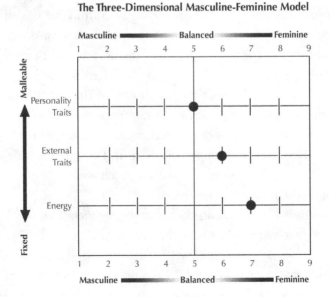

The key to this model, however, lies in the dynamic relationship among these three dimensions. If you ask a man to complete this profile after the parking ticket scenario mentioned above, the profile will veer toward the masculine. If he has just comforted a child who has skinned her knee, you would see a profile veer to the right—depending on his energy and masculine-feminine intelligence (MFI). The more MFI he possesses, the more fluid the personality traits become. The less MFI, the more this profile remains the same in different circumstances.

This fluidity forms the foundation of gay men's gifts to the world. Our decidedly more feminine energy, and our ability to move in and out of masculine and feminine personality traits as the need arises, enable us to serve humanity in profound ways.

Let's consider another example of how a personality trait can manifest differently depending on a man's energy. Both heterosexual and gay men are equally capable of embodying the decidedly masculine trait of competitiveness. Heterosexual men tend to manifest competitiveness more aggressively—with alpha energy. Think Wall Street, the corporate boardroom, and the military. They often manifest competitiveness with toughness and even ruthlessness. Gay men compete just as much, but tend to do so less aggressively.

Malcolm McLaren's song, *Deep in Vogue* illuminates this difference succinctly. In it, he includes a voiceover by the voguing dancer Willie Ninja, who explains the phenomenon of the fiercely competitive culture of balls among gay men of color in New York City in the late twentieth century: "Instead of fighting, they take it out on the dance floor."[13] Gay men's more feminine energy results in competitiveness without aggressiveness, a jockeying for position and prestige without the undercurrent of violence. This energy, as illustrated here and throughout the distinct gay male gifts, provides humanity with a much wider set of competencies through which to solve problems.

Masculine-feminine intelligence imbues gay men with the flexibility and fluidity that the world needs now more than ever. In 2013, John Gerzema and his colleague Michael D'Antonio published the results of a 13-country study involving 64,000 people regarding masculine and feminine traits. The authors conclude that, "*Feminine values are the oper-*

*ating system of 21ˢᵗ century progress...*This shift toward the feminine does not mean the end of men, but it does suggest a natural balancing that vastly increases the capacity of both men and women to solve problems and create a good life." In fact, 81 percent of respondents agreed with this statement: *"Man or woman, you need masculine and feminine traits to thrive in today's world."*[14]

The problem with masculinity, as most cultures currently understand it, is that it requires that men remain *inflexible*—to meet every circumstance with the same limited tools. In patriarchy, heterosexual men are allowed no counterbalancing feminine within themselves; women are expected to play this role, and they can only do so from afar. This is why the masculine shadow—aggression, violence, domination, and subjugation—runs our systems of governance, and why we could tip toward self-destruction. The current era challenges humanity to embrace balance, which requires restoring the feminine to its place of honor.

Gay men live between the masculine and feminine, embracing and employing them both. We have this balance hard wired, which is why our leadership is so essential to restoring balance to the planet. We can serve not just as models for this balance, but teachers. To the extent that personality traits are malleable, one can learn compassion, sympathy, understanding, and so on. As such, gay men can teach all men how to access their feminine as well as their authentic masculine (the masculine without the shadow). Heterosexual men may never embody the kind of fluidity that gay men possess, due to a stronger presence of the masculine energy, but they can learn to access those parts of themselves that our patriarchal culture has told them are off limits. When straight men release their fear of the feminine, they will find their lives greatly enriched.

Masculine-feminine intelligence has enormous utility, as we will see in the following chapters, but it also makes the road for gay men more challenging to traverse. For this intelligence upends patriarchy—and the patriarchs aren't happy about it.

Embracing the Feminine and Masculine

Gay men have a complicated relationship with the feminine. While we possess more feminine energy as a group, we live in a society that tells us that this core essence of ourselves is wrong. We may have confronted the taboo of homosexuality and turned it into pride, but we still wrestle with the feminine within each of us—our energy, our personality traits, and most of all, our external traits. The feminine remains the last taboo for gay men to overturn.

For effeminate men, this road is both shorter and more painful. When one is instantly pegged as gay based on external traits, the closet becomes less a hiding place than a temporary SRO. Effeminate gay men cannot hide like men who have more masculine appearances. And as such, they have led the way. The drag queens have given us the permission to embrace, appreciate, and love the feminine. Effeminate gay men are owed a debt of honor and gratitude for this leadership.

For many gay men, denial around the feminine still runs deep. Open any gay dating website or application, and you will see a preponderance of ads professing and expressing preference for masculinity. Yet, for all of our struggle, gay men are miles ahead of heterosexual men when it comes to embracing the feminine within. As the following chapters will illustrate, we are on intimate terms with the feminine, and in many ways honor and employ it with great aplomb.

As members in one of my groups determined, when gay men embody the full integration of masculine and feminine, we reclaim our authenticity. We recover the joy that we knew and gave freely as little boys. The path ahead requires just as much forward-thinking vision as it does reclaiming the essence of who we were when we entered this world as children.

Serving and Healing

Chapter 5
A Gentle, Collaborative
"Social Orientation"

G ay men exhibit a range of characteristic traits that emerge well
before puberty—sensitivity, gentleness, kindness, peacefulness,
non-violence, empathy, and a collaborative, cooperative orientation. We tend to be considerate and accommodating. As Harry Hay
described it, "What begins as an unformed disposition toward non-aggressiveness, favoring homosexual orientation, ends in a special form
of consciousness. It is this consciousness...that is the source of social
contribution of gays."[15]

From an early age, gay boys are fundamentally different. Because
children's work is play, these traits tend to show up in the ways that
young gay boys like to play. Most gay boys, when allowed to express
themselves freely, will either gravitate toward play typically associated
with girls or engage in gender-typical play in a gentler manner. For gay
boys of my generation, that meant choosing Barbie over GI Joe, an
Easy-Bake Oven over a toy gun. These seemingly simple choices be-
lie the very different "social orientation" that gay boys come equipped
with—we gravitate toward gentleness and nurturing, not aggression.

Even when we engage in play associated with heterosexual boys, our
more feminine energy changes how we participate in those activities. A
typical gay boy who plays with Matchbox cars, for instance, will play
more gently and thoughtfully, while a typical straight boy will demonstrate more aggressiveness. In team sports, the typical gay boy tends to

exhibit less aggression and sometimes even displays confusion about his role in the game.

Consider the characteristics of gay boys who are drawn to historic preservation, as described by Will Fellows in his book, *A Passion to Preserve: Gay Men as Keepers of Culture*:

> "The profile of the boy who is not like other boys emerges in one after another of these men's stories. He is unusually sensitive, gentle, well-mannered, mature, attracted to reading and other quiet activities, to music and art, to homey things and homemaking activities."[16]

Give or take a trait, this descriptor could easily apply to the majority of gay boys. Indeed, this range of traits implies what is missing in the typical gay boyhood—interest in competitive sports. In fact, the widespread lack of interest in competitive sports among gay boys is one of the more apparent manifestations of our more collaborative social orientation. Because the feminine traits of compassion and empathy come naturally to us, achieving victory over another in competitive sports means that we end up hurting another. Being forced into this form of competition is so antithetical to most gay boys' social orientation that gym class often becomes a source of considerable pain, discomfort, and alienation in the typical gay boy's childhood. Rather than achieve dominance over another, which competitive sports call for, we would rather get along.

In what is almost a side note, David Halperin, in his book *How to Be Gay* [17], affirms that the experience of being gay *precedes* sexual awakening. He devotes a chapter to gay men's affinity for musical theater, citing D.A. Miller's 1998 book, *Place for Us*. In this chapter, he explores how, especially for the pre-Stonewall generation, this art form gave gay boys growing up in the 1950s a "figurative language in which to give systematic...expression to 'those early *pre-sexual* realities of *gay* experience.'" Fellows' preservation-minded gay men echo these sentiments as well. As I have observed personally and through reports from men in my groups, the gay experience—and the feeling of being profoundly different—begins at a very young age.

As with all generalizations, exceptions and variations always exist. Some boys with same-sex attraction manifest behaviors that more closely match those of boys with opposite-sex attraction. Some gay boys and men enjoy competitive sports, for instance. Some boys who gravitate toward more gentle pursuits will grow up to be heterosexual. Introverted and technically-oriented boys are a good example here. Heterosexual men who embody gay men's egalitarian social orientation are highly prized by and sought after by heterosexual women—they are the exceptional men many a straight woman hopes to find. The key is noticing the sum total of their behaviors and the underlying energy. Often, the clues will predict homosexuality—but again, not always.

So let's explore these behaviors and traits as they appear in gay men as adults. Men in Gay Men of Wisdom groups had this to say:

- We are good listeners.

- We are understanding.

- We have good communication skills.

- We are attuned to our intuition.

- Gay men are consensus builders.

- We tend to be more egalitarian.

- We have a deeper understanding of difference and diversity.

- We possess sensitivity to difference and a greater acceptance of other ways of being.

- We have a greater awareness of and sensitivity to difference in other people, and we value it.

- We have a greater openness to diversity and difference—not just tolerance.

- We have a shared understanding of what other minorities experience—and an interest in understanding them.

- We have a curiosity for people who are different.

- We have compassion and empathy; we are more empathetic.

- Gay men are loving, familial, nurturing, and supportive.

- We are sensitive and more emotional.

- We have emotional intelligence. (Wikipedia defines this as the ability to monitor one's own and other people's emotions, to discriminate between different emotions and label them appropriately, and to use emotional information to guide thinking and behavior.)

- We are less competitive. When we compete, we do so differently.

- We don't use our power to control others. Rather, we guide and develop the talent and potential in others. We inspire, teach, and lead collaboratively.

- We see people's potential. We empower others.

- We are willing to show our feelings, and willing to negotiate.

- We are oriented toward treating others equally.

- We see vulnerability as a strength.

- Part of the change that takes place is that we see things differently. Without us, valuable change does not happen.

- Many gay men lack interest in things associated with heterosexual men, like sports.

Two men described these traits as they manifest personally:

- "My leadership style is very consultative."

- "Aggressiveness is not the first way I operate with others."

David Nimmons, author of *The Soul Beneath the Skin: The Unseen Hearts and Habits of Gay Men*, captures the peaceful essence of gay men when he describes us as having "the least publicly violent male culture in the world." He supports this assertion through analysis of police data in areas where gay bars are located. Among police, the peaceable nature of gay men is well known. Brawls practically never happen in gay bars, so police know that they do not need to deploy the resources that are required to deal with violence in heterosexual bars. The only violence that occurs around a gay bar is usually outside, and at the hands of gay bashers. Considering gay boys' natures, this would stand to reason: these traits carry through to adulthood.

The Houses of New York

One of the best ways to understand gay men's different and gentler social orientation is to observe us in our "native" habitat: those places where we create unique, gay male social structures free of interference from the heterosexual world. In Chapter 14, we will consider how gay men's cruising patterns intersect with our attunement to the beauty of the natural world in places like Provincetown and Fire Island. Here, let's examine a social structure that gay men created in one of the least gay-hospitable environments.

During the violent crack epidemic of the 1980s and early 1990s in Harlem, African-American and Latino gay men and transgender people created a world that revolved around extravagant, competitive balls. As captured in the beautiful and poignant 1991 film, *Paris Is Burning*, performers in drag and all manner of artifice (known as "realness") paraded, walked, and vogued on the floor, aiming for prestige, respect, and top honors. While the crack epidemic unleashed unprecedented theft, violence, and murder around them, gay men in the inner city *created culture*. They used their talents to impress and dazzle each other, and to transcend the hopelessness and despair of poverty, violence, and pain from the homophobic families who discarded them.

These gay men created houses—families of choice headed by a "mother," who served a nurturing and responsible function for the men and trans people in her charge. To become a house mother, one had to establish a distinctive style and reputation for excellence on the floor at the balls. Gay men chose their house based on the mother whom they related to and respected most. The film's interviews with the house mothers conveyed the love that they had, and the care that they took of their members. These chosen families had a distinct matriarchal and feminine quality, characterized by love, care, mutual support, and non-violence.

While these houses may have had fierce rivalries with each other, and the queens developed creative ways of insulting each other ("throwing shade" and "reading," for example), they channeled these rivalries into art and creative expression. Even in this competitive setting, organizers created a seemingly endless array of categories, giving as many participants as possible a way to demonstrate and gain recognition for their talent. This type of inclusive competition represents an important contribution to humanity: rather than perpetuate the painful—and ultimately patriarchal—dichotomy of total victory and crushing defeat, we can acknowledge exceptional talent and still honor what each person has to offer.

The ball culture and the house structure serve as remarkable displays of the resilience of gay men living under extremely difficult circumstances. They provide some of the clearest evidence of gay men's more collaborative, gentle social orientation—and a reminder that, because we show up in every group in the human family, these traits have global implications.

You'd Never Suspect He Was Gay

With this deeper understanding of gay men's social orientation, let's consider how typically "heterosexual" traits might manifest among gay men. A gay man may be just as athletic and competent on the field as a heterosexual man, for instance, but off the field he may be the consensus-builder on the team. He may exhibit a sweetness and friendliness that endears him. Or he may be the boy who listens to and serves as a confidante for others. This seems to be true even among those boys who actively hide their gentler social orientation through bullying and acting "straight."

Consider Michael Sam, the first openly gay player in the National Football League. He has been widely and deservedly lauded for his incredible courage in coming out—indeed, for overcoming immense hardships in his life. The media have devoted less attention to other elements of his character, but a 2014 *New York Times* article provides intriguing insights. The article recounts the story of when Sam came to the aid of a longtime friend who had been punched in the mouth outside a local mall. When Sam saw his friend hurt, Sam found and confronted the attacker not by hurting him, but by lifting the offender into the air to scare him. As the article stated, capturing the consensus among his friends, Sam is "a natural peacemaker."[18]

An article on the website *Bleacher Report* acknowledges the dual elements of Sam's personality:

> Sam may also be the poster child for the dichotomy between who a player is on the field and who he is off. The warrior, the monster, the animal is also the comedian and the singer. He's the guy who "creates a remix to any song," defensive end Shane Ray said, and will spend an entire practice belting it out. He's also the teammate who recognizes that football is just a game. He interacted with Missouri fans and alumni, consistently kept teammates relaxed and loose during practice and played with an infectious joy.[19]

Seeing Michael Sam speak and smile, one can't help but notice a sweetness and a kindness to him. This trait inspires others. In interviews, people who know him praise his leadership style, speak glowingly of him, and use a word rarely heard in the world of professional sports to describe their feelings for him: "love." Here, we see how a gay man can defy gay norms and still possess a different social orientation. He may be competitive on the field, but he is not moved to violence. He may be loud and boisterous, but he is friendly and kind. Indeed, Sam appears capable of engaging his masculine and feminine masterfully, giving permission to everyone around him to be themselves.

When gay men own and honor our differences, we will give parents the cultural permission to become more aware of and attuned to what constitutes classic traits of gay boys—even if their social orientation appears more subtly, such as it appears to in Sam's case. As the Outreach Program for Children with Gender-Variant Behaviors and their Families at the Children's National Medical Center advises, we know that most boys who manifest strong and persistent gender-variant behaviors will grow up to be gay adults.[20] With this knowledge, parents can normalize these traits and create permission for their boys to be exactly as they are—whether they awaken to heterosexuality or homosexuality. Our expanded identity can give parents the permission they need to create pathways to this discovery, and even coming-of-age rites. Imagine a world in which parents anticipate the discovery of whether their boy is gay or heterosexual as much as they do their sex at birth—for parents will know that their gay sons' social orientation will carry through to adulthood and manifest in special and distinct gifts to the family and humanity.

Subject-SUBJECT Consciousness

In 1976, Harry Hay presented a new theory about what makes gay people different: subject-SUBJECT consciousness. This theory, which synthesized Hay's long-held Marxist convictions with his growing sense of gay consciousness, has at its core an observation he made about feeling different as a gay child: "Boys seemed to consider girls merely as sex objects, to be manipulated into giving in, and the girls, for that matter, seemed to think of the boys as objects, too. But HE whom I would *love* would be another ME—not an object, but another *subject*."

Hay therefore proposed that, "The egalitarian bond of love and sex between two similars [subject-SUBJECT]…went on to pervade all the relationships of a gay person." Heterosexuals, in contrast, who experience those they desire sexually as others— as "objects"—manipulate and coerce each other in order to obtain what they want (subject-OBJECT). This tendency translates into behaviors outside of romance and sex.

Will Roscoe, who edited Harry Hay's writings, provides insight into this theory that also seems to temper it: "In a society founded on the inequality of the genders, relations *within* genders tend to be where ideals of equality are developed and practiced...Not oriented toward the opposite sex the way our peers are, we sometimes escape indoctrination into the habit of viewing others as objects, sexual or otherwise."[21]

Hay's theory speaks to gay men's distinctly different social orientation. Men in Gay Men of Wisdom groups made similar observations— that gay men relate to other people and view the world in ways that are more collaborative and egalitarian. We have a characteristic gentleness, compassion, and non-aggressiveness. In fact, these traits typically emerge in gay boys before puberty, providing the first clues for parents that their son might be gay. With this understanding, we can argue that *social and sexual orientations constitute two distinct and characteristic manifestations of gay boys and men.* Parents can't definitively know that a boy is gay until he reaches puberty, but if they understand the concept that some boys have a different *social orientation*, they can create pathways that normalize and allow him to express it. This has the potential to influence parenting styles for future generations.

In a society that honors sex—and does not demonize it, like ours does—gay men's social orientation would appear much more clearly and visibly to us. I envision that, in the future, gay men will be known perhaps more for their social orientation than for their sexual orientation.

The Implications of a Tribe of Peaceful, Collaborative Men

Gay men are a global presence. We are born into families in every society. As adults, we may choose to move into cities and locales where the social climate is friendlier and where we can thrive. But the fact is that gay men populate every society in the world. To my mind, this dispersion is no accident. Without our leadership, masculinity and aggressiveness run amok. We are humanity's naturally occurring peacemakers, dispatched to help every society achieve balance.

Consider the ripple effects of a tribe of peaceful, gentle men who value collaboration, cooperation, and differences. The more gay men come out, and the more freely we express our innate gifts, the more peace and collaboration spread. Differences are appreciated rather than crushed. One of the most potent ways nations could advance peace would be to ensure they have a flourishing gay male community. This would mean creating a welcoming environment, establishing basic protections that all members of the majority enjoy, and actively seeking openly gay men for leadership positions.

As the world shrinks, sensitivity, kindness, gentleness, collaboration, and cooperation become even more important to human survival and welfare. While heterosexual men ponder ways to introduce emotional intelligence into the corporate world—and pat themselves on the back for their innovativeness—most gay men come pre-wired with this trait. Our sensitive, cooperative orientation makes us superb leaders. As John Gerzema's research points out, leadership in today's world requires not just emotional intelligence, but the masculine-feminine intelligence that gay men naturally possess.

Kirk Synder captures this in his book, *The G Quotient*, which he discusses in an article on *The Huffington Post*. "After recently completing a five-year research project spanning more than 3,000 working professionals all over the country," he writes, "I found reported levels of job engagement, job satisfaction and workplace morale among employees reporting to white-collar gay men to be upwards of 35 percent higher than nationally reported statistics."[22] He posits that openly gay male managers and executives offer a specific and effective model of leadership characterized by seven principles: inclusion, creativity, adaptability, connectivity, communication, intuition, and collaboration. These create higher levels of job satisfaction and workplace morale among employees of gay managers.[23]

In typically male-dominated fields, for instance, gay men's social orientation, which rests upon masculine-feminine intelligence, brings balance to environments where collaboration is often last on the agenda. We shift perspectives, open minds and hearts, and make these environments more agreeable for everyone. My partner, who works in construction and real estate development—an unmistakably macho field—is known for maintaining high expectations and holding his colleagues and contractors accountable. But he takes the time to listen to people, to allow them to have their feelings, and to compromise when needed. Like Michael Sam, he is the peacemaker, collaborator, consensus-builder, and leader. Most heterosexual men in his line of work adhere to the typical "my-way-or-the-highway" pattern of business. As a man with masculine-feminine intelligence, he introduces new ways of relating to others in this male-dominated industry.

Here, we see how gay men have more impact when they come out and give themselves permission to express the whole range of who they are. While it would be impossible to conduct such a study on closeted gay men, we can conjecture that, similar to what men in the Gay Men of Wisdom groups self-report, leaders who are closeted about their sexuality would tend to be more guarded, dimming expression of any traits that might give them away. We could imagine that closeted gay male leaders would likely have less of an impact on employee satisfaction and morale. Taken further, those in the grip of self-hatred might turn these traits into their opposites—much like the closeted politician who votes against gay rights.

A gay man who embraces his different social orientation sets a powerful example for all those around him. When he claims it solidly and without need for explanation or apology, people around him respond to his certainty. When we embrace these more feminine ways of being, we project the masculine traits of confidence and assertiveness. People around us take notice, even if they are not consciously aware of what they are picking up on. The gay man who fully owns these traits projects his gifts more powerfully, and has a greater impact on those around him. Our gentle, collaborative social orientation illuminates how gay men possess a vast, untapped resource for solving the world's problems.

Chapter 6
An Orientation toward Service

"How many of us are schoolteachers, shamans, prie§ts, and mini§ters; how many of us are in service capacities? An enormous number, completely disproportionate. When I marched with Martin Luther King and worked in the civil rights movement, I met so many gays."
—Malcolm Boyd, openly gay Episcopal priest[24]

We have explored how gay men's masculine-feminine intelligence forms the basis for nearly every distinct gift we bring to the world. We have established that gay men possess not only a different sexual orientation, but that we have a distinct *social* orientation that counteracts and provides an alternative to patriarchy. Here, we explore gay men's orientation toward service.

Gay men care for, serve, and heal the world. Our skills in the feminine traits of empathy, intuition, sensitivity, and mastery of emotions—and our masculine gifts for decisiveness, taking action, delivering on promises, and making thing happen—make us both highly attuned to people's feelings and skilled at responding to them. We not only sense people's needs, we possess the desire and aptitude to meet them. In our work lives, gay men's intuitiveness and assertiveness combine to make us supremely able to anticipate and meet customer, client, and patient needs. This balance—inherent in masculine-feminine intelligence—enables us to seamlessly move from the feminine to the masculine and back again at a moment's notice. For these reasons, gay men are masters of the service industry.

Viewed graphically, this mastery looks as it appears in the chart below. (Note that only the first feminine trait and the first masculine trait directly relate to each other.)

Traits that Make Gay Men
Masters of the Service Industry

Feminine Traits	Masculine Traits
Ability to sense and anticipate people's needs	Ability and desire to respond to people's needs
Ability to be a confidante	Ability to organize, bring order, direct processes
Attunement to beauty, creators of beauty	Accountability: holding ourselves and others accountable
Capacity to understand and validate people's emotions	Assertiveness
Collaborative orientation	Best-little-boy-in-the-world approach to excellence
Empathy	Decisiveness
Intuitiveness	Delivering on promises
Nurturing	Desire to make things better for others
Providing a non-judgmental mirror/seeing people for who they are	Making things happen/taking action
Sensitivity	Mastery of a given service profession or field's competencies

Gay men's service orientation manifests most visibly in the fact that we are a disproportionately large presence in professions that center on taking care of, nurturing, and healing others. It appears in more subtle forms as well. Gay men bring healing into the most pedestrian of services, and into careers that do not necessarily call for service. It extends into every facet of gay men's personal lives. In the nuclear and extended family, gay men often become caregivers for their elderly parents.

This pervasive service orientation arises from two things: 1) the unique position that we occupy in the human family—the place between the masculine and feminine, and as outsiders in society and even in our own families of origin; and 2) a genuine and strong desire to do good in and for the world. Below, I'll explore this unique position and our desire to do good.

In Between and Outside

Gay men occupy the place between the masculine and feminine. We are men, but we know the feminine intimately. This gives us unique access to the inner worlds of heterosexual men and women, without the need for a translator. Thus, we are the bridge between men and women. From this in-between and outsider place, we see men and women for who they are, and we mirror that back without judgment. This gift brings healing into our every human interaction.

As Christian de la Huerta notes, "As outsiders, queer people help society to more accurately perceive itself."[25] As Harry Hay put it, "Because we Queers need nothing from either Hetero men or Hetero women, we have learned to see them as *they would like to be seen*—in make-up, in hairdress, in design, and in tailoring, for instance.... We have learned over the centuries *to listen to them non-judgmentally*."[26] Gay men are humanity's sounding board.

Men in Gay Men of Wisdom groups had this to say:

• Gay men provide a non-judgmental mirror for others—for women, especially.

• Our in-between/outside perspective allows us to see others for who they are.

• We look at the world in a fundamentally different way. This enables us to produce innovations.

• We understand men's and women's side of things.

• I can help both sides see each other's side—gently—and I help them see the larger picture.

• I have the gift for reflection. I want to share that with others.

• We are the people who can look at "both/and," not just "either/or."

• It is easy for us to help straight men understand women. We can talk to men because we are men. We can talk with women because we understand them intrinsically. We are the bridge.

• Straight men have questions about women—they don't understand them. Men and women process things differently. Women have to talk things out. We understand women.

• We are the counselors and mediators between men and women.

• We have the kind of access to women that straight men are denied.

• Our dual natures give us understanding of both men and women. This has made us particularly effective therapists. It is a very useful perspective to help deal with problems.

• I model how to find the middle ground. I help people see the world differently. I help them see that you can control your reactions to things.

• We have an inherent in-betweenedness.

• We are nurturers and populate the caring and helping professions: nursing, therapists, hairdressing, flower arranging.

• The kind of person who gives care to others is not the kind that wants to wage battles or wars.

• We are the confidantes (the listener, the priest). A gay man is someone you can cry to.

• Gay men demonstrate the "Best Little Boy in the World" syndrome.

• Gay men are the organizers.

• Gay men are caretakers/caregivers. Our response to the AIDS crisis was one manifestation of that impulse.

• We are the counselors.

• We are trustworthy.

• We create a psychic space for others in which to be themselves. We create room for people. We allow them to be themselves.

• We are renovators of people.

• In the family constellation, gay men often become caregivers for their elderly parents. Many are supremely gifted here.

• Who do you want to speak to when you really need to talk? A gay man, naturally.

A Desire to Do Good: The Best Little Boy in the World

In 1973, Andrew Tobias published the now-classic tale of growing up gay, *The Best Little Boy in the World*, under the pen name John Reid. This book named a phenomenon that gay men knew all too well—the desire among so many gay men to overcompensate in excellence as a means of proving themselves, winning the world's love and approval, and, more importantly, combating the self-loathing of internalized homophobia. Forty years later, this phenomenon still resonates with gay men, and it even surfaced in Gay Men of Wisdom discussion groups.

Without a doubt, gay boys' and men's overcompensation originates from and reinforces anguish: once excellence is achieved, the voice of self-loathing returns to find a new target for self-doubt, thus perpetuating the cycle. Until the underlying internal criticism and self-hatred are resolved, the pattern continues.

Gay men are not the only ones to suffer from this syndrome; it is common among many African-Americans, who learn from white society that there is something inherently wrong with them and that they must be exceptional in order to be deemed acceptable. Even today, women still face barriers in the work world that leave them behind, giving contemporary credence to the old saying, "I have to work twice as hard to get half as far." Gay men, African-Americans, women, and anyone else who finds themselves on the lower rungs of the hierarchical ladder all wrestle with negative judgments of their self-worth, and thus remain susceptible to this phenomenon.

But there's something different about the way gay boys and men manifest the best-little-boy-in-the-world syndrome, and the gusto with which we embrace it. Who strives to be more perfect than an over-compensating gay boy? Gay boys and men *want* to excel. Among many of us, there exists a drive toward perfection, or at least very high standards. It shows up in the exquisite beauty that gay men create; in the way we care for our bodies; in our fastidiousness; and in the trends in fashion and style we set.

The popular ABC television show *Modern Family*, which began airing in 2009, features a gay couple, Cam and Mitchell, who adopt a girl. The show lampoons Cam and Mitchell's perfectionism—whether it means having to throw the most fabulous parties or being the most flawless parents for their adopted daughter. The joke always lands squarely on Cam and Mitchell for being incredibly uptight—though their perfectionism usually results in a display of excellence, whether that be hosting a party or parenting. But lest we dismiss this depiction as merely a caricature, a 2014 op-ed by Frank Love in *The Advocate*, the national LGBT news magazine, bristles against gay men's perfectionism when it comes to parenting. This "meme," as he describes it, pressures gay men to leave the bars and clubs behind so that they become the best possible parents. Love rails against this idea, seeing no dissonance between having a life and being a responsible parent. "Does being a dad mean I also have to be perfect?" he asks. "Why do gay parents have to live up to a ridiculous standard created by the gay community?"[27] Here, the best little boy in the world grows up to be the best gay father in the world.

When gay men's drive for perfection meets our social orientation, it produces exquisite service, caregiving, and healing for others. Apart from the desire for love and acceptance, this drive speaks to how *gay men truly want to excel and be of service*. We *want* to do good in the world and make it a better place. At its productive core, the best-little-boy-in-the-world phenomenon highlights the gay male orientation toward service excellence.

While this syndrome seems a natural fit for so many gay boys, it is worth noting other potential responses to feeling less-than: bullying, acting out, entering gangs, being self-destructive, taking risks, staging a mass shooting at one's high school, and so on. While some gay boys might take these routes, these responses fall outside the typical gay boy's orientation. Instead, for so many gay boys, we see an adaptive and very telling response: a widespread pattern of excelling in the direction of service. Gay men's gentler, collaborative social orientation, it seems, primes us to not only be attuned to others' needs but also predisposed to wanting to help others meet them.

Mastery in Professional Service

As men in my groups began to articulate, gay men fill the range of healing arts and services. Many of these fields require the feminine gifts of having an attentive listening ear—the art of being a confidante—along with the masculine trait of providing service. Gay men excel in both. We disproportionately fill the ranks of:

- Therapists

- Social workers

- Psychiatrists and psychologists

- Coaches

- Personal trainers

- Chiropractors, massage therapists, and body workers

- Opticians

- Physicians, physician assistants, and nurses

- Healers of many types

- Teachers

- Mediators

- Priests

- Hair stylists

- Flight attendants

- Event managers

- Realtors

- Flower arrangers

- Interior designers

- All the hospitality professions, including waiters, maître d's, hotel managers, bed-and-breakfast proprietors, and so on.[28]

As with all generalizations about the 14 Distinct Gay Male Gifts, exceptions abound. Gay men are not the only ones to fill these career roles. We are not the only ones who can and do heal. And, of course, not all gay men possess these gifts. Our disproportionately large representation in these professions, however, speaks to commonalities and visible trends. *How* we fill these roles—and the drive to fill them in the first place—speaks volumes about who gay men are.

Men with a gentle, collaborative social orientation fill professional service roles differently from those with more traditional, hierarchical, patriarchal values. I want to hire the realtor who will listen to my needs, for instance, rather than the man (or woman) who is only interested in the sale. A teacher who understands, nurtures, and encourages his students—yet holds them to high standards—will have a far greater positive impact than the strict, demanding teacher who remains emotionally aloof. Anyone can work in a service industry, but only masters possess mastery. Only healers can heal. This requires a firm grasp of both the feminine and masculine.

Some of the service fields gay men fill draw more from the feminine than the masculine, and some require the gift of attunement to beauty in order to achieve mastery. Chiropractic and massage therapy, for instance, require a fairly equal balance of feminine and masculine traits, with no specific requirements for attunement to beauty. Floral arrangement and hair styling demand attunement to beauty, and draw heavily on feminine traits. Running a successful business in these fields necessitates as many masculine traits as feminine.

As a life coach, I have been captivated by this profession's personal development tool, which owes its modern form to the work of Thomas Leonard, a gay man. With an action-oriented focus, life coaching requires equal balance between the masculine and feminine—as much empathy and intuitiveness as accountability and ability to respond to a client's needs. Not surprisingly, coaching draws large numbers of gay men and straight women—a common phenomenon in service-oriented professions.

In my gay men's coaching circles, I have colleagues who coach heterosexual male corporate executives and CEOs—and they are exceptionally good at doing so. These coaches give their clients what they cannot get from the men in their lives: the emotional intelligence to validate their experience; the permission to have and express their feelings; and the chance to be vulnerable with another man. At the same time, these coaches hold their clients firmly accountable and help them deliver the kind of leadership that the corporate world requires. This leadership, as Kirk Snyder and John Gerzema point out, requires both masculine and feminine traits. Who better to teach these to heterosexual men than gay men?

In this instance, gay men's service orientation resembles the model presented in *Queer Eye for the Straight Guy*, the Bravo television show that ran from 2003 to 2007—without the tongue in cheek or the cringe factor. In the executive coach role, gay men lead and serve (without the ironic implication) straight men—as only another man can do. It is a role that gay men will play more of—and more consciously—when we become aware of our unique gifts and roles in the human family. Indeed, gay men have the capacity to help straight men heal. When we do so—and when we honor our capacity to heal and lead all men—we will heal ourselves. This will draw straight and gay men together, helping us honor our respective roles in the world and discover our commonalities.

The Wounded Healer

Masculine-feminine intelligence and our gentle, collaborative social orientation prime gay men to be natural healers. Our woundedness makes us especially competent in this role. The outsider position we occupy, compounded by our painful journey to survive, along with the death and rebirth we experience coming out, equip gay men to help others along their journey to healing.

Men in Gay Men of Wisdom groups had the following to say about this:

- Coming out made me evolve and grow. Healing the wound of being hurt for being gay allows me to have more compassion for others. I can empathize more easily.

- I show empathy for people in pain. I give support to others.

- I have the inclination and ability to help those who need help.

- We have a gift for being able to validate non-normative experiences and relationships people have. Because we have had the experience of being not recognized, we can witness those experiences in others.

- We assist people in normalizing their experiences—people who feel alone, who feel like they are the only one, and who feel crazy. We say, "I can understand how you would feel that way."

• I've had to hold myself up. I learned how to tell the truth about myself. This made me sensitive to injustices.

• I'm more me, which gives people permission to be more them.

• Sharing our vulnerability by coming out is very healing.

• Woundedness makes us especially insightful healers.

• The deepest truth is that I am not wounded. I have been given a journey to learn from.

The Gay Hero's Journey is a modern-day initiation into a contemporary form of shamanism. Today, gay men play roles similar to the sacred and healing functions that shamans played historically in native cultures. Thanks to the work of gay scholars, we now know that men whom we would consider gay today occupied many of these roles in native cultures historically and throughout the world. Denise and John Tully Carmody offer this insightful definition of a shaman:

> One who is a specialist in ancient techniques of ecstasy. The shaman normally is a functionary for a non-literate community, serving as its healer, intermediary with the gods, guide of the souls of the dead to their rest, and custodian of traditional tribal lore. The typical shaman comes to this role through either heredity or having manifested idiosyncratic traits (epilepsy, sexual ambiguity, poetic sensitivity, dramatic dreams). Psychologically, shamans depend on an ability to function in two worlds, the ordinary reality of daily life and the extraordinary reality they encounter through their ecstatic journeys. As well, they serve their tribe as a defense of meaning, by incarnating a contact with the powers thought to hold the tribe's destiny.[29]

The path to shamanism varied greatly from culture to culture. Will Roscoe points out in his book *Jesus and the Shamanic Tradition of Same-Sex Love* that throughout northern Eurasia, "individuals became shamans as a result of a crisis—a life-threatening illness or injury, a dream, a vision, or in its most extreme form, a seizure." The initiation of the shaman involves "suffering or torment resulting in symbolic death followed by rebirth."[30] This initiation mirrors the suffering and torment that the people who come to the shaman for help are experiencing. His journey gives him the tools to lead others to healing.

Shamanism is simply an older set of healing modalities. Common features can be observed between it and contemporary modalities. In his book, Roscoe includes anthropologist Claude Lévi-Strauss' analysis of a South American Indian curing ceremony. Lévi-Strauss found remarkable similarities between it and psychotherapy. In this ceremony, the shaman makes patients conscious of their psychological experience by portraying their suffering through symbols and myths. By making this suffering explicit and giving it meaning, the shaman is able to validate patients' emotional situation, make the pain that they are enduring acceptable, and help them achieve "release of the physiological process" they are experiencing. The shaman then reintegrates the experience of illness back into a meaningful whole.

In this ceremony, as in psychotherapy, the practitioner "seek[s] to establish communication between conscious and unconscious mind, although in psychotherapy, the patient provides his or her own myth, while in shamanic healing this is provided by the shaman." As Roscoe states, "identification with others is essential to empathy—the ability to sympathetically feel the experience of another—which is recognized as one of the most important skills of therapists."[31] In this native ceremony, we see the parallel between ancient and modern forms of healing.

Randy Conner's book *Blossom of Bone: Reclaiming the Connections between Homoeroticism and the Sacred* describes how gay men have been shamans throughout the ages.[32] We have endured initiation rites that have varied over time and cultures, always reflecting some core need in a given society and time period. Homophobia gives us our contemporary initiation into the shaman's journey. Through it, we process humanity's deepest wounds, which result from patriarchy: the devaluation and subjugation of the feminine, the dishonoring of sexuality, and violence. When we triumph from our personal death and rebirth journey, we become more able to heal others, just as the shamans of native cultures and past societies did.

Even after homophobia fades, gay men will likely always play the role of the outsider and shaman. Our rites of initiation will change with the times, but they will always reflect some core human need or lesson. Our position in the human family makes us intimate strangers with those in the majority—we know them better than they know us. By nature of being outside and in between, we will always need to learn how to navigate within the majority, in ways that the majority will never have to consider. This virtually ensures that, even in the best of times, gay men will experience some type of wound—which may change with the times—necessitating the shaman's journey of descent, death, and rebirth. Our predisposition to service means that from a very young age we will be primed and trained to help humanity learn its core lessons.

The Diminished and Devalued Role of the Gay Male Priest

The sad irony of gay men's orientation to service is that, while we are ideally suited for religious service, and gay men are a major presence in the ranks of religious leadership, the teachings of most religions explicitly reject us. Mark Thompson reminds us that gay men's relationship to Christianity has essentially been one of betrayal: churches have used our energies and gifts to fuel the spirit of religious service, and have burned, persecuted, and expelled us.[33]

This creates the unfortunate circumstance of intense secretiveness and a life of fear for gay men within religious ranks. If we use the Coming Out Continuum as a model to gauge impact on others, religious homophobia robs participants—and the world—of the benefits of gay men's unique gifts. This fundamental and flat rejection by the world's religions has fueled the Gay Hero's Journey for many gay men. The descent, death, and rebirth we have experienced have produced innovations in spirituality that can revive and refresh religion, making it once again much more relevant to humanity. Chapter 7 explores this further. Religious homophobia, however, produces much of gay men's pain—for lay people and those in leadership.

In *Gay Spirit: Myth and Meaning*, Malcolm Boyd, Mark Thompson's life partner, recounts his harrowing experience as a closeted gay man in the Episcopal priesthood from the 1950s to the 1970s:

> "Hiddenness was the name of the game…it was deadly for a priest to be open in the underground homosexual community of his city or town. Blackmail was a ready weapon; the insinuation of the possibility was even worse. Many gay priests were beloved within their parishes for their sensitivity, androgyny, gaiety of spirit, wisdom, wit, and sophistication…. Yet at the least suggestion of homosexuality, they could be simply and peremptorily dismissed."

And yet, Boyd pointed out, the church contained within it an unusually high proportion of gay men—a third or more of the hierarchy and clergy, according to his sources.[34] Boyd displayed remarkable courage when he came out in a 1976 *New York Times* interview. In recent years, the Episcopal Church has become one of the most LGBT-friendly Christian denominations, but it remains an outlier among the major churches. As the next chapter explores, religion remains the next frontier in the LGBT movement.

Chapter 7
Religious Reformers and Spiritual Leaders

For our ancestors, the worlds envisioned by their myths were obvious. The great bear was a god; the corn maiden was a goddess; the Sun was God....There was no conflict between observation and belief. The myth was the way to make sense of what was observed.

Today many religious world views disagree with observation. The major religion of the United States, Biblical-based Christianity, for instance, denies the fundamental discovery of science, in contradiction to evidence, that life evolved on Earth over a vast period of time. That's got it backward. The popular myth ought to incorporate evolution and give it a spiritual meaning, not deny it. How can a religion give guidance when it isn't in touch with reality?
—Toby Johnson[35]

Religion is notoriously resistant to change. In fact, most religions are purposefully designed to preserve and perpetuate a given creed, and to resist new developments that would call into question that creed's teachings. Religious leaders and faithful followers see it as their duty to maintain the integrity of those teachings and, in many cases, to convert "nonbelievers" to their creed. History is rife with epic battles between those seeking religious reform and resistant religious hierarchies; evangelical crusades by zealous missionaries to convert "non-believers"; and the use of armies, inquisitions, and other means to consolidate a religion's power and squelch change. While times and tactics may have changed, the intransigent nature of religion—and often the drive for wealth and power, disguised as evangelism—persists.

The mass liberation of gay men and lesbians presents for religion its newest and most potent challenge. Many of the world's creeds—developed centuries ago when the world looked very differently—explicitly or implicitly prohibit homosexuality. And yet, the presence of gay men and lesbians living openly demonstrates our humanity, our inherent goodness, and our essential contributions to the world. As understanding grows about natural variations in sexuality, and as people come to see gay men and lesbians as equal human beings, will religions revisit their doctrines, or will they continue to resist change? Will they use their power to expand understanding and inclusiveness, or will they use it to perpetuate judgment, exclusion, and harm? This question—and the conflict playing out within religions right now—forces a fundamental question about a religion's essence: Is it about love, or is it about power and control? A religion's actions—not its words—provide the answer.

Coming out has always been about freely expressing love—in its many forms. With courage and heart, gay men and lesbians expand humanity's definition of love. This has much more power than we realize—and we are much more powerful than we comprehend. Our enemies understand this better than we do. The Religious Right in the United States fights us with such vehemence and vitriol because they know we have the potential to drive religious reform—to tip the scales away from power and decidedly toward love. The fundamentalists will do everything in their power to stop us. And yet, history will reveal their ruse, making them seem as ridiculous as the Catholic Church for finding Galileo guilty of heresy for advancing the idea that the Earth revolves around the Sun. Since the gay liberation movement began in the 1950s, we have made considerable and, in some cases, astonishing progress toward religious reform.

At the same time, gay men's exile from mainstream religions—due to judgment, exclusionary doctrines, and hatred—has produced extraordinary spiritual innovation. By experimenting with spiritual paths that honor intuition, the body, sex, and the Earth, gay men are remaking spirituality. These innovations hold immense implications for spirituality, and they could remake religion.

Driving Religious Reform

Considering religion's intransigence, the effectiveness of gay men and lesbians in advancing religious reforms since the 1950s is nothing short of amazing. This portends greater shifts in the future—not just for LGBT inclusion, but for the wholesale rethinking of religious doctrines. It's worth considering a few highlights from these efforts.

Gay theology. Not long after the founding of the Mattachine Society in the United States, the earliest rumblings of a gay theology began to emerge. In 1955, Anglican Derrick Bailey published scholarly work that showed how errors of translation and emphasis had mistakenly cast the Sodom story as being about homosexuality, when it was actually about inhospitality.[36] In 1959, Church of Christ pastor Robert Wood published *Christ and the Homosexual*, which proposed that homosexuality might be nature's own check for overpopulation, and endorsed gay sex as probably necessary to self-expression.[37] According to scholar Rollan McCleary, the next decade would see an emerging gay theology characterized by assimilationist sensibilities. This wave, he says, "appealed for charity and consistency in Christian practice, and sought to mediate between the gay community and the church." As the gay rights movement became bolder, so too did gay theology, which increasingly called for equality in the face of refusal to ordain gay clergy.[38]

Reforms within Judaism. While many reform efforts emerged during early gay liberation, Judaism was the first major religion to respond to gay theology, beginning with the founding of the Beit Simchat Torah synagogue in New York in 1975. This was followed by the establishment of the World Organization of Gay and Lesbian Organizations in 1980. As McCleary states, "Jewish adaptation has been fast and remarkable, especially with regard to gay-specific Passovers, liturgies, and prayer books, and there has been theological support from gay and non-gay rabbis." The Reform branch of Judaism has increasingly questioned the original biblical prohibitions against homosexuality and has widely accepted reinterpretations of those texts.[39]

Metropolitan Community Church. In 1968, a year before the Stonewall riots, the former Pentecostal minister Troy Perry founded the Metropolitan Community Church (MCC). While not the first gay-centered church, it became the largest and fastest growing such church. Perry's autobiography, *The Lord Is My Shepherd, and He Knows I'm Gay,* gained considerable attention when it was published in 1972.[40] MCC now has 172 congregations throughout the world.[41]

The Roman Catholic Church. In 1969, Father Patrick Nidorf founded what became DignityUSA, a group advocating respect for LGBT people in the Catholic Church. This group, which specifically calls for change in the Catholic Church's teachings on homosexuality, has local chapters throughout the United States.[42] Stymied by the Vatican's refusal to reconsider church teachings against homosexuality, DignityUSA faces an uphill battle. Pope Francis' considerably more open position on gays, when compared to his predecessor, is a hopeful sign. For instance, in July 2013 the new pope garnered international attention when he said during an interview, "If someone is gay and he searches for the Lord and has goodwill, who am I to judge?"[43]

The pope's notably more compassionate statements toward gay men and lesbians won him the distinction as *The Advocate*'s 2013 Person of the Year. In October 2014, Pope Francis convened "an Extraordinary General Assembly of the Synod of Bishops on topics related to the family and evangelization." A draft report from this synod initially urged pastors to be more welcoming to gays, who have "gifts and qualities to offer to the Christian community." Conservative bishops derailed this greater openness in the final report, however. While this battle seems far from over, Pope Francis' greater openness has yet to translate into specific doctrinal changes.

Episcopal transformation. In 1974, Dr. Louie Crew founded Integrity, a group that advocates full inclusion of gays and lesbians in the Episcopal Church. Fast-forward to 2003, when Gene Robinson was elected as the first openly gay bishop in the Episcopal Church. This set off a storm of controversy, and the Episcopal Church received a rebuke from the Worldwide Anglican Communion the following year. Despite this pressure, in 2009 the Episcopal Church opened all orders of ministry to baptized LGBT members of the church and allowed bishops to bless same-sex unions at their discretion. In perhaps the most open, welcoming statement from any major Christian denomination, the Episcopal Church's website includes this unequivocal statement: "To our lesbian, gay, bisexual, and transgender brothers and sisters: 'The Episcopal Church welcomes you!'"[44]

Unitarian Universalists. With principles that widely embrace spiritual traditions from many sources and faiths, the Unitarian Universalists were early and natural advocates for inclusion of LGBT people. In 1970, the General Assembly of the Unitarian Universalist Association (UUA) passed its first resolution on the topic, urging all people and all member churches to end discrimination against homosexuals and bisexuals. This resolution addressed both church life and broader issues of discrimination in housing, employment, and the granting of federal security clearances and visas. Since then, the UUA General Assembly has passed numerous resolutions supporting LGBT issues, and in 1989 it created a Welcoming Congregation program. As of May 2012, there were 697 UU Welcoming Congregations in the United States (64 percent of U.S. congregations), and all but three Canadian congregations are recognized as Welcoming (94 percent).[45]

Voting with their feet. While LGBT people have pressured religions from within, and have experienced some success, a considerable number of people have left religion altogether, sending a very strong message to religions about their future viability. According to the Public Religion Research Institute, 37 percent of LGBT Americans are now unaffiliated with any religion, compared to 21 percent of Americans overall. Tellingly, 58 percent of Americans, and 70 percent of the Millennial generation, agree that religious groups are alienating young people by being too judgmental on gay and lesbian issues. Among Americans who left their childhood religion and are now religiously unaffiliated, about one-quarter say negative teachings about, or treatment of, gay and lesbian people was a somewhat important (14 percent) or very important (10 percent) factor in their decision to leave. Among Millennials who no longer identify with their childhood religion, nearly one-third say that negative teachings about, or treatment of, gay and lesbian people was either a somewhat important (17 percent) or very important (14 percent) factor in their disaffiliation from religion.[46]

Clearly, the gay issue is not the only factor driving people away from religion, and LGBT people are not the only ones leaving. In fact, Gallup polls found that the segment of Americans who said that religion is "not very important in my life" grew from 12 percent in 1992 to 22 percent in 2013.[47] Considering the staunchly religious nature of the United States, the fact that one-fifth of adults claim no religious affiliation points to the diminishing capacity of religion to provide meaning. In Europe, the trend away from religion is even more pronounced. In the Czech Republic, for instance, more than 60 percent of people say they never attend religious services, with the exception of special occasions, such as marriages and christenings; in France, Britain, and Belgium, this figure exceeds 50 percent. In The Netherlands, Spain, Sweden, Germany, and Estonia, church non-attendance levels range from 33 to 50 percent.[48] Within the birthplace of Christendom, religion is losing its hold.

When taken together, these developments speak to the power that gays and lesbians have to influence religious reforms, and to win allies to support these efforts. Religion's hierarchical and non-democratic structure, however, portends a longer struggle than in the political and legal realms. But the changes within religion are telling.

As more people leave religion entirely, spiritual movements have gained prominence. Unlike religion, spirituality lends itself to near-endless variation and personalization. Some spiritual paths contain organizing principles, while others do not. Within spirituality, no central authority exists. In this still-evolving and difficult-to-define realm, gay men have distinct contributions to make and leadership roles to play.

Spiritual Leadership

Spirituality presents a challenge to explore. While it speaks to a persistent human yearning, it is also deeply personal. It seems the term has as many definitions as there are people. Yet, to present a coherent discussion of spirituality, we need a definition that is both broad and inclusive. I like this one, drawn from the nursing literature:

> Spirituality is that which gives meaning to one's life and draws one to transcend oneself. Spirituality is a broader concept than religion, although that is one expression of spirituality. Other expressions include prayer, meditation, interactions with others or nature, and relationship with God or a higher power.[49]

This definition includes three important elements: 1) a search for meaning; 2) the desire to experience some form of transcendence; and 3) a practice, or form of expression. Harry Hay's original questions for the Mattachine Society—"Who are we? Where do we come from? What are we for?"—could thus be viewed as spiritual: they prompt a search for meaning. The intense repression and harsh legal climate of the 1950s would not support full-on gay spiritual inquiry, however. It would really not be until the first conference of Radical Faeries in 1979, which brought together all three elements and launched a distinctively gay male spiritual movement, that gay spiritual concerns gained national attention. Since then, explorers and teachers of all varieties have forged their own paths. While these paths contain wide variation, gay men's spirituality has distinct characteristics, which have broad implications for human spiritual exploration:

Discovering the self through group ritual. Gay spirituality began as an effort to discover gay men's true nature and purpose. In contrast with assimilationist thought, which holds that gay men are not appreciably different from anyone else—nor should they want to be—gay spirituality originally sought to discover or connect with those differences in the context of group activities, rituals, and transcendent experiences. These elements remain integral to gay spirituality, and many groups foster this search, as discussed below. This exploration has produced an unanticipated result: It has created a cadre of aware, loving, and spiritually advanced gay men. By discovering who we are on a deep level, gay men who follow these paths have become spiritual adepts, leading others to deeper appreciation of and value for themselves. Our path to self-discovery has made gay men spiritual leaders for humanity.

Honoring the body and sexuality as vehicles for transcendence. While Western religions teach the inherent sinfulness of the body, Eastern religions have long engaged the body as a vehicle for transcendence. Yoga and meditation, for instance, use the body in different ways to expand a person's consciousness. Gay men's spirituality borrows from Eastern traditions and provides a decidedly updated, sexually liberated, and unique gay male perspective on them.

Ready embrace of the Earth as a source of spiritual or divine essence. In Western religions, followers look to the heavens for their source of divinity, and creeds teach that God has spread the Earth before humans for the taking. This has produced rapacious environmental practices that now threaten the Earth's ecosystem. Indigenous spirituality honors and integrates the Earth as a source of life and divinity. Several gay male spiritual paths explicitly or implicitly honor the Earth and seek connection with it, borrowing from indigenous traditions. Through combining reverence for the sacred masculine, as represented by male sexual energy, and the feminine, as represented by the Earth, gay male spirituality has the potential to help humanity re-establish balance.

Our exile from religion and society produces deep reflection and a generous spirit. So many gay men have left religion due to rigid dogmas, judgmental religious leaders, and intolerant followers. This exile has forced gay men to question basic religious assumptions and to discover and create our own authentic spiritual paths. In the wake of the spiritual crisis that this exile imposes, gay male spirituality has produced a generous, loving, open-hearted, and inclusive ethos.

Flair for the theatrical. Gay men have long commented on how our flair for the theatrical shows up in organized religion, particularly in settings such as the Catholic and Episcopal churches, whose priests wear elaborate vestments and whose rituals contain dramatic elements. To see this drive in its native habitat, unfiltered and uncensored, one need only look to gay male spiritual practices. Gay men engaging in group spiritual inquiry use all of the gifts of drama and theater at their disposal. These gifts lend themselves to creating transcendent experiences and harken back to our roles as shamans in indigenous cultures.

Even though just a subset of gay men feel called to engage in specifically gay male spirituality, it remains difficult to capture the range of expression this realm involves. Because spirituality lends itself to personalization and individual experience, a complete overview would fall outside the realm of this exploration. Instead, by providing some highlights, I hope to capture the range and flavor of the gay male path to spirit, and its implications for human spirituality.

Radical Faeries. The first Spiritual Conference of Radical Faeries, held in Arizona in 1979, represented the culmination of Harry Hay's vision for gay men. The flyer for this event, which took place over Labor Day weekend, featured the headline, "A Call to Gay Brothers." It promised a blend of the spiritual, the radical, and the faerie, suggesting a synthesis of spirituality and politics, "beyond Left and Right," and assuring gays that they had a place in the paradigm shift of the New Age. In giving the inaugural speech, Hay invited the more than 200 participants to "tear off the ugly green frog skin of Hetero-male imitation…to reveal the beautiful Fairy Prince beneath."

This gathering set the tone for much of gay spirituality that would come later. The "Heart Circle," one of the few organized activities of the event, has since become a staple of nearly all gay male spiritual gatherings, representing, as Hay and his co-leaders Don Kilhefner and Mitch Walker proposed, a non-hierarchical, egalitarian sharing of feelings, concerns and intimacy. In the Heart Circle, men are allowed to speak openly and freely of themselves and their interior lives without fear of judgment or interruption. Stuart Timmons, Harry Hay's biographer, wrote of the event: "At the first Radical Faerie Circle...a spontaneous theme of paganism emerged. Invocations were offered to spirits; blessings and chants rose and fell. Some people shook rattles or clusters of tiny bells." Participants invoked spirits as varied as Peter Pan, Marilyn Monroe, "The Shadow of My Former Self," and even Kali. A spontaneous mud ritual emerged when more than fifty naked men went to a river hollow, made mud, and poured it on one another. They erected a large earth phallus on a man who was lying down and placed laurels on his head. They lifted the man in the air and began a procession in which they chanted "Om." The procession gave way to an extended period of ecstatic dancing, eventually ending with a baptism-like washing off of the mud. This ritual, participants reported, evoked a sense of returning to the gay male tribe of earlier eras.[50]

This first gathering launched the Radical Faerie "movement," a word that perhaps misrepresents faeriedom, but serves as the closest descriptor. Now, at Radical Faerie sanctuaries in rural settings around the world, and in local faerie circles, gay men gather to pursue this distinct form of spirituality. As Rollan McCleary observes, "Because there is an anarchic, consensual quality to the Radical Faeries, with considerable diversity of expression among different circles and no binding creed, it is hard to make a fair general assessment of their ideas and practice whether from published material or direct experience. It is almost easier today to say what Radical Faeries are not and don't believe than what they are and do believe."[51]

Christian de la Huerta describes the Radical Faeries as "gay men who share some basic neopagan beliefs such as the sacredness of nature and a respect for different paths to the Divine...The movement is flavored by Native American spirituality, and its members include a diverse bunch of Wiccans, Druids, and other traditions...Rituals are varied and incorporate elements from different pagan traditions...The celebration of life is a common theme; rituals often involve dance, music, meditation, fire, prayer, ritual music, sweat lodges, drumming, mud pits, [and] nudity... Sexuality and sensuality are honored and celebrated."[52]

Circles remain at the heart of gatherings, along with a near-universal (McCleary describes it as virtually compulsory) androgyny through drag. According to Bill Rodgers, known by his Faerie name Willow-fey—Faeries encourage each other to take on a "magic" name—"The faeries see that the principle of androgyny in members counteracts the need for male-female balancing…On a practical level, drag becomes ritually important, as a means of expressing the divine Androgyny in a physical form. The wardrobe becomes important for some faeries at gathering."[53]

The purposeful formlessness and anarchy of the Radical Faeries to-day, and their mysteriousness even to most gay men, make it difficult to gauge the implications and impact of this gay spiritual path. Certainly, the Faeries embrace and invite a wide diversity in gender identity, gen-der expression, and sexual orientation. The Faeries' often androgynous tribal rituals that loosely invoke indigenous and genderqueer sensibil-ities make this path a laboratory for deeply personal and communal exploration. Intriguingly, the Faeries' loose, non-specific, non-hierar-chical, egalitarian, and consensus-driven ethic also characterized the Occupy Wall Street movement that erupted in 2011. As with the Oc-cupy movement, the form (or lack thereof) itself may be the Faeries' greatest contribution today—a playful experimentation with models of human relations that provide alternatives to patriarchy.

The movement that began with the Radical Faeries has evolved into a diverse series of spiritual paths—groups and gatherings, organizations, and even individual practitioners bringing their unique gifts to gay men and the world. Consider a few examples:

Sisters of Perpetual Indulgence. The most closely related to the Radical Faeries of the various gay spiritual paths, the Sisters of Perpetual Indulgence applies and stretches drag's ability to both skewer and express sincere admiration for a given subject (a trait that I explore in Chapter 11). At first glance, this group seems to be a drag parody of nuns. Upon closer inspection, it becomes clear that it is something altogether differ-ent and entirely unexpected. The Sisters mix the conventions of drag—humor and nuns' habits being particularly pronounced—with sincerity in the form of a distinct mission. Its website states, "The Sisters of Perpetual Indulgence® is a leading-edge Order of queer nuns. Since our first appearance in San Francisco on Easter Sunday, 1979 [just prior to the first conference of Radical Faeries], the Sisters have devoted ourselves to community service, ministry, and outreach to those on the edges, and to promoting human rights, respect for diversity, and spiritual enlightenment. We believe all people have a right to express their unique joy and beauty and we use humor and irreverent wit to expose the forces of bigotry, complacency, and guilt that chain the human spirit."[54] This group has Orders around the world, though each has its own "Habits, cultures, and rules." Public performance, which blurs the lines between entertainment and provocation, along with service, characterize their activities.

The Sisters of Perpetual Indulgence provide another example of innovation and experimentation in gay spirituality. Indeed, one could argue that discussion about the Sisters should have been included elsewhere in the 14 Distinct Gay Male Gifts. I struggled with this: do the Sisters belong in the discussion on drag? A "Gay" Spirit? An Orientation toward Service? Herein lies evidence of gay men's prolific creativity—our ability to combine the unexpected, to embody paradox, and to bend convention in ways that create altogether new ways of being in and seeing the world.

The Body Electric School. While I discuss Body Electric in detail in Chapter 13, it deserves a mention here too, for as with the Sisters of Perpetual Indulgence, the Body Electric School integrates disparate experiences into a new whole. This school, founded by the former Jesuit Joseph Kramer, invites participants to experience spirit through sex, transcendence through the body, personal meaning through group ritual. It embodies the essence of gay male spirituality for its honoring of the body as the gateway to the transcendent. The Body Electric experience invokes the brotherhood of the gay male tribe by teaching participants how to stimulate spiritual experience through non-ejaculatory genital massage. This takes place in a loving group setting, placing participants at the intersection of communal and individual, sex and the sacred. It could be seen as a sexual church, a mass that channels the sacred by tapping into the intensity of sexual energy. This has the potential to unleash participants' personal power and open their hearts. Many of the men I know who follow this path embody the essence of spiritual leadership: they live open-hearted, big, bold, loving lives in service to humanity.

Easton Mountain. This retreat center, community, and sanctuary located near Albany, New York, does not promote one type of spiritual path; rather, it creates a container for spiritual growth to happen. Founded by John Stasio, who refers to himself as an "independent 'post Roman' catholic priest," Easton borrows elements of its communal structure from the monastic model, yet it has a distinct countercultural sensibility. It offers a range of programs that foster personal, spiritual, sexual, and creative growth. Some programs simply offer community in an inclusive, loving setting. The circle, which the Radical Faeries embrace, provides the common bridge for all of its programs. Circles form before mealtimes, at events' closing times, and any time men gather with intention. Without advancing any one approach to personal and spiritual growth, but by creating the laboratory for the extended community to develop new approaches, Easton Mountain provides a haven for gay men who are seeking deeper answers. It helps men find those answers and return to the world stronger, more healed, and with the skills and fortitude to serve humanity. In a deep and profound way, Easton Mountain develops gay men into spiritual leaders.

Other venues. Numerous other venues, groups, and paths promote gay male spiritual development, such as The Wildwood Retreat Center in Guerneville, California, and Gay Spirit Visions, based in Atlanta, Georgia, which holds conferences and gatherings. While listing every group or venue falls outside the scope of this discussion, the proliferation of options speaks to the energy that the First Conference of Radical Faeries embodied.

Gay men's search for meaning, and the ways we choose to embrace this exploration, have produced a generation of gay men who are uniquely suited to provide spiritual leadership and guidance for all people. We bring a new spiritual paradigm, which holds tremendous appeal, for gay men's spirituality is sex-positive. It is inclusive and open-hearted.

It invites individuals to explore their own paths toward meaning, and to release negative messages from religion and society. Gay male spirituality is characterized by an egalitarian ethic that promotes no central dogma or hierarchy, even as practitioners of every variety use their skills and talents to teach specific practices.

Consider the flourishing of gay men offering spiritual service practices, such as meditation, yoga, and body work of all kinds; ministries such as the Bodhi Spiritual Center in Chicago, a self-proclaimed "spiritual, not religious" community founded by Mark Anthony Lord, a gay man; teachers such as Christian de la Huerta, who brings breath work and personal exploration into his spiritual programs; and Reverend Yolanda, who uses drag and performance as a vehicle for her interfaith ministry. Robert Barzan established the *White Crane Journal of Gay Men's Spirituality* in 1989 as a newsletter for the meetings he was holding in his home in San Francisco.

Gay men have emerged as spiritual leaders, whether directly offering healing and sustenance, or more subtly by living in the world as men of purpose and substance. Gay men's orientation toward service primes us to heal others. Our wisdom, gained through the painful process of societal and religious rejection, and the resultant deep spiritual introspection, has transformed us into the open-hearted spiritual leaders that humanity needs to make its transition from patriarchy to The New Way Forward.

Men in Gay Men of Wisdom Groups had this to say about the gay male "window" into spirituality:

- Spirituality is what religion should be.

- Gay men see religion from the outside, because we have been excluded.

- Being gay gives me a unique window into spirit from a two-spirit perspective.

- Spirituality is a process of waking up, of becoming more aware of our inner nature, and our connectedness to everything around us.

• Being kicked out of religion has helped me find a more authentic path to spirit.

• We have to come up with our own paths.

• Being a gay man at this time in history—we are shifting consciousness.

• Spirituality is a search for meaning that is deeply personal.

• We don't experience the polarities that most people in the world see, such as masculine/feminine, good/evil. These kinds of divisions come out of a heterosexual world view, which sees the opposite sex as "other." We are more inclined to see others as same. We don't see polar opposites. We see connection, wholeness.

• Not having children—something most gay men experience—gives us a different view. Monastic life supports this vision. It's why the monks remain childless.

• Not having children: we chose this path to be stewards of compassion. We are healers. We know how to love people. I believe we choose this path in this lifetime.

• Not having children gives us a different sense of the future. That future is not in children. There's a sense of being present in the moment now. We bring that freedom, because we are not concerned with imagining the future.

• Being gay makes me ask the questions that make me go deeper.

• Being alone as a gay child fostered a more contemplative experience.

• Having suffered rejection, we come to be at home in ourselves.

• Our outsiderness forces us to think critically.

• Our purpose is to bring wholeness to the world. We can see connections where others cannot.

• We become happy when we develop a sense of self-love. To become whole and healthy, gay men have to work hard at it. It is the task of all humanity. Others see how we empower ourselves, and this serves a powerful example to everyone.

• We are a gift.

• We are out in front of the shift in human consciousness.

• Gay spirituality means that we are part of the bigger idea of saving the Earth.

Chapter 8
Teachers of Compassion, Generosity, and the Authentic Masculine

AIDS cracked open the closed human heart. By suffering and dying on such a mass scale, and at so young and prime an age, gay men exposed the biases, the willful neglect, and the outright desire for gay people to disappear—a view held among so many, and a view still held in many quarters. It made visible the fact that people who consider themselves to be good and upstanding commit heinous atrocities with great ease. The AIDS virus unleashed tremendous suffering. Good people's indifference, disdain, and religious righteousness multiplied this suffering, turning gay men into sacrificial victims.

We can look back on the early years of the AIDS epidemic and ask with horror, "How could the United States have turned its back on its gay men? How could people have been so hateful?" And yet, we could ask that same question of white slave owners and complicit Northerners prior to the Civil War. We could look back at segregation with similar questions. Unexamined assumptions, an unwillingness to question, and closed-hearted religious doctrine turn people into monsters. As Martin Duberman puts it, "Hostility can always find its own justification."[55]

The greatest irony about AIDS is that it served the gay cause more than any political protest could have achieved. The gruesomeness of the disease, and the swath of vitality that it obliterated, jarred people into recognizing gay men's humanity. When a group suffers and dies on a massive scale, the society of which they are a part is being called to have compassion for the people it discards. Whether and how it answers this call speaks to that society's character. Consider The Holocaust: the unfathomable suffering of the Jews shocked the world into defending this persecuted group's intrinsic humanity. This sentiment toward gays, also a target of Hitler, would need to wait more than forty years.

During the AIDS epidemic, gay men unwittingly became teachers of compassion. Gay men's suffering and dying illuminated our hearts and loves. Sickness forced parents of gay men to confront their deeply held judgments, to question rigid dogmas, and recognize the goodness in their dying children. Impending death has a way of helping one appreciate the preciousness of life. By suffering in such widespread fashion, the gentle men of our tribe provided a lesson to the majority about what happens when hearts harden and a society decides that certain of its people are expendable. The gay men who died from AIDS bequeathed humanity an expanded understanding of what it means to be human.

A Telling Response

With AIDS decimating the community, gay men had no choice but to act. Any major crisis prompts the instinct to help and care. AIDS demanded a heightened, intense, and prolonged response. What is most telling is not the fact that we responded to AIDS, but *how* we responded.

A crisis tests the character of an individual or group. In the cauldron of AIDS, gay men's gifts shone in dramatic and unprecedented ways. Gay men's response to AIDS provides one of the clearest and most profound examples of the gifts explored in this book: our masculine-feminine intelligence; our peaceful, collaborative social orientation; our orientation toward service; and even our gift for creating and preserving culture. We demonstrated to the world that gay men do something altogether unique and special.

Far from serving as merely an exercise in history, an exploration of gay men's response to AIDS tells us who we are today. Let's begin with gay men's initial response: to provide care, comfort, and support.

Caregiving and service. Gay men's service orientation shone during the AIDS epidemic. Along with our stalwart and selfless allies—lesbians—gay men created entire *systems* of care. Beginning with the first group created in response to AIDS—Gay Men's Health Crisis, founded by Larry Kramer, in New York City—we built organizations that reflected the best values and heart of gay men. GMHC offered buddies, information and resource-sharing, practical and emotional support, meals, financial assistance, and legal help. It would serve as the model for AIDS service organizations everywhere; in fact, GMHC would devote considerable resources to helping other groups replicate the model.

GMHC had an unspoken and, in my opinion, unsung quality. As an employee myself from 1991 to 1993, I can attest that the GMHC staff and volunteers brought a distinctive and non-judgmental love, caring, sensitivity, empathy, and nurturing to this organization. Indeed, through GMHC and other organizations, gay men—as masters of the service industry—gave this instinct its most heightened and precious treatment in the post-liberation era. I marveled at the sheer generosity that they demonstrated to the people they served.[56] While there were few effective HIV treatments at the time, people came to GMHC and received the kind of caring, service, and inner healing that only an environment steeped in gay male values could provide. Clients knew they would be nurtured, cared for, and helped to the best extent possible. GMHC was just one of many organizations and efforts driven by gay men and lesbians, whose response created the AIDS service infrastructure.

In *The Soul Beneath the Skin*, David Nimmons, who served as president of the New York City LGBT Community Center and deputy executive director of GMHC, describes how this heightened orientation toward service found expression in gay men's tremendous levels of voluntarism—both formally at organizations like GMHC, and informally for their friends and partners. He cites a 1994 study from the Center for AIDS Prevention at the University of California, which found that 54 percent of men sampled in central-city gay neighborhoods had cared for other men ill with AIDS. He states, "There is no [other] known example where more than one in two men took time to care for others unrelated to them by blood, family, or clan ties. Let alone kept doing it for more than a decade."[57]

The sheer level of response, and the qualities with which we responded—with love, care, and generosity toward each other and others who had HIV—illuminates gay men's service orientation. In creating an unprecedented culture of male caregiving, gay men demonstrated our extraordinary capacity to heal humanity.

Non-violent political theater. Considering the willful indifference to and neglect of the AIDS epidemic on all levels of government, it is remarkable that gay men's anger never turned violent. No IRA-style bombings, no shootings, no riots or arson—just organized, focused, and highly effective political action. In gay men's political response to AIDS (with enduring support from lesbians), we channeled our anger positively, demonstrating the masculine principle without violence.

Watching HBO's 2014 adaptation of Larry Kramer's play *The Normal Heart,* and the 2012 film by David France, *How to Survive a Plague,* I was reminded of history I nearly forgot. Time has a way of erasing the most painful memories. The latter film explores in detail how ACT UP meticulously, persistently, and intelligently moved the government's bureaucratic and intransigent research system into high gear, paving the way for the life-saving protease inhibitors that would transform AIDS from a death sentence to a chronic, manageable disease. What's even more remarkable is that gay men are not surprised that this movement—driven by such intense despair—never turned violent. Even Larry Kramer's vitriolic rants never crossed that line. Through ACT UP, gay men expressed the masculine traits of: assertiveness, competence, confidence, courage, daring, decisiveness, forcefulness, independence, leadership, logic and analysis; being outspoken, being proud and strong, defending one's own beliefs, and having the willingness to take a stand and take risks. Without any violence. Astonishing. In fact, the only violence that occurred at ACT UP demonstrations was perpetrated by the police.

In addition to non-violence, AIDS activism in the era before protease inhibitors and combination drug therapy bore another distinctive gay male characteristic: a flair for the theatrical. I can attest to this; I attended many protests. These events contained an air of high drama and excellence. They were well organized and stage-directed. So you don't want to get arrested today? Move here, grab a sign, and join the legal march. Want to demonstrate civil disobedience? Go over there, and here's what you can expect when you get arrested. Demonstrations proceeded flawlessly, like well-rehearsed choreography.

Consider the action that ACT UP took at the New York Stock Exchange. The following is an excerpt from Swarthmore College's Global Nonviolent Action Database:

> On September 14, 1989, seven members of Power Tools [an ACT UP sub group] entered the New York Stock Exchange using faked credentials. Five of them entered the VIP balcony overlooking the trading floor, chained themselves to it and unfurled a banner that said "SELL WELLCOME." As the stock exchange began to function for the morning, the protestors sounded marine foghorns that drowned out the traders, leading to a five minute pause in trading. About an hour after the chained protestors were removed and arrested, 1,500 protestors arrived to cause pandemonium at the Stock Exchange.[58]

ACT UP mastered the art of political theater. This included striking visuals that conveyed its political messages and reflected a distinct design sensibility. After ACT UP member William Orlander curated the New Museum's "Let the Record Show" exhibit in 1987—which included the now-iconic "Silence = Death" visual, artists formed the collective Gran Fury.[59] The group's arresting posters and images defined the era. One featuring a bloody handprint proclaimed, "The government has blood on its hands. One AIDS death every half hour." A poster featuring three couples—one male, one female, and one male/female, read, "Kissing doesn't kill. Greed and indifference do." The artist Keith Haring produced activist works with his signature combination of graffiti and playfulness. One poster, which features three figures pantomiming, "See no evil, hear no evil, speak no evil," pronounces, "Ignorance = Fear,

Silence = Death, Fight AIDS, ACT UP." The brilliant works of this era synthesized esthetics, communications savvy, and political punch.

It took gay men to create a body of artwork around a life-threatening illness. In 1987, the NAMES Project undertook the creation of the AIDS Memorial Quilt, combining caregiving with a democratic approach to art. Visual AIDS launched in 1988, directing the creative impulse to raise awareness about AIDS. The Tamarand Foundation, founded by my friend Joseph Mondello and his late partner Bruce Detrick, created the Hope Garden: A Living AIDS Memorial in New York City's Battery Park City. This foundation brought gardens to hospitals, AIDS service organizations, and other public places to benefit people with AIDS.

Implications of Gay Men's Response to AIDS

The AIDS epidemic forced gay men against a metaphoric wall. Forged in the fire of crisis, we expressed our gifts in the most exquisite, visible, and powerful fashion to date. In the worst of times, we showed the world the best of who we are.

When pushed to our limits, our collaborative social orientation produced an unprecedented culture of male caregiving and an entire AIDS service infrastructure. Our nonviolent nature manifested in political protest in which no one but the demonstrators themselves came to harm. Marrying the authentic masculine principles with the gifts of theater, gay men moved intransigent bureaucracies, overcame inertia and hostility, and fast-tracked life-saving HIV medications. Our gifts for creating beauty shone through art and design. At our most desperate hour, we exhibited one of the most resilient displays of masculine-feminine intelligence in our movement's history. And as sacrificial offerings, gay men who died opened closed human hearts.

In many ways, AIDS provided a training ground that primed gay men for the greater and more profound level of service that the world needs now. Those who survived the plague emerged as modern shamans, having literally experienced death and rebirth. Those who came of age after the protease inhibitors inherited a permanently altered gay male culture.

At the most basic level, young gay men now enter a milieu where AIDS leadership, the success of political action, and a service infrastructure created by gay men are all givens. While younger gay men may not have experienced the kind of caregiving that took place in the 1980s and 1990s, they encounter and learn from older gay men an ethic of communal care. As David Halperin illuminates in *How to Be Gay*, older gay men transmit and "teach" gay culture to those who are younger, through powerful informal networks.[60] Thus, through myriad encounters, the lessons and experiences of AIDS become ingrained in gay culture through successive generations.

While the depths of the AIDS epidemic have passed in the industrialized world, gay men remain primed for service to the world. Gay men still teach compassion and generosity. We manifest the authentic masculine principle. We expand love. And we widen the circle of humanity.

Gay men's response to AIDS provides the strongest evidence yet of the critical healing and balancing function that gay men serve in the human family. Conversely, it provides a cautionary tale to societies that persecute and kill their gay men. When these societies kill or drive out their peaceful men, they consign themselves to violence. When they silence their gay men, they stifle creation of culture, innovation, and hope for the future. When they disown the caregivers among them, they allow suffering to take root. Societies thrive when they recognize the precious assets they have in their gay men.

Chapter 9
Models of Forgiveness

"When we forgive, we set a prisoner free and discover
that the prisoner we set free is us."
—Lewis B. Smedes[61]

For a group that is as hated as we are, gay men have ample opportunities to practice one of Christianity's most treasured virtues:
forgiveness. Most of us grow up in families and communities that,
to a greater or lesser degree, harm us. We are fed a pernicious lie. We
endure immense pain until we determine for ourselves that those who
claimed to act in our best interest have been misguided at best, and
vicious at worst. Gay men bear the brunt of homophobic attacks—a
distinct vitriol fueled by men's fear of the feminine. We face attacks—
both physical and otherwise—due to our free sexual expression and because of AIDS. Most of us have experienced rejection from the people
with whom we should feel safest and most nurtured—our families and
friends—and from communities and religious institutions where we
should feel most affirmed.

For many gay men, rejection can continue long after we come out.
Some of us never fully come out because of intense homophobia in our
families and communities. This is particularly common among African
Americans and in many Latino cultures, and for those who come from
staunchly conservative religious backgrounds. Despite the hurt, the rejection, the hurdles, and the pain, so many gay men do come out. We
teach love and acceptance to our families—difficult lessons that most

people resist. And in the end, many gay men forgive the people who hurt them the most deeply.

We might not be perfect here—we may forgive some while with-holding forgiveness from others. We may retain anger at some of the institutions that have excluded and marginalized us. But overall, gay men tend to forgive. Our predisposition to *want to forgive* and reconcile is central to the character of the tribe.

Gay men could feel fully justified to live in rage against those who have harmed us. Some gay men choose this path. Most do not. Consid-ering what we endure, gay men's propensity to forgive is nothing short of remarkable. It speaks to the healing role we play in the world. We don't forget, for forgiveness is not about forgetting, but about coming to peace with what happened. We acknowledge past hurts as well as the inherent humanity of the persons who harmed us. We extend love to those who hurt us.

For as common as this phenomenon is, we rarely acknowledge it. Ask yourself: Who have you forgiven? Among the gay men you know, how many have forgiven family members and friends for past hurts? How many have reconciled or attempted to reconcile with family and friends? In contrast, how many gay men do you know who have with-held forgiveness and reconciliation? I suspect that, when we really think about it, most of us will identify much more forgiveness—on our part and among the gay men we know—than lack thereof.

We should honor and acknowledge this gift. Forgiveness rarely makes the front page of the newspaper. It happens in the privacy of one's heart and usually between two people. Forgiveness bridges divides, heals rifts. Even when forgiveness does not accompany reconciliation—whether because the offending party refuses it or has died—the one who forgives frees himself. Forgiveness lacks the drama of conflict, yet it deserves attention as the healing force that unifies. We should celebrate our propensity to forgive as much as we cheer on the expansion of civil rights.

Gay men model this most challenging virtue. We can teach this skill. If we can forgive the grievous hurts that our families, commu-nities, and religions have inflicted on us, others can forgive those who have hurt them. The road to peace is paved with forgiveness. Without it, peace remains impossible. Forgiveness begets forgiveness. In yet another way, gay men model the best instincts for everyone.

Men in Gay Men of Wisdom groups had this to say about forgiveness, and gay men's propensity to forgive:

• What will it take for us to go from victims to teachers? We can tap into this place of forgiveness. We can forgive others for doing things that weren't true to themselves. We can acknowledge that we have been a persecuted people, and that we still are, but we can start forgiving.

What does forgiveness mean?

• Forgiveness used to be about discharging my anger. Now it's much more about myself and my ability to move on.

• Forgiveness is the first step to healing. When we forgive, it opens up a place in our hearts and allows wholeness to happen.

• It recognizes that we can't change what happened. Forgiveness is an opportunity to become more than who we are currently.

• Holding onto hurts becomes a mirror into ourselves: we keep ourselves in a victim state when we do so. Forgiveness releases us from victimhood.

• When I don't forgive, there is something in myself that I have disowned.

• Forgiveness is the letting go of the victim state. It is the reclaiming of the ability to act. It enables you to see yourself honestly in a situation.

• Forgiveness is compassion for oneself—by forgiving another person and giving them the space to be human, you give yourself that same permission.

• Forgiveness is about breaking the cycle of oppression. Carrying anger is toxic. Releasing it is a great gift.

• Self care = forgiveness. Forgiveness = self care. Lack of forgiveness leads to depression, anger, and hurt.

• Forgiveness allows my heart to be open.

• Forgiveness allows us to be a compassionate witness. It requires strength—to step back and compassionately understand another person.

Who do gay men forgive, and for what hurts?

• Gay men excel at compassionately understanding other human beings.

• We forgive our mothers. They have the biggest effect on us.

• Our fathers, for their human frailties.

• When I forgave my father, I found myself remembering so many great moments with him, instead of those few when I thought he was against me. He was always coming from a place of love. Forgiving my father was one of the most important events in my life.

What can the world learn from us about forgiveness?

• The world could be better if it had one less gay man who is angry.

• Liberation comes from forgiving.

• We have no choice. We have to forgive. We are the ones who suffer when we don't.

• Freedom to forgive is the freedom to be oneself.

• We forgive a world that doesn't understand us.

• We forgive you because we know that love is the answer. That demonstration will open hearts.

• Despite all the obstacles in our path, we still have the strength to make contributions to society. Ours is a path that can apply to any group that is attacked, constrained, or persecuted.

• We are good examples of fortitude.

• Forgiveness is empowering. It is a way to take our power back.

• Forgiveness frees our energy to use for other, better purposes.

Reinventing Manhood

Chapter 10

Friends, "Soul Mates," and Co-Revolutionaries with Straight Women

There is no friendship quite so comfortable, harmonious, and enduring as the bond between gay men and straight women. This bond manifests in all realms, bringing gay men and straight women together in personal friendships, family relationships, and career and avocational settings. This friendship pattern is so common and well understood that women who love gay men have even been given their own affectionately derogatory moniker: "fag hag."

This close bond defies the traditional ideas about men's and women's capacity to relate with one another. As Robert Hopcke and Laura Rafaty posit in their delightful book, *A Couple of Friends: The Remarkable Friendship between Straight Women and Gay Men*, "In an era when men and women are supposed to be from 'different planets,' and unable to communicate with each other, gay men and straight women seem able to communicate effortlessly."[62] To gay men, this bond makes intrinsic and perhaps unexplainable sense. Here, I attempt to make sense of it.

Gay men and straight women share a remarkable set of traits in common:

- Similar energies

- Masculine-feminine intelligence

- The same objects of sexual desire

- A more collaborative social orientation

- An orientation toward service

- Common sensibilities and interests

When gay men and straight women encounter each other, we experience a recognition that requires no explanation or discourse from either party: We see the same configuration of energy and traits that lives within us, only in mirror form. Gay men see it reflected back in a female body, and straight women see it manifested in male form. Thus, we simply *understand* each other.

Similar energies. If we revisit the Three-Dimensional Masculine-Feminine Model and ask straight women to complete this assessment, I suspect we would see results that trend closer to those of gay men versus other men. This is a strong hunch; I have not yet attempted to measure this. But the lived experience as a gay man has taught me that heterosexual women and gay men share remarkably similar energies.

Masculine-feminine intelligence. Up to this point, we have discussed how gay men possess masculine-feminine intelligence. Women, of course, possess it too. Even in traditional roles, women have been called on to be both nurturing and decisive, caregivers and protectors. Women learn to navigate in a man's world, where masculine traits are the most valued. And through the women's movement, women have claimed the right to embrace a much wider range of traits and roles, many of which involve the masculine. Freedom to have a career and determine one's sexual and reproductive destiny requires exertion of the masculine traits of decisiveness and personal power, both collectively and individually.

For the most part, while claiming the masculine, women have generally not forsaken the feminine, at least in their personal lives. The women's movement was about freedom, not restriction, after all, and straight women wish to be desired by their male mates. A 1981 television commercial for the fragrance Enjoli neatly summarizes this element of women's liberation with its sung lines: "I can bring home the bacon, fry it up in a pan, and never let you forget you're a man. I can work 'til five o'clock, and come home and read you [a child] tickety-tock [a children's book]."[63] Here, before a national audience, a woman celebrates her ability to move into the masculine and back to the feminine, and back to the masculine and returning to the feminine—all with grace and ease.

In many male-dominated work environments, women still need to emulate men to get ahead, even if doing so risks being labeled a "bitch." And yet, this response to adopt the masculine in certain environments seems more adaptive than fixed. I have a female friend in the construction trades who strikes fear in men on the job through her unyielding and domineering work style, then goes home to her knitting and frilly home decorating. Even women in male-dominated industries have the ability to move in an out of the masculine and feminine, and therefore navigate gender expression intelligently.

The same objects of sexual desire. Gay men and straight women love men—sexually and emotionally. Whereas we may have a different relationship to our sexuality, given our difference in biology and social conditioning, attraction to men creates a strong common experience around which our bond can deepen. When we commiserate about our boyfriends/partners/husbands, we really understand each other's experiences. Gay men can give their straight women friends advice about the men in their lives because we are not only men, we partner with them. How many brunches, lunches, and dinners have served as proxy therapy sessions between gay men and straight women about their love lives?

A more collaborative social orientation, and an orientation toward service. Gay men and straight women share similar and overlapping social roles, which is rather remarkable when one considers the differences in life experience among men and women. It's no mystery that women are generally more collaborative and gentle than heterosexual men, or that they are more oriented toward service. Feminine traits lean heavily toward the collaborative and, as we explored earlier, they are required to master service to others. When straight women encounter in men—namely, gay men—the same configuration of traits that they themselves possess, they discover the men of their dreams (minus one generally important quality).

Common sensibilities and interests. For most gay men, the close bond with women began with our primary relationship—our mother and other females in our family. Gay men share an unusually close bond with their mothers—often more so than with their fathers. Mothers who sense their child is gay might be more likely to act protectively toward their offspring, as they might toward a child with some other form of difference, which could account for some of this closeness. But much more than that, gay men share a natural affinity for their mothers, and vice versa. As boys, this can manifest in interests typically associated with girls—often around activities in the home—which forms a strong bond between a mother and her gay son. While heterosexual boys may bond with their fathers around typically male activities, such as team sports, gay boys often find themselves drawn to activities that they and their mothers enjoy and do together. This speaks to common sensibilities among gay boys (and the men they become) and women.

Michael C. LaSala, Ph.D., Director of the MSW program and associate professor at Rutgers University describes this phenomenon among the families he interviewed for his book *Coming Out, Coming Home: Helping Families Adjust to a Gay or Lesbian Child*. "Perhaps it is not surprising that mothers and their gay sons often describe their relationships as close," he explains. "Compared to fathers, mothers typically have an advantage whereby they usually interact more with their children. However, being gay might be a factor that makes some mothers and sons even closer. This was found to be true for many of the mothers and sons I interviewed."[64] One architectural historian profiled in Will Fellows' *A Passion to Preserve* states pointedly, "I was the daughter she always wanted...I enjoyed learning to sew and making doll clothes."[65]

For these reasons, gay men and straight women share an instant, deep, and enduring connection. We are each other's best friends. And while straight women might take their relationship with gay men to the margins by occasionally falling for gay men, gay men take their love for straight women to dramatic heights. We adore and idolize strong women. Our drag queens imitate them. Gay men's icons include a string of strong, highly visible women in movies, television, music, and pop culture—mostly heterosexual. For instance, while gay men may like k.d. lang, we *love* Madonna. There's a fundamental difference in sensibility and energy between these two performers. We see ourselves in strong heterosexual women, and we adopt their creative contributions into our gay culture. Straight women's culture is gay culture, and vice versa—because we are mirror images of each other, manifesting in different physical form. It is for these reasons that we can watch *The Golden Girls* and feel like we're one of the girls.

This affinity finds its way into our vocations and avocations. In whatever field one finds concentrations of gay men, chances are straight women appear en masse. At the National Trust for Historic Preservation, people joke that it is staffed by gay men and divorced women, which is not so far from the truth.[66] This pairing shows up in many service industries. Consider, for example, flight attendants, hair stylists, social workers, and therapists. It shows up prominently in the arts, such as in theater and interior design. In the development offices of most nonprofit organizations, it seems, one will find a predominance of heterosexual women and gay men.

Above all, the friendships between gay men and straight women bring joy, validation, and comfort to each other. They are based on mutual admiration, a shared outlook, and a lack of tension and competition. For many gay men, their friendships with women provide respite from the fraught relationships with other gay men—the rejection, the pressure to conform to bodily and fashion standards, and the insecurities that can accompany sexual attraction among gay men. Similarly, for women, without the sexual pressure, they can enjoy a man's company and receive the kind of understanding and validation they don't always get from straight men. This is one relationship where gay men feel at home, and straight women feel relieved.

Participants in Gay Men of Wisdom groups had this to say about gay men's friendships with straight women:

• We have a beautiful relationship with straight women. Straight men look on it with wonder.

• We have a closeness with our mothers, with straight women. We are best friends with straight women.

• We relate a lot to feminism, to the struggle that women have had—women who have had to be daring.

• Our relationships with women are that of equals. They are non-sexual. We make friends with them. Straight men struggle to do that.

• We model how women and men can be friends.

• I can see how women work in a way that straight men don't.

• We relate to women instinctively.

• We have non-threatening connections with women.

• We admire women.

• We recognize the strengths, talents, and power of women.

• We have strong maternal bonds.

The Implications of the Strong Gay Male-Straight Female Bond

Gay men and straight women enrich each other's lives with friendships that endure, go deep, and imbue life with rich meaning. We share a comfortable connection that gives each of us relief from the pressures of our respective worlds. Gay men adore straight women, and straight women reward gay men with their loyalty and devotion. We are, as Hopcke and Rafaty point out, the best of friends.

In addition to the immeasurable joy we create through our relationships, gay men and straight women are engaged in a revolution that has broad implications for human evolution. The way we interact with each other has already changed—and will foster greater changes between—

all men and women. Our partnership, along with gay men's conscious leadership, will help heterosexual and bisexual men discover the liberation that we already enjoy.

The women's movement was all about liberation—freeing women from the bonds of enforced servitude and empowering women to have choice in all areas of their lives. While inequalities persist, and glass ceilings have yet to be smashed in many areas, girls growing up today take for granted that they can choose their destiny, whether that be becoming an athlete, a scientist, or a stay-at-home mom. Among certain segments of society disdain for feminism may run deep—a product of the historical amnesia that typifies Americans—but the fact remains that young women in the West today enjoy freedom that their grandmothers only dreamed of.

The gay liberation movement, which exploded after the Stonewall Riots and not long after the emergence of the women's movement, similarly freed gay men and lesbians from centuries of negative messages and persecution. With an explosion of courage, determination, and anger—on top of the groundwork carefully laid by the movement's early activists—gay men and lesbians asserted their power to live with authenticity. That the women's and gay liberation movements emerged sequentially (in the 1960s and roughly the 1970s, respectively), speaks to the similar sensibilities that each advanced, and the bond discussed here.

Heterosexual and bisexual men have never experienced such a movement on a mass scale. Certainly, a men's movement has existed for some time. The California Men's Gathering, which began its annual events in 1978, and the Mankind Project, which started in 1985, make notable contributions here. But these and other groups—and their ideas—have so far not won over the majority of heterosexual men. The Mankind Project's statement about what it means to be a modern, mature man rings of masculine-feminine intelligence: "Building and supporting the emotionally mature, accountable, and compassionate male role models that our communities need."[67] Anything invoking the feminine scares off most men, however, because of society's rigid gender roles for men. Fears of being seen as feminine, less than a man, or—worst of all—gay, keep most men locked into a narrow version of manhood wherein mas-

culine traits are deemed the only acceptable option. Feelings, communication, empathy, sensitivity, and affection with other men remain foreign
territory. Fear of the feminine keeps many gay men trapped in "straight
acting" roles as well. (While I explore this topic further in Chapter 12, I
include it here for the relevance it holds to this discussion.)

This is, of course, a sweeping generalization. Not all heterosexual
and bisexual men buy into rigid gender roles, and not all gay men possess exquisite interpersonal skills. But this pattern describes the typical
American heterosexual man. Gay men, by and large, offer a stark contrast to this pattern, creating for straight women proof and validation
that men can do better. Our close relationship with straight women exerts pressure on heterosexual men because, in gay men, straight women
see the men of their dreams. And having experienced what is possible,
straight women are much less willing to compromise. How many heterosexual women have chosen to remain single rather than enter or stay
in unfulfilling relationships? I know of at least seven in my life. How
many do you know?

A humorous video in support of gay marriage made a splash on the
Internet when it was published in 2012. Entitled "Gay Men Will Marry
Your Girlfriends,"[68] the video cites the list of straight women's frustra-
tions with straight men. Men in the video threaten (very tongue-in-
cheek) that if straight men don't drop their opposition to gay marriage,
they will marry straight men's girlfriends. Because, as the video states,
"we know what she wants."

Here are a few excerpts from the video script:

> "We'd be the best husbands ever… We'll go to the
> gym with her, and afterwards, we'll get Pinkberries as
> a reward. Not to mention, we dress better than you.
> While you were spilling Manwich on your cargo shorts,
> we were inspecting our Oxford shirts for the craftsman-
> ship of their gauntlet buttons… What do you make
> your girlfriend for breakfast? Burnt scrambled eggs?
> We'll make her a quiche—a mother fucking quiche."
> And so on.

While the video is hilarious—thus its wide appeal and viral spread—it points to the gap between what heterosexual women want, and who straight men are. It highlights, unwittingly, the impact that generations of openly gay men have had on women's expectations. Many straight women want their men to master both the feminine and masculine. They want a strong man who will listen and be sensitive. They want men who can be providers and nurturers, just like they can—and just like their gay male friends can. Heterosexual men, however, often fall far short of women's expectations.

The persistence of rigid gender norms—and most men's perpetuation of them—has a detrimental impact on more than just straight men's romantic lives. It is eroding men's economic potential, their self-worth, and even their place in the world. Consider the growing gap in college enrollment and graduation rates among women and men. A 2013 book, *The Rise of Women: The Growing Gender Gap in Education and What It Means for American Schools*, explores this trend and its causes. [69] Prior to 1970, many more men completed bachelor's degrees than women. But with the changes brought about by the women's movement and the civil rights movement, women began surpassing men. Between 1970 and 2010, men's rate of B.A. completion grew by just 7 percent, rising from 20 to 27 percent. In contrast, women's B.A. completion rates almost tripled, growing from 14 to 36 percent. In the 1970s, boys led girls in taking advanced courses to prepare for college; today, more girls than boys take these classes. In students taking these advanced courses, girls score an average of two-tenths of a GPA point higher than boys.

The book's authors found a surprising and disturbing reason for this gap: society's gender norms. Boys involved in extracurricular activities such as music, art, drama, and foreign languages have higher levels of school engagement and get better grades than other boys. These activities, however, are often denigrated as un-masculine by pre-adolescent and adolescent boys, who absorb and reflect the cultural assumptions of their parents and communities. The authors found that this was especially prevalent among boys in working- and lower-class backgrounds. They cite examples from sociologists C.J. Pascoe and Edward Morris, who found that boys who strive for good grades are labeled as "pussies" and "fags" by their peers. Of course, gay boys do number among those who engage in these extracurricular activities—making them more likely to succeed.

This phenomenon illustrates how deep fear of the feminine runs for men. They would rather erode their economic potential, their futures, and their standing in the world than be labeled as "fags." Yet the world is growing increasingly interdependent, and success in the twenty-first century requires mastery and integration of the feminine and the masculine. Without it, straight men face the prospect of falling further behind, and behind their women. I wonder how often resentment about this gap fuels violence toward women—how often straight men who disown their feminine react using the only tools they have given themselves permission to use.

The alliance between straight women and gay men highlights a problematic gap, but it also points to opportunities. When gay men become conscious of our masculine-feminine intelligence, we can teach all men how to honor and integrate the masculine and feminine that lie within them. As we will explore in Chapter 12, by helping straight men heal their wounds around the feminine—and the authentic masculine—we will heal our own wounds and take our honored place in the world. With our gifts for empathy, compassion, and non-judgmental mirroring; our orientation toward service; our peaceable, non-violent natures; and our life experience as men, gay men may be the only ones who can help straight men achieve masculine-feminine integration.

Chapter 11
Esthetic Outsiders and Gender Tricksters: The Art of Camp and Drag

Among gay men, a complex and distinct sensibility developed in response to homophobia: camp. This unique way of responding to injustice—which heavily engages esthetics—exists at the intersection of two distinct gay male gifts: our fine attunement to beauty (Chapter 14) and our orientation to service, particularly as this orientation relates to our propensity to heal (Chapter 6). Among its several functions, camp employs esthetics to demonstrate value for that which is, and those who live, on the margins of society. In this sense, it expresses solidarity with outsiders and welcomes them into the gay fold. One of its most popular forms of expression, drag, embodies a sophisticated duality and challenges gender roles—as well as any other topic in its path. Camp and drag demonstrate how gay men have employed creative means to survive in a world that has not loved us. At the same time, these responses illustrate the duality that characterizes so much of gay men's roles in the human family: our caring, gentleness, and heart on the one hand, and the subversive way we challenge convention on the other.

Camp

As Susan Sontag observes in her essay *Notes on Camp*, "To talk about camp is to betray it." [70] Indeed, any description of camp immediately dilutes its essence—for camp is both a sensibility and a unique form of social expression.

Rooted in the minority experience of being a gay man, camp is a filter through which gay men experience and make sense of the larger world. Expressed with characteristic effeminate flair, camp applies humor to, revels in, and exalts that which is outlandish and over-the-top. As film scholar Richard Dyer describes it, camp is "a characteristically gay way of handling the values, images, and products of the dominant culture through irony, exaggeration, trivialization, theatricalization, and an ambivalent making fun of and out of the serious and respectable."[71]

Over-the-Top Creative Expression = The Outsider = Gay Men

For all of its drama, bluster, humor, irony, feigned indifference, and sarcasm, camp originated as a coping mechanism. It provided a way to deflect and deflate the injustice of being a hated minority. Gay men have always trained their sleuthing senses to recognize each other—those who, like them, remain hidden in plain sight. Camp uses this recognition ability to crack the dominant culture's code—to instantly discern that which contains gay sensibilities, and thus to see ourselves. Gay men hone in on the exaggerated, the over-the-top, the unloved, and the unexpected as the esthetic equivalent of the outsider—a cultural representation of us.

Those people who express distinctly gay sensibilities become the biggest camp icons. Consider Judy Garland's camp appeal, for instance. As Dyer describes it: "She was imitable, her appearance and gestures copiable in drag acts...her later histrionic style can be welcomed as wonderfully over-the-top; her ordinariness in MGM films can be seen as camp."[72] Garland's personal struggles—her sensitivity and fragility—resonated deeply with gay men. Garland became the consummate outsider playing an insider's game.

This ability to sense the outsider extends to artistic expression. Sontag points out that Art Nouveau provides one of the best examples of camp art. The difference in design between an art nouveau lamp and a standard lamp could be described as "excess" or "over-the-top." This "excess" represents that which falls outside the norm—again, the esthetic equivalent of gay men. Elevating the value of creative expression that exists outside the margins serves to express our solidarity with the *ideas and people* who exist there. When we say that a movie is "so bad, it's good"—an inherently campy sensibility—gay men recognize the inherent outsiderness of that work. We see ourselves reflected, and we give it our loyalty. Through camp, gay men assign value to that which—and those who—the majority overlook.

Few films capture "over-the-top" and "outsider hidden in plain sight" as well as *Mommie Dearest*, the 1981 Paramount Pictures movie of Christina Crawford's tell-all autobiography of growing up as actress Joan Crawford's daughter. David Halperin devotes a chapter to Joan Crawford in his book, *How to Be Gay* ("The Passion of the Crawford") and includes a detailed explication of how the film became one of the best short-hands for camp.[73] A still from the film that he reproduces shows Faye Dunaway as the enraged Crawford, pancaked with near-clownish makeup, eyes and mouth wide open in a maniacal expression, strangling Christina for having the audacity to scream at her, "I AM NOT ONE OF YOUR FANS!" Most gay men of a certain age know this scene, and can quote the line from Joan that provokes Tina's outburst: "WHY CAN'T YOU GIVE ME THE RESPECT THAT I'M ENTITLED TO?"

The scene is actually quite violent—Joan has to be pulled off Tina before she causes her serious harm. To the average heterosexual viewer, this scene would read as "horrifying." To the average gay man, it reads as "funny"—the epitome of camp. Tina's defiance and Joan's outrageous narcissism create a catfight that tickles the gay male funny bone. Camp filters out the tragedy and exposes the humor, which most people in the majority cannot readily recognize.

While this scene alone makes *Mommie Dearest* campy, Joan's esthetic perfectionism ensures the film's permanent position in the camp hall of fame. How many gay men *don't* know what the line "No wire hangers!" refers to? Of course, it references another of Joan's rages, where she castigates Tina for placing her expensive dress on a wire hanger. For gay men, this reaction reads as darkly comic and truly funny.

So why do we laugh? On some level, we relate to Crawford's attention to esthetics—because it is *so gay*. We appreciate that wooden or padded hangers would treat a garment more gently, and we find humor in the absurd lengths she goes to in order to enforce her esthetic standard. It is as if only a pathological gay man could commit such an act. In fact, this perfectionism appears throughout the film. For instance, at one point, she says to her housekeeper… "It's not you I'm mad at, it's the dirt."

This film operated on two levels: as a widely distributed, mainstream movie and, due to its exaggerated content and Faye Dunaway's over-the-top performances, an esthetic outlier. Gay men recognized this outlier pattern. We saw ourselves represented in its code and we embraced it.

Camp invokes feminine esthetics. Gay men often express camp with exaggerated effeminacy. Camp's propensity to identify with the ideas, creations, and people who lie outside—especially when others fail to see it—illustrates an inherently feminine trait: compassion and empathy for people's pain and misfortune. In camp, we recognize the heart of gay men as caregivers—for those who live on the outside, and for the outsiders who masquerade as insiders. Camp also illustrates gay men's ability to recognize the beauty that others overlook. This gift shows up in our propensity to restore old, abandoned, and decrepit homes and neighborhoods, which I explore in Chapter 14. As men in Gay Men of Wisdom groups have said, "Gay men renovate people, houses, and neighborhoods." Camp provides a clear, wide window through which to view this gift.

In addition to functioning as a way to identify with—and to spot—outsiders, camp delivers a unique type of expression that challenges social conventions and gender roles, in the form of drag.

Drag

Drag expands, blurs, and redefines boundaries. It serves as the most visible tool through which gay men consort with the feminine. But drag never claims to tap into the authentic feminine. Rather, it offers a camp version—an illusion of womanhood characterized by exaggeration, artifice, theatricality, irony, and, often, humor. This illusion, or artifice, creates the vehicle for drag's expression. Because each drag queen expresses and interprets drag uniquely, one must examine the *vehicle* of drag to consider its distinct social implications. Drag invites a range of expression that challenges convention as it entertains. Since drag can take so many forms, here I will focus on its most popular—men adopting women's dress.

The Vehicle of Drag

The container that drag creates drives its unique power and social implications. Let's explore this further:

Drag never takes itself seriously, yet often gleefully skewers convention. Drag expresses the essence of camp, which deflates and defuses seriousness. A drag queen may take herself seriously, but drag itself never does. This light-hearted medium allows the drag queen to disarmingly deliver messages that contain a punch. Drag's artifice gives the queen broad permission to level social critique (crassly, if she wishes), make her audience smile, and keep them thinking long after the performance. Much like comedy, drag allows the queen to poke fun at nearly anything and get away with it. As men in my groups have observed, there is wisdom in humor.

Drag embodies dualities: masculine/feminine and reverence/parody. When a man dons a dress, applies makeup, puts on a wig, and wears high heels, it is an act of courage and solidarity with the feminine. When a man transforms himself into a "queen," he locates himself the closest to the female, the feminine, and womanhood that a man can approximate. This transformation is an act of reverence. Drag queens may imitate, parody, skewer, and present absurd, exaggerated, and ridiculous versions of womanhood, but the container of drag intrinsically honors its subjects and objects.

A drag queen may parody Cher, for instance, but she does so because she admires and reveres Cher. For instance, in Season Six of the Logo Channel's reality television series *RuPaul's Drag Race*, Bianco del Rio gave an exaggerated impersonation of Judge Judy that left the audience in stitches. The audience laughed at Judge Judy because Bianca del Rio offered *herself* as the object of ridicule. The imitation originated in the drag queen's admiration for Judge Judy and the characteristics that make her a strong woman—traits that gay men greatly admire.

Gay men master the ability to embody duality; drag provides a theatrical format to express it. Drag and its dualities can easily be misread as misogyny. But drag does not apologize or pander: it expresses a sophisticated and quintessentially campy sensibility, and it requires that sensibility of its audience. In fact, drag's inherent parody and exaggeration call attention to the oppression of women. High heels, for instance, make women vulnerable—they can't run away. Makeup forces them to spend large amounts of time disguising themselves to please men's standards of beauty. By donning heels and applying makeup in exaggerated style, drag queens highlight the ridiculousness of these standards while, paradoxically, embracing their pleasures.

Drag aerates and expands gender roles for men. In return for stepping into the feminine, drag grants its queens access to—and the unique ability to consort with—the feminine. Through drag, gay men playfully experiment with unique configurations of the feminine and masculine, purposefully blurring the distinctions between the sexes. While much of drag can be experienced as entertainment, drag itself is subversive. It upends gender roles, permitting a greater range of gender expression.

Similar to how transgender people expand notions of fixed, binary male and female, gay men use drag to expand notions of what it means to be a man or a woman. As men in Gay Men of Wisdom groups have observed, "We're hyper masculine as men and we're hyper feminine as women. We take gender roles to an extreme—as a reaction or backlash to prohibitions on gender fluidity." In a patriarchy that insists on a narrow definition of manhood, gay men use drag to counterbalance, aerate, and expand rigid gender roles for men and prevent these roles from hardening.

Drag requires an audience. Gay men may informally dabble with drag, but true drag is theater. A drag queen commands attention and requires an audience. This container immediately establishes a distinction between the drag queen as performer and everyone else as audience. The audience willingly gives its consent to witness a performance and accept what the performer has to offer. Thus, this container gives power to the queen to not only run the show, but deliver subversive messages in the form of entertainment.

Camp and drag serve subtle, sophisticated, and dual ends: Camp at once exposes gay men's caring heart for those who live on the outside. Drag, one of camp's most visible expressions, upends expectations, subverts gender roles, and issues social critique that no other form of expression could manage. Drag provides one of the most complex illustrations of the duality of gay men's roles. It provides an innovative way to level cultural critique without diminishing the person(s) or object(s) being critiqued. In fact, it can both level critique *and* express affection or affinity.

This duality—holding the space for gentle ridicule and expressing genuine affinity—represents a complex contribution to the world. This propensity shows up in gay men's intrinsic ability to understand both men and women without the need for a translator, and in our ability to serve and heal humanity. Indeed, we see this duality reflected in our foundational gift: masculine-feminine intelligence. Camp and drag provide another angle from which to view gay men's ability to heal, to provoke, and to drive human evolution.

Chapter 12
Modeling Sustainable Manhood

"We cannot solve our problems with the same thinking
we used when we created them."
—Albert Einstein[74]

Masculine-feminine intelligence bestows upon gay men an innate flexibility to access the masculine and feminine. Most gay men do not need instruction to access their emotions, to demonstrate empathy, and to act cooperatively. Sensitivity and intuitiveness often come naturally. At the same time, because we are men, and because we are socialized with all the expectations of manhood, we have broad access to the masculine.

Male gender norms restrict men's repertoire of expression. The emergence of an emboldened gay male community around the globe counteracts that rigidity. By our very nature, gay men challenge patriarchal structure. When we become aware of our impact and our potential, we can use this gift to advance change where it is needed most: expanding male consciousness.

Prisons of Their Own Making

By coming out, gay men and lesbians have made enormous contributions to global consciousness. As Chapter 16 explores, we serve as models of authenticity and courage, and we cleanse shame for humanity. Additionally, and very consequentially, coming out created a new rite of passage. It says, "I now choose to live according to who I am instead of what society wants me to be." This public declaration emboldens us to choose authenticity in all areas of our lives, well beyond our sexuality. We have bequeathed this rite to future generations, creating a lasting ripple effect.

Coming out, of course, represents just the first step in our journey to authenticity. Gay men spend considerable energy questioning and re-writing society's rules about what it means to be a man—and recovering from the emotional violence these rules and their messengers inflicted. But gay men are not the only ones whose spirit becomes crushed by society's wholesale prohibition on the feminine for men. All boys and men suffer from it.

To explore this prohibition further, let's revisit the Three-Dimensional Masculine-Feminine Model from Chapter 4. On two of the measures most amenable to fluidity—personality traits and external traits—society's expectations enforce considerable rigidity to qualify as a "real man." Nearly every feminine trait on both scales is off limits. To scientifically test my theory, I asked a group of men in one of my weekend programs to complete a masculine/feminine trait assessment based on what society *expects of men*. The men in the group looked at me with puzzled expressions, then one man blurted out, "Duh! It's the list of masculine traits." We all agreed.

Of course, differences exist between society's expectations of men and their actual behaviors. Many men choose to express feminine traits and consider it a sign of strength. For instance, the last few decades in the United States have witnessed an expansion of men's permitted behaviors and traits, a rise in stay-at-home dads, and increasing gender parity. The women's movement largely influenced these expansions in gender norms. Among the Millennial generation, men embrace a much wider set of permissible expressions than do their parents. For this generation, which came of age at a time when gay men had already been living openly for years, gay men's model of manhood has no doubt had an influence.

Even the most macho men give themselves permission to express at least some feminine traits under certain circumstances, such as with female partners or their children. It is also important to note that different societies define masculinity and femininity differently than in the

United States. But the generalization about gender-norm restrictions carries weight—and not just in this country. Patriarchy exerts tremendous pressure on men to conform to a given society's definitions of manhood. In most parts of the world, the worst thing a man can be is like a woman.

This restriction places half of the human experience off limits for men. In terms of personality traits, society pressures men not to express: affection, caring, compassion, communicativeness, collaboration, cooperation, eagerness to soothe feelings, emotions, empathy, a family or inward orientation, flexibility, gentleness, helpfulness, intuitiveness, kindness, nurturing, passivity, patience, reasonableness, responsiveness, sensitivity, sexual submission, shyness, soft-spokenness, sympathy, tenderness, understanding, yielding, and warmth—among others. In terms of external traits, societal expectations keep men confined to rigid body posture and movements, narrow permissions for dress, and vocal inflections in the lower octaves. One misplaced hand gesture or the wrong crossing of legs leaves a man open to receiving the worst insult: being labeled a fag or a sissy.

When considered in this light, the restrictions on men ring with insanity. And yet this insanity rules and drives much of men's behavior. Because men control the levers of power, denial and repression of the feminine within themselves translates into denial and repression of the feminine and feminine principles globally. Considered slightly differently, men devaluing swaths of themselves translates into men devaluing swaths of humanity. We see this imbalance in stratification, hierarchy, and racism. It shows up in the way governments repress; armies slaughter; corporations subjugate, exploit, and pollute; and politicians steal power. Religions perpetuate this imbalance in teachings that assign women lower status. It manifests as emotional and physical violence toward women; cut-throat business practices; and the perpetuation of income inequality. It results in the careless destruction of Earth's environment, which could in the not-too-distant future extinguish us all. When the dominant force in the world denies half of the human experience, it becomes all too easy for this group to deny the humanity in others.

The sad irony of men's entrapment within a rigid, narrow range of expression is that this prison is entirely of men's making. Men maintain control of and perpetuate these restrictions on male norms. Women have little say in it; they may exert pressure on their men to integrate their masculine and feminine, as we explored in Chapter 10, but this goes only so far. (Of course, some women actually support and reinforce gender rigidity.) In some ways, heterosexual men become more permanently wounded than gay men, because they have no rite of passage that can help them "come out" and throw off these limiting conventions. Herein lies the paradox for straight men: If you belong to the dominant culture, who do you rebel against? What do you reject? What is your foe? Women could throw off men's values and reclaim their personal power. Gay men and lesbians could reject society's messages that tell them being gay is inherently wrong. But if you live amid and benefit from the power of the dominant group—like the proverbial fish that can't recognize water, how would you even grasp the prison you live in?

For those of us outside of this prison, the view inside seems awfully bleak. Consider a life where pressure to conform to the narrowest range of human expression keeps one constantly on guard. A colleague of mine shared insight into the straight male experience as he and I talked about the unfortunate prevalence of gay men's preference for "straight acting" sexual partners. "'Straight acting,'" he said, "is an act. Straight men are scared shitless to be seen as anything other than manly, so they adopt an act."

Sociologist Michael S. Kimmel supports this assertion. In his article, *Masculinity as Homophobia*, he describes the interior state of the typical U.S. male:

> The great secret of American manhood is: *we are afraid of other men....* Our efforts to maintain a manly front cover everything we do. What we wear. How we talk. How we walk. What we eat. Every mannerism, every movement contains a coded gender language. As adolescents, we learn that our peers are a kind of gender police, constantly threatening to unmask us as

feminine, as sissies.... As young men we are constantly riding those gender boundaries, checking the fences
we have constructed on the perimeter, making sure that
nothing even remotely feminine might show through.
The possibilities of being unmasked are everywhere....
Even the most seemingly insignificant thing can pose a
threat or activate that haunting terror.[75]

Nathan Palmer, a sociologist at Georgia Southern University, engages his students in class discussions around Kimmel's work, where they
discover the inevitable implications of a narrow definition of manhood.
He describes this process in his blog Sociology Source.org:

After we have clearly discussed how gender is socially constructed and defined what masculinity as
homophobia means, I ask my students to brainstorm
the consequences men and women experience because
of this narrowly defined masculinity. My students are
quick to point out that many men do "stupid" risk taking behaviors to show they are tough. Students draw
the obvious connection to the shamefully high levels of
male violence toward women. Many men, they typically
say, are hostile or even violent to gays and lesbians because a narrowly defined masculinity sees any non-com-
pliance as an affront to their own masculinity. After this
students usually go quiet.[76]

Palmer's students make the obvious connection between toxic male
shame and violence. According to a 2013 World Health Organization
report, 35 percent of women worldwide have experienced either physical and/or sexual intimate-partner violence or non-partner sexual violence. [77] This violence turns inward as well. The American Foundation
for Suicide Prevention reports that suicide rates among men are nearly
four times higher than among women, and have been for many years.[78]

On a more subtle yet pervasive level, fear of other men keeps men
disconnected from each other. Homophobia creates intense fear of even
platonic displays of affection among men, unless they fall under strict

contexts—such as celebratory hugs and pats on the butt during sport-
ing events. The male hug—with hands clasped and arms crossing the
chest to prevent full-on body contact—delineates the line that cannot
be crossed. Whereas friendships among men were once celebrated even
in the United States, homophobia created a distance among men, keeping them starved of authentic male friendship and platonic affection.

A life lived in fear, shame, and inner violence creates external manifestations of these conditions. Fear, shame, and violence become projected onto others—and sometimes onto oneself. The metaphor is inescapable: the interior of the average American man—and men around
the globe—is as toxic an environment as the one into which we are rapidly transforming the Earth. Men's rejection of the feminine has created
a human and ecological disaster.

Claiming Our Gay Manhood as a Model for All Men

It seems no accident that at precisely the moment in history when our
technology has turned men's disavowal of the feminine into a human
and ecological disaster, large numbers of gay men have come out of
the closet and demonstrated a balanced form of manhood. Gay men
represent the future of manhood. We show how to live as men who
integrate the masculine and feminine. We live as free men—because we
have chosen to open ourselves to the entire range of human expression
and, therefore, to humanity. We are teachers of men. Gay men model
sustainable manhood for all men. It's time we claim this leadership and
consciously use it to benefit all men—and all people.

One man in a Gay Men of Wisdom discussion group raised a compelling objection to this concept when I proposed it. "I struggle with
the question of what it means to be a man because I see it as negative,"
he said. "I don't fit the stereotype of what it means to be a man, and as
a result my experience with manhood has been on the receiving end of
anger and violence from the hands of men. Men use power, violence,
aggression, and domination. These are things I don't want to be associated with."

His comments reflect a common gay male reality: we experience
violence—emotional, physical, or both—at the hands of men and learn

to associate that with manhood. The gravity of this wound cannot be overstated. It is important to distinguish between the masculine and manhood, however. While our culture considers them synonymous, they are in fact two different things. Masculinity includes those traits and energies a society determines to be masculine, while manhood encompasses the ideal set of traits that men should possess. When manhood consists of only the masculine and little to no feminine, aggression and violence—masculinity's shadow side—take over. This describes the state of manhood in most parts of the globe. The authentic masculine, however, provides a positive energy that makes a contribution to society equivalent to that of the authentic feminine.

Another man in the same group explained this as follows: "The masculine has tremendously beneficial contributions to make: holding a place of service to others; strength; being a light for people we know; taking action; giving back; sacrificing to benefit others; leading; being leaders; honoring our world; being protectors; taking responsibility for oneself and one's own actions. Men have a different strength from women, and heterosexual men have a different strength than gay men."

When I began leading gay men through explorations of the masculine and feminine, I fully expected that I would run into the greatest resistance around the feminine, and that men would sail through the assessments and discussions about the masculine. Much to my surprise, the opposite took place. This prompted me to rethink my assumptions and observations of gay men. It became clear to me that the real challenge lay not in the struggle with the masculine or feminine per se, but on a deeper level, in our struggle with manhood.

The notion of gay manhood does not exist. To some, the words "gay manhood" even sound funny. In them, I hear the echoes of the kind of masculinity presented in Robert Bly's *Iron John*—straight men trying their hardest to be sensitive, strong warriors. We don't have a notion of gay manhood, because we don't feel like men. We don't feel entitled to claim manhood for ourselves—as if heterosexual orientation provided the key to this kingdom. We still believe, on some level, that we are less than other men. All the evidence, of course, points in the other direction. We are the strongest men on the planet, because we have done the unthinkable: we have challenged all men to look inside and recognize the feminine within them. Only an army of loving men could ever have the nerve, guts, and masculinity to accomplish this. We are men who are giving all men the key to unlock the prison gate.

We have begun redefining manhood whether we intend to or not. When we claim our manhood as gay men—and honor the balance it contains, in all its variations, from the nelliest queens to the butchest daddies—we will begin our deep healing work. When we proudly proclaim ourselves as men who embrace and honor the feminine, and who embody and express the masculine—and know that deep within ourselves—we will become whole. We will become the strong teachers that all men look to for guidance, because we will possess a strength that speaks to them.

Some of us may simply choose to live with this awareness. That alone will change how we interact with others, and it will change how men see us. Others of us will choose to consciously apply this awareness in what we do in our workplaces, in our families, and our communities. For some, it will mean literally entering into some form of service to men, such as a therapy practice focused on helping men heal, or a spiritual or religious ministry. Some may choose to become involved in men's groups and take active leadership roles. And some gay men may create new services, such as "coming-out-from-the-masculine-shadow" rites of passage, or other experiences specifically for straight and bisexual men. The possibilities will expand beyond our current conceptions, for we as gay men will have stepped fully into our leadership role, modeling and teaching sustainable manhood for all men. When we heal other men, we will complete our own healing journey.

Gay Men of Wisdom on Gay Men and the Masculine

Gay Men of Wisdom groups have produced rich discussions about gay men, the masculine, and the feminine:

- We are not afraid to be confrontational; we have used the masculine to create political power: ACT UP, gay rights. We have channeled the masculine to useful ends.

• Gay men are tough as nails.

• Gay men have a strong work ethic. That feels very masculine to me.

• Gay men care about their physical appearance and enjoy their masculinity.

• We have demonstrated strength and perseverance. We have survived and overcome the odds of lonely, difficult childhoods.

• Acceptance of gay culture allows people to be bisexual, which will create an American culture that is less warlike. There will be less pressure on men to be so hyper-masculine.

• As a gay man you're forced to make peace with your feminine side.

• We break barriers. We have helped redefine sex roles, especially for men. We help break the hardening of sex roles.

• We are not afraid to physically express our feminine side, such as through gestures, flairs, fashion, and trend setting.

• Our culture has crushed the feminine out of straight men; gay men can help restore it.

• We have created permission to be intimate without being sexual, affectionate without being sexual. We have given men a broader set of permissions. Heterosexual men have little of this available to them. We have created models for authentic male-male friendships.

• Some gay men form close and authentic relationships with heterosexual men. More of this will happen in the future. This is where we are headed.

• It's easier for us because we don't have to worry about not being manly enough. This puts tremendous pressure on straight men. We have much less pressure on us. This allows us to be ourselves.

• We're automatically models of manhood. The appearance of gay people in the world causes people to feel differently. This gives heterosexual men the permission to see themselves differently and more expansively.

• We give men permission to be affectionate without being sexual. We model this.

• We expand definitions of masculinity.

• The shadow damages straight men just as much as it damages gay men.

• We have led men in this area, and are suited to lead them further.

• We can teach straight men that women are human beings. If you are strong in yourself, you won't have an issue with a woman being in charge.

What is different about how gay men embody manhood?

• On the surface, we appear the same, but inside we are different.

• We don't have the same pressures as straight men. We don't relate to women sexually.

• We are feminine and masculine, depending on who we are with. We don't have to play a role.

• For gay men, masculinity means being sexually attractive, not being dominant over others. It means wanting to be loved.

• We define masculinity by sex, but we can get lost in it.

What can we teach heterosexual men about being men?

• Allow yourself to feel. Be okay with it.

• It's okay to cry.

• Being physical/sensual is not the same as being sexual. This is a distinction most heterosexual men are too afraid to make.

• We expand notions of what it means to be a man.

• We can teach straight men how to understand women.

• It's okay for straight men to see each other.

• Be who you are.

• Find that strength in yourself to be who you are.

• Find the courage to speak up and create change. That's the power men hold.

• It's okay to have feelings. Strength is not in not having feelings, but in facing and harnessing them.

• We can teach men to love themselves, because, while we still have a ways to go individually and collectively, we have done this for ourselves.

• We can teach straight men how to feel.

• Gay and straight men can learn from each other about what it means to be a man. We can create a new definition of what it means to be man together.

Freeing and Enriching
the Human Spirit

Chapter 13
Sexual Leadership

*"Sex is one of the most profound ways that our life
force gets expressed. For many people, sex is actually
equated with life."*
—Michael Shernoff[79]

Perhaps no group of people is more closely associated with sex than
are gay men. Part of this dates back to 1869, when German psychologist Karoly Benkert coined the term "homosexuality."[80] This
opened the door for the medical professions—and society at large—to
pathologize those we now call gay people, and especially men who have
sex with men. Part of this identification also relates to our conscious
choice. The gay rights movement reclaimed homosexual identity and
turned it into something positive. Post-Stonewall gay liberation was inextricably linked to sexual liberation. This enthusiastic, unapologetic,
and free embrace of sex has placed gay men at odds with most religions
and cultural conservatives—including some conservative gays. But missing from the usual gays-are-degenerates-because-they-love-sex diatribe
is consideration for how this embrace of sex contributes to the vitality of
the human family. Because sex is such a hot-button topic in a country as
driven by religion as the United States is, it rarely receives consideration
as a beneficial, adaptive force—other than for procreation.

Because gay men have sex for pleasure, not for procreation, we break
every rule. And in doing so, we rewrite those rules. While heterosexuals
may have launched the sexual revolution years before Stonewall, gay
men made up for lost time and assumed leadership of it. In *Coming Out*

Spiritually, Christian de la Huerta explores how gay men have played the role of "consciousness scout" for humanity. Echoing other gay thinkers, he proposes that we "go first" by "discovering new paths [and] searching out new answers."[81] In fact, we can view many of the 14 Distinct Gay Male Gifts from this perspective. Gay men's sexual expression provides one of the more potent and visible manifestations of this role. Through it, we demonstrate sexual leadership.

What do I mean by sexual leadership?

Since Stonewall, gay men have innovated ways of expressing sexuality that hold tremendous implications. We demonstrate sexual leadership by:

- Modeling inner-motivated sexuality based on the embrace of pleasure, personal freedom, choice, and authenticity

- Rejecting all external control over our sexuality, including shame

- Approaching our sexual partners as equals

Gay men's sexual leadership produces far-reaching benefits for the human family. It:

1. **Fuels our social innovations and creative contributions**. How we express our sexuality, and the quantity of sex many of us have, informs the distinct and critically important social and creative contributions gay men make.

2. **Creates sexual and relationship models based on authenticity and self-determination**. Gay men's sexuality serves as a laboratory, yielding innovations that result in greater sexual freedom and self-determination for all people.

3. **Brings bisexuality out of the closet**. By giving permission to bisexual men to express their same-sex desires, gay men pave the way for this largely silent but potentially powerful allied group to help expand understanding and acceptance of human sexual fluidity.

4. **Provides an antidote to global violence.** The presence of a core group of men-who-love-men provides an essential counterbalance to male aggression and violence, bringing peace and love to the planet.

5. **Reconnects sexuality and spirituality.** Free expression of sex yields explorations that re-establish the link between sexuality and spirituality.

Let's explore each in detail.

1. Fueling Social Innovations and Creative Contributions

In 2012, the Leslie-Lohman Museum of Gay and Lesbian Art in New York hosted an exhilarating exhibit entitled "The Piers: Art and Sex along the New York Waterfront." Through photos, films, and narratives, the show focused on "the relationship of the uses of the Hudson River docks by artists and a newly emerging gay subculture."[82] In short, the show explored how gay men used the piers for cruising and sex, and artists used the piers to create art—often inspired by or about sex. I found myself mesmerized by Ivan Galietti's film, *Pompeii New York*, in which the piers serve as the backdrop for gay men's cruising rituals. When I realized that the filmmaker was standing behind me, I struck up a conversation with him about New York and gay liberation in the 1970s versus gay life now. "Today, we talk about marriage," he summed it up. "Back then, gay liberation was all about the freedom to fulfill one's sexual desires and fantasies with as many partners as one wanted."

The Leslie-Lohman Museum's exhibit illuminates the inextricable link between gay men's sexuality and our creativity. In the piers, all manner of sex took place, while artists created all manner of art—photography, murals, installations, and film. While it is likely that gay men used the piers for sex because they were deserted, this phenomenon illustrates how, when gay men are free to create communities without interference from the heterosexual world, we invite both sexuality and creativity to flourish.

The ancient tradition of Tantra made this link centuries ago. In Tantra, the second chakra, where the genitals reside, is associated with both creativity and sex, with passion, play, and sensuality. In fact, the

Body Electric School's Celebrating the Body Erotic workshops teach men Tantric practices in which they learn to harness sexual energy by drawing it up through the body—without achieving ejaculation. This process enables the practitioner to use sexual energy to enliven himself with vitality and creativity. As one teacher I know put it, "Imagine living your life horny."

As Tantra implies, when individuals free their sexual energy, they innovate. When a community of individuals frees its sexual energy—and releases the societal shame that attempts to control it—they produce even greater innovation, as creative ideas reverberate throughout and become amplified in that community. As perhaps one of the sexually freest groups of people, gay men disproportionately innovate, both socially and culturally. This is no accident. The outsize contributions we make owe their character to the unique nature of gay male sexuality. In this chapter, I will explore the social innovations that gay men produce as a result of our relationship with sexuality and our sexual expression. In the chapter that follows, I will explore our outsize contributions to the creation and preservation of culture, and the link to our sexuality.

As a side note, it is intriguing to consider how such sexual vitality and creativity could thrive in an environment as decaying as the Hudson River piers. One cannot fathom heterosexuals using spaces this way. The flourishing of sex and art in decrepit spaces points to the role of renewal that gay men play. Gay men see the beauty and potential in decay, and we set our energies into revitalizing abandoned and neglected areas and neighborhoods. I explore this role of cultural and neighborhood renewal further in the following chapter.

Gay Male Sexuality = (Male Sexuality)²

Much of the distinct energy that gay male sexuality unleashes results from male sexuality meeting male sexuality. The male sex drive contains distinct elements. According to Lisa J. Cohen, Ph.D., psychologist and associate professor of clinical psychiatry at Beth Israel Medical Center and Albert Einstein College of Medicine in New York City, research shows that, compared to women, men experience sexual desire more spontaneously, are more reactive to visual cues, masturbate more, and use more pornography. Psychologist and author Roy Baumeister proposed that men have a fixed, biologically-determined sex drive that is relatively insensitive to context. Women, on the other hand, have a much more variable sex drive, which is far more responsive to the surrounding circumstances.[83] In other words, men's relentless sex drive makes them ready to go at a moment's notice. Women like to be wined and dined to get in the mood. This may oversimplify complex mechanisms and gloss over exceptions, but these generalizations tend to hold up.

When a heterosexual man's intense sex drive encounters that of a woman's, it becomes necessarily moderated. To obtain what he wants, a man must learn and appeal to a woman's desires, which may be considerably different from his. This speaks to Harry Hay's subject-OBJECT theory: men and women must navigate their differences when it comes to sex. Because they often approach sex from different perspectives, men and women learn techniques to manipulate the other to obtain what they want. For men, navigating this terrain most often puts the brakes on their desires. If all men could have their way sexually, they would behave like gay men. Thus, to truly understand male sexuality, one needs to consider gay men's sexuality.

When gay men meet each other with the same relentless sex drive, and that ready-to-go-at-a-moment's-notice energy, explosive, often instant encounters result. There are few speed bumps in sex between men. Because we understand each other's desires and have similar needs, sex tends to occur easily, frequently, and creatively.

Men in Gay Men of Wisdom groups had this to say about this phenomenon:

- We understand what you want. We know your anatomy.

- We have a lot more sex—more than most.

- Gay male sex: everywhere, all the time.

- We're not shy about sex. It's out there for everyone to see.

- We have anonymous sex. We have more group sex.

• Gay men have sex for pleasure versus procreation; there is a freedom in it that brings benefit to oneself and others.

• Sex without worry of procreation is freeing; it produces joy and gives one a way of being alive.

• We are sexually generous. We have lots of partners.

• Sex among men is like ordering coffee at Starbucks.

• We create sexual subcultures—new ways for men to relate and connect non-violently.

The Role of Cruising

Men find physical beauty irresistible, and we can't get enough of it. Gay, straight, or bi, nothing pleases a man like gazing at someone he finds sexually attractive. It's why we use porn more than women. Heterosexual women refer to this trait as "the roving eye," and it can provoke intense jealousy on women's part. That's because women know that what men see can easily stimulate their relentless sex drive and…fidelity be damned.

While heterosexual and bisexual men's roving eyes may get them in trouble with women, gay men—apart from jealous lovers—tend to appreciate and enjoy this trait in each other. We return another's gaze with similar intensity. We love beholding beautiful men, and we love the thrill of sexually connecting with them. And so we engage in a distinct social hunting pattern: cruising.

Cruising could well be named the official gay male pastime. We have raised cruising to creative heights, devising myriad ways to connect—or simply to enjoy the erotic entertainment of the search. Mobile applications and dating websites dangle the thrill of instant and plentiful hookups—or more often, as it turns out, virtual cruising. The name of one site emphasizes this primal urge: "Manhunt." Video stores and sex clubs feature maze-like corridors, feeding the male desire for sexual conquest. Popular magazines and websites parade beautiful men as a means of attracting and retaining reader interest.

Whether we engage in cruising with the intention to connect sexually, or simply for the thrill of the hunt, cruising lights a fire that drives gay men. It has no equivalent among heterosexuals or lesbians, because it derives from the distinct male-on-male sex drive. (Bisexual men can certainly engage in it with men.) For cruising to happen, it must be mutual, mutually enjoyed, and based on equality among participants. Strip shows—a favorite of many heterosexual men—are not cruising, as they contain an inherent power differential.

From the Hudson River piers of the 1970s to contemporary bathhouses, from back rooms to movie houses, from street cruising to sex clubs, to outdoor cruising and sex amid nature, gay men connect with each other sexually in ways and quantities that have no parallel in the larger human family. And so, our sexual patterns create a distinct social network and range of relationships that also have no parallel elsewhere. While AIDS may have cast a chill over this sexual landscape in the 1980s, it re-emerged with the advent of safe sex and remains a major component of the gay experience today.

Through the course of a gay man's life, his sexual repertoire may include:

• Hundreds of sexual connections with men he meets just once each—many of which can be sweet, hot, beautiful, or otherwise simply intimate.

• Friends with benefits whom he meets regularly.

• Boyfriends, partners, or husbands with whom he has monogamous, open, or polyamorous relationships.

Throughout this repertoire, we create intimate relationships of short to long duration. For many gay men, as men in my groups have pointed out, sex becomes the way we make friends. When the sexual attraction wanes and transforms into friendship, the two have already laid the groundwork for a closeness and mutual appreciation that heterosexual men could never experience. Gay men's prodigious sexual connections with each other create a network—indeed, a brotherhood—that links us together, bringing us from our disparate families of origin into a new family that transcends geographic boundaries. By continually relating to each other sexually—whether this involves actual sex or just visual cruising—we innovate new forms of human relationships and keep ourselves open to greater love.

Gay men rarely consider the social value of the vast and intricate network that we create due to our patterns of sexual connection. If anything, we spend time hiding, denying, or judging it. To consider this concept, let's explore a less charged form of large-scale social interaction: the continual interplay that takes place among people living in cities. Something profound happens when people gather in high-density urban areas: commerce, art, music, ideas, sex, friendships, services, and innovation blossom. Human interdependence flourishes. People mix on a daily basis, which creates an enlivened energy that gives a city its character.

Consider one of the most obvious examples of this phenomenon: the City of New York, where people literally bump up against each other every day on the street, in the subways, cafes, stores, restaurants, and parks. This mixing creates a dynamic energy greater than the sum of its parts. Anyone who visits New York experiences and becomes part of the city's inescapable energy. The interchange that takes place in the city fosters ideas, social movements, and events that affect the world. It inspires all manner of creativity and innovation.

Songwriters pen passionate songs about New York's vitality, the most recent of the genre being Alicia Keys' "Empire State of Mind." In it, she proclaims how the city's streets provide inspiration and renewal for those who strive. New York City is a triumph of complex, consistent social interchange among people, most of whom remain anonymous to each other, but who interact with, affect, change, and inspire each other. Indeed, I doubt I would be writing this book if it were not for the dynamic exchanges I experience in New York City.

Thus, social innovation is less likely to happen in small towns than it is in dense cities like New York, San Francisco, Chicago, and Los Angeles. Mixing produces vitality. It is one reason the United States has remained so vital a force in the world; successive waves of immigrants not only fill the low-wage jobs that Americans born here won't take, they bring economic and cultural vitality.

If social interaction drives innovation, what happens when we add something as potent as sex to the mix? To consider this, let's explore what happens on an individual level. Oftentimes, when we reflect on sex we have had, we think about it as it relates to ourselves, as we might assess the meal we just ate: Was it good or great? Was it satisfying? Was it "meh"? Was my partner present or distracted?

But what gifts does a sexual exchange give to our partner? When I asked this question in my groups, it provoked puzzled looks and head scratching at first; it's not a question most of us are used to asking. Ultimately, the men concluded that mirror experiences usually take place: each partner feels a sense of connection and worth, and feels attractive and desirable. I would add that we engage and exchange life-force energy with each other—sharing forms of "love of man" with each other, the depth of which can vary based on our relationship with that man. As Tantra suggests, the flow of sexual energy opens us to our innate creativity and frees us to listen to our inner voices. When we connect with another person sexually, we deepen our connection with ourselves.

When we consider these personal impacts in the context of gay men's prodigious patterns of sexual connection, we can appreciate the potent and large-scale innovations that our sexual leadership produces. How we express ourselves sexually corresponds closely with how we express ourselves socially. And so the qualities that characterize gay men's sexuality show up in how we live our daily lives. For gay men, sexuality is a social laboratory in which we experiment with ways of relating to each other, and we then channel that learning out to the human family. Consider these statements from men in Gay Men of Wisdom groups about what makes gay men's sexual expression unique (left-hand column), and the corresponding social innovation.

The Gay Male Sexual Leadership Laboratory

Traits that Make Gay Men's Sexual Expression Distinct	Social Innovations/ Contributions
Sexual openness and generosity	Openness and generosity toward others
We have sex as equals	We treat people as equals and model the equal valuing of all human life
We like role play	We bring playfulness to our daily lives
Versatility	Masculine-feminine intelligence, flexibility, cooperation
We have more open and polyamorous relationships; we are relationship innovators	We are open to new ideas; we innovate socially and culturally. We model honesty and authenticity in intimate relationships.
We are more open to exploring sexual experiences	We are open to a range of human experiences and perspectives
We are more open about and to sexuality	We are open to others' authenticity and sometimes hidden truths
We play with sex roles	We challenge conventional thinking
We are communicative and show respect	We communicate and demonstrate respect
Cruising	We desire to connect with other people and be of service
We engage in sex for connection and transcendence	We bring a sense of spirit into our lives and share it with others
We have the ability to separate love from sex when we want to. We can enjoy sex without deep love for another person.	We possess openness to love and accept others for who they are. We readily express "love of mankind" for others.
We have fewer rules	We challenge conventional thinking
We give ourselves permission to be wild	We make new rules
We are more creative, experimental, and open when it comes to sex	We bring creativity and new ways of thinking into every facet of our lives and the larger world. We inject honesty into what we do and model it for the world.
We create sexual subcultures when we want variety or when we are dissatisfied with the status quo	We replace the status quo with ways of being that are based on authenticity
We've developed rich sexual communication.	We are gifted communicators
We created the hanky code	We are gifted communicators
We take sexual fetishes to a new level	Willingness to experiment, try new things, and forge new paths

The Gay Male Sexual Leadership Laboratory (continued...)

Traits that Make Gay Men's Sexual Expression Distinct	Social Innovations/ Contributions
We engage in sex as a purely physical act	We bring sensuality and appreciation for beauty to the world
We view sex as vitality	We bring vitality to our lives and others'
We have sex that is motivated by pleasure and joy	We bring pleasure and joy to those around us
We are honest when it comes to sex	We model honesty
We engage in sex for pleasure	We encourage others to live life fully
We rebel against conformity	We challenge conventional thinking
We are teachers of pleasure	We model the enjoyment of pleasure in all its forms
We model sex without shame	We teach others how to free themselves of shame
We normalize taboos	We model authenticity and courage
We have the capability to love— to express ourselves to a wider audience	We express and share love freely
We create positive connections with other men	This puts out positive energy, which leads to happiness, and greater acceptance of others
We express sexuality free of shame	We model a life lived without sexual shame
...I would add:	
Playfulness in sex	Playfulness in life
Sexual freedom	Personal freedom
Sexual creativity	Cultural creativity

As men in Gay Men of Wisdom groups point out, gay men carry erotic energy into our daily lives. Our free expression of sexuality injects fresh energy into nearly everything we touch. Though we may not reproduce literally, we channel vitality into the human family. This gives birth to a range of innovations, which show up in many of the 14 Distinct Gay Male Gifts. This speaks to the powerful role that gay male sexuality plays in advancing human evolution.

The freedom and energy that gay men bring appeal to those around us, giving us greater influence than we realize. It is the primary reason why many religious leaders and cultural conservatives fight us so much: because we undermine their power over others. As this exploration illustrates, sexual freedom yields personal power and innovation. It advances love and understanding, forges connections, and invites challenges to stale conventions. It weakens patriarchal structures, diminishing religious leaders' and cultural conservatives' control over people's autonomy and self-determination. Gay men's free sexual expression drives a wedge into patriarchs' power by freeing and enriching the human spirit. Indeed, gay men are the patriots of the sexual (r)evolution.

2. Creating Sexual and Long-Term Relationship Models Based on Authenticity and Self-Determination

In his 1998 book, *The Pleasure Principle: Sex, Backlash, and the Struggle for Gay Freedom*, Michael Bronski proposes that "heterosexuals will be...drawn to more flexible norms that gay people, excluded from social structures created by heterosexuality, have created for their own lives. These include less restrictive gender roles, non-monogamous intimate relationships and more freedom for sexual experimentation; family units that are chosen, not biological; and new models for parenting. But most importantly, homosexuality offers a vision of sexual pleasure completely divorced from the burden of reproduction: sex for its own sake, a distillation of the pleasure principle."[84] We can see ample evidence that this prediction is already proving true.

Consider the prevalence of "friends with benefits" among heterosexuals, which followed the innovation of "fuck buddies" among gay men. The popular HBO show *Sex and the City* introduced this concept to the world in a September 1999 episode in which Samantha, Carrie, and Miranda school Charlotte about the ins and outs of fuck buddies. As Samantha summed it up with her characteristic gay-man-like frankness, "It's like Dial-a-Dick."[85] Gay men needed no explanation of this concept; we invented it. We laughed because the straight world was finally catching up.

In addition to friends with benefits, gay men's predilection for no-strings sex has shown up as the new norm among young adults. In 2012, researchers at the Kinsey Institute for Research in Sex, Gender, and Reproduction published a comprehensive article entitled "Sexual Hookup Culture: A Review." In it, the authors state that "'Hookups,' or uncommitted sexual encounters, are becoming progressively more engrained in popular culture, reflecting both evolved sexual predilections and changing social and sexual scripts.... These encounters are becoming increasingly normative among adolescents and young adults in North America, representing a marked shift in openness and acceptance of uncommitted sex."[86]

Cathy Crimmins, in her book *How the Homosexuals Saved Civilization*, points out how "much of the diversity and innovation in straight sex lives today is due to…gay influences. Straight America is more comfortable with oral and anal sex, pornography, bondage, sex toys, and bisexuality than ever before."[87] Syndicated sex-advice columnist Dan Savage serves as one of the more high-profile transfer points for gay men's sexual leadership, sharing advice with heterosexuals from a free, open, and distinctly gay male perspective.

The Role of Equality

Gay men's sexual leadership extends into the long-term relationship models that we pioneer, which are characterized by the same inner motivation, authenticity, honesty, flexibility, and inherent equality as our more casual forms of sexual expression. Our equal standing with each other, and lack of a rulebook and established roles, free us to explore what works for each partner. Certainly, we are not the only ones who are experimenting with alternative long-term relationship models, but among gay men, alternative structures are the norm. In *The Soul Beneath the Skin*, David Nimmons reports on a range of studies that confirm that about 75 percent of gay male couples in stable, long-term relationships are consensually non-monogamous, while only about 10 to 25 percent of opposite-sex married couples are.[88]

For heterosexuals, sexual freedom ostensibly ends with marriage. While monogamy may work for many opposite-sex couples, it creates enough misery—and enough cheating scandals—to call into question its utility for everyone. Data on sexual infidelity for opposite-sex couples varies, but according to the General Social Survey—sponsored by the

National Science Foundation and based at the University of Chicago—in any given year, about 10 percent of married people (12 percent of men and 7 percent of women) report having sex outside their marriage. In 2006, University of Washington researchers found that the lifetime rate of infidelity for men over 60 had increased to 28 percent, up from 20 percent in 1991. For women over 60, the increase in their lifetime infidelity rate was more striking: to 15 percent, up from 5 percent in 1991.[89] As these things go, people who have secrets to hide generally underreport them, so we can assume these figures are underestimates. But even if they describe things accurately, they illustrate the fact that compulsory monogamy does not work for everyone.

While some gay couples may feel pressure to conform to the heterosexual model, it is telling that a large majority does not. Even the difference in language used by gays and straights points to our different expectations. Colleen Hoff of San Francisco State University, the principal investigator for the Couples Study, a study of long-term male couples in non-monogamous relationships, points out that, "With straight people, it's called affairs or cheating, but with gay people it does not have such negative connotations."[90]

Gay couples choose the relationship model that works for them, based on their values and needs. David Nimmons reports that, for about 25 percent of gay male couples, that choice is monogamy—because it works best for both parties. It reflects their style, their relationship to sexuality, and the way they define commitment. But this choice can change with a relationship's longevity. For instance, among the 86 gay male couples who participated in the Couples Study, 42 percent began their relationships with an agreement to monogamy. Of these couples, 49 percent opened their relationship in the first year. Among the rest of the couples, the median time it took to open their relationships was five years.[91] Other research shows that approximately two-thirds of long-term male couples who have been together for five years or more are honestly non-monogamous.[92] The 1984 book *The Male Couple* reported that all of the 156 long-term couples participating had opened their relationships after five years.[93]

While the exact figure seems hard to pin down, research clearly shows that the vast majority of gay male couples create open relationships, which have as many variations as there are couples. Because gay men often separate sex from love, couples can draw distinctions between emotional and sexual fidelity—with emotional fidelity often being the line that they cannot cross. Ground rules can include how much information, if any, they share with each other; allowed or disallowed sexual acts; safe sex requirements; time and place of allowed liaisons, and so on. Some couples adopt a "Don't ask, don't tell," policy; others allow liaisons only when they play together. Open relationships typically rely on honesty, communication, and commitment to certain shared ground rules. Some couples choose polyamory, which involves multiple committed relationships with the full knowledge and consent of all partners. Polyamorous relationships require entire sets of agreements, given the multiple parties that can participate.

In all, open and polyamorous relationships require an advanced set of ethics: because no external body, like a divorce court, will issue sanctions for rule-breaking, partners become responsible solely to each other. This raises the stakes and requires a level of conscious commitment and personal responsibility. As David Nimmons suggests, open relationships require "extraordinary inventiveness and imagination," and constitute "one of our most significant affectional and ethical innovations."[94]

Gay men's relationship innovations offer models for opposite-sex couples where one or both partners craves sexual variety but wishes to sustain the integrity of the commitment. Religious, legal, and societal pressure, however, keeps most opposite-sex couples tethered to an externally-imposed relationship model which fails to account for real human needs, rather than one driven by authenticity. If compulsory monogamy worked for all couples, infidelity would not exist. In fact, in one study comparing deception within gay and straight couples, gay men were found to be "significantly more truthful" than heterosexual men, and straight men and women were found to respond deceptively more often than gay and lesbian couples.[95] Men in my groups echo this sentiment, expressing the idea that gay men serve and can heal humanity because we tell the truth about real human needs. Gay men create relationships based on negotiated ethics, which have implications for the evolution-ary development of all committed relationships.

Joe Quirk, author of the best-selling relationship book *It's Not You, It's Biology*, maintains that the kind of transparency that open relation-ships require can make them stronger. "The combination of freedom and mutual understanding can foster a unique level of trust," he says. Quirk describes traditional American marriage as being in crisis, stating that, "we need insight. If innovation in marriage is going to occur, it will be spearheaded by homosexual marriages."[96]

It is unlikely that most gay men who choose marriage will adopt a lifelong monogamous model. As gay marriage becomes more common-place and expands to all fifty states, gay men will remake this institution by introducing innovations tested in our community. Foes claim that gay marriage will damage traditional marriage. More likely, gay men will breathe freshness, vitality, and authenticity into marriage, saving it for everyone.

3. Bisexuality: Come Out, Come Out, Wherever You Are

Cathy Crimmins observes that gay men's free sexual expression has laid the groundwork for greater acceptance of bisexuality. Our presence and example alone create validation for men who are sexually attracted to both women and men to explore or at least consider their attraction to men. More than that, in the 1990s, gays and lesbians did something remarkable: we formally welcomed bisexuals—along with the transgen-der people who had always been in our midst—into the umbrella of our communities, creating the now-ubiquitous letter word, LGBT. It is telling that it was homosexuals, not heterosexuals, who created a safe, supportive, and empathetic place for bisexuals.

Despite this welcome, most bisexuals remain in the closet. John Syl-la, one of the founding members of the American Institute of Bisexuality, explains in the *New York Times* that, "Most [bisexuals] are in convenient opposite-sex relationships." As a result, homosexuals and heterosexuals often question—not without grounds—whether proclaimed bisexuality serves to conveniently hide homosexuality. The fact remains that many gay men have used the relative cover of bisexuality to hide their true orientation—or as a stepping stone to coming out. The title of the *Times* article in which Sylla was featured captures this widespread skepticism: "The Scientific Quest to Prove Bisexuality Exists."[97]

And yet, research indicates that bisexuals might actually outnumber homosexuals. According to a 2009 survey reviewed by the Williams Institute—a policy center specializing in LGBT demographics—3.1 percent of American adults identify as bisexual, while just 2.5 percent identify as gay or lesbian. While these figures cannot account for discrepancies between behavior and identity—and presumably if one factors behavior, these figures would jump considerably—they give a strong indication that there are many bisexual men out there.[98]

This has considerable implications, as connections among gay and bisexual men serve as transfer points for ideas, shared understandings, innovations, and sex. Most of this remains in the realm of possibility, but if gay men's influence on the larger society is any gauge, we can expect the development of a greater alliance between gay and bisexual men. The Millennial generation's much more accepting attitudes toward LGBT rights portend this shift.

Already, there exists a considerable transfer of information and energy between gay and bisexual men that neither group fully acknowledges. Open any gay dating application or website, and ads from bisexual—or, again, presumably bisexual—men abound. Consider the many venues gay men have created in which to meet each other; one can reasonably expect that a sizable number of bisexual men participate in them. Though I am not sure any studies have measured the intermingling of gay and bi men, given the size of the bisexual male population, and the lifetime likelihood of infidelity in opposite-sex marriages, it is safe to assume that some number of gay and bisexual men are having sex with each other.

The mere social proximity of gay and bisexual men creates opportunities to expand gender norms for all men. As we expand permission for inner-motivated sexuality, awareness of alternatives to limiting definitions of manhood are likely to find their way into the mainstream through bisexual-gay male contact. Movements such as the Mankind Project, the California Men's Gatherings, and a host of other welcoming environments for gay and bi men will no doubt speed the cultural transfer of gay men's innovations to all men. Indeed, the quiet alliance between gay and bisexual men holds perhaps some of the greatest potential to influence heterosexual adult males and the next generation of boys. Perhaps, as we see with the considerably more liberal attitudes among Millennials, this transformation has already begun.

4. The Global Antidote to Violence

Sex is one form of love. The sex-negativity of American culture makes it easy to forget this. Our religions, cultural conventions, and laws attempt to limit and proscribe sex, and wily shame serves to internally reinforce these external methods of control. Sex is powerful and empowering. It returns power stolen by external "authorities" to where it belongs—the individual. Sex is one of the most powerful ways of connecting with another human being. As the slogan from the 1960s suggests, it literally "makes love."

The presence of a significant group of men-loving-men changes the energetic state of the planet. Gay men—and the bisexual men we connect with—form a network around the Earth in which we bring the energy of love to a planet that is consumed with violence. If any other group of people engaged in global practices that channeled love into the world, they would be revered, but because we engage in sex as one means of doing this, we have been hated. The people most prone to act violently are those who are most homophobic, because homosexuality—especially among men—is the global antidote to violence. It threatens patriarchy, because it literally creates a more loving, more egalitarian world.

When gay men freely express our sexuality, we engage in a planetary transformation. We serve as grounding rods, neutralizing and counteracting men's knee-jerk rush to violence. Men in Gay Men of Wisdom groups had this to say about it:

- The tenderness of men loving other men provides another way for men to relate—one which is not hurtful or destructive. This provides a needed counterbalance to the male tendency to possess poor conflict resolution skills, and the quickness with which men turn to violence.

• There is an energetic difference that we may not have language for yet. Remember that we chose the term "gay." The original reclamation of this term contains hints of this energy.

• When we have sex, we create a connection with another person, a different way of communicating.

In creating this field of loving energy throughout the planet, gay men provide all men with alternative ways of being, offering some of the greatest hope for peace on Earth.

5. Restoring the Link between Spirit and Sex

No-strings sex has become so old-hat for gay men that many—including men in my groups—have expressed "hookup fatigue." The endless accessibility of free sex can create a sense of emptiness and disconnection; one man's freedom is another's prison. And so, in characteristic gay male fashion, when we become dissatisfied with the status quo, we innovate.

Men in Gay Men of Wisdom groups said this about this phenomenon:

• Our understanding of sexual liberation has evolved. We have expanded the notion of what this means, so liberation has become not limited to just sex with anonymous or multiple sex partners, but encompasses the full range of our desires.

• Many gay men tire of sex without meaning. Sexual desire can often signal a deeper desire, often for intimacy.

• Gay men are expanding the definition of why people engage in sex—for pleasure, and to meet deeper needs, including intimacy. We are winning the right to be intimate.

For many gay men, sexual liberation has become the search for fulfillment and deep connection with each other, which may or may not occur with multiple partners. We have expanded permission to become intimate with each other, which may or may not even involve sexual contact. Long-term relationships have always provided a haven for connected, meaningful sex, but not all gay men are in such relationships, and gay men in open and polyamorous relationships desire meaningful connections with other men as well. Gay men's innovations in this area borrow ancient ideas and give them a decidedly modern, gay spin.

Toby Johnson, in his pioneering book, *Gay Spirituality*, reminds the reader of the harm done by Western religions' separation of spirituality and sexuality. By depriving individuals of the direct connection with spirit that comes from the sexual experience, religious teachings contradict the lived experience of sex. As he puts it, "Our having sex is God's way of experiencing joy in creation. And our being loved by another is our way of experiencing God's love for us. God's love manifests as our beloved. In a way, all sex is sex with God."[99] Indeed, anyone who has exclaimed or considered exclaiming the words, "Oh, God!" during orgasm understands this experience.

In true consciousness-scout fashion, gay men have been seeking ways to imbue sexuality with spirituality—whether with each other or alone. Mentioned above, the Body Electric School, founded by Joseph Kramer, provides an excellent example of this type of innovation. This school's workshops teach Taoist/Tantric techniques, which help gay men look beyond the surface-level physicality that drives so much of our sexual dialogue, and connect with the erotic energy within. These techniques help participants discover and honor the sacredness in each other through sexuality. The school's varied offerings remain immensely popular and have created an entirely different kind of discussion about sexuality in the community and beyond. Indeed, while Body Electric began with a focus on gay men, it serves people of all genders and sexual orientations.

The Erotic Engineering Male Mystery School, created by Bruce P. Grether, provides another example of this line of inquiry. Its Mindful Masturbation practice helps practitioners use masturbation to reach higher states of awareness. Blue Tyger, an Erotic Engineering student-teacher, created a video course entitled *Heartgasm*, which demonstrates how one can achieve self-love through such masturbation. "Loving yourself isn't just something you tell yourself," he explains in the video trailer, "It's something you can actually physically do."[100] In the larger culture, we hear messages of shame around masturbation. It takes gay men to restore love to this universal male experience.

Kirk Prine, who describes himself as a body story expert, leads the Flesh & Spirit Community, based in San Francisco. Flesh & Spirit, founded in 1992, is "a community of queer men on an ecstatic path of transformation...Liberating ourselves to be more whole and thus in greater service to the world." In a characteristically gay male approach to spirituality, Flesh & Spirit holds as a central principle the "healing, integrating, and celebrating [of] queer men's bodies and the erotic as sacred." The community offers programs and services that weave ideas, concepts, and practices from many sources: Buddhism, Tantra, Taoism, African and Native American spiritualities, Christianity, Wicca, Judaism, Sufism, energy medicine, body-oriented therapies, and more.[101]

In retreat centers such as Easton Mountain and Wildwood, and at community centers and in groups throughout the United States, gay men who have grown dissatisfied with the status quo of sexual liberation have created an entirely alternative structure for exploring the deeper potential for sexual and spiritual connection. Twenty years from now, we can fully expect to see the ideas and practices that grow out of these explorations take root in the larger society.

Further Comments from Gay Men of Wisdom Groups about Sexual Leadership

• Culturally, we bring up the issue of sex as pleasure—sex as having no reason. If heterosexuals saw sex as pleasure, they would begin to behave sexually more like gay men.

• We are willing to talk to women about sex. This provides a safe way for women to explore, gather information, and apply it.

• We allow others to see that you can be yourself and go for what you want/desire.

• We've made heterosexuals take a good look at their sex life. What do they see? That they're allowed to enjoy their sexuality. Some see how unhappy they are, which gives them the power of choice.

• We allow all other groups to think about sex in a different way than how it is defined by religion and society.

• Sex is one more way of connecting with another human being.

• Sex can be seen in terms of a developmental process. When we are young, it makes sense to want to experience a lot of sex with different partners. When we get older, we may want less sex, and/or to connect on deeper levels. This could explain many older men's dissatisfaction with random or no-strings sex and a desire for deeper intimacy.

• A man who comes out late in life might go through his adolescent sexual stage. This could be entirely developmentally appropriate, as he's making up for lost time.

• Gay men bring a refreshing perspective—modeling what it looks like to live without sexual shame.

• Gay men serve as sexual leaders because we are willing to embark on a conscious journey. We might not have all the answers, but we are willing to explore and discover those answers.

• Sexual leadership requires acceptance of who we are, awareness of what we want, and the courage to be out.

The Authority of Sexual Leadership: Modeling Freedom and Responsibility

In many ways, gay men model that most cherished of American values—self-determination. By insisting on sexual expression free of external constraints, we test ways of relating sexually that spring from within. This leaves open the possibility to change our minds and our course.

Gay men lead humanity when it comes to sexuality not because we have all the answers, but because we are willing to continually discover what healthy and free sexual expression means for each of us.

With freedom comes responsibility. Our relationship innovations require a level of consciousness, communication, and truthfulness that does not exist in the traditional heterosexual relationship model—for when an external authority calls the shots about a relationship's rules, neither party has to think for themselves. While the traditional model may offer structure and safety for some, it creates misery for many. Gay men serve as sexual leaders because we model values of both freedom and personal responsibility. And as we see from our influence on the larger culture, the human striving for freedom cannot be constrained forever.

Chapter 14
Fine Attunement to Beauty, Creators and Keepers of Culture

"Our most fundamental experience of pleasure is essentially sexual in nature. The pleasure of a concert, a painting, a play, a movie, all relate in some way to our sexuality. Things we feel, see, hear, and touch enter our consciousness through the physical senses but they become part of our lives…through what they mean to us. Our experience of the material world in all of its forms and manifestations is profoundly sensual."
—Michael Bronski[102]

As we explored in the previous chapter, gay men's sexual leadership fuels the social innovations we bring to the human family. The principles of Tantra illuminate the close relationship between sexual and creative energies—energies that gay men excel at summoning and expressing. There is another force that propels gay men's drive to create: our fine attunement to beauty or, synonymously, our sensuality. As Michael Bronski observes, sexuality shares a close relationship with sensuality. If we imagined them as colors, they would sit side by side on the color wheel, each bleeding into the other.

Fueled by our sexual and creative energies, and our fine attunement to beauty, gay men make outsize contributions to culture. Christian de la Huerta describes this in his archetype of gay men as Keepers of Beauty: "Throughout history, queer people have been responsible for creating, promoting, and supporting much of the world's beauty, and have done so disproportionately to our numbers."[103] This gift has never received serious consideration by or appreciation from the gay community at large. Even men in my groups have given it little more than a tongue-in-cheek nod: "Gay men make things pretty." But culture is no small matter; it creates the ideal conditions for the human family to thrive. As keepers of culture, gay men play a critical supporting role in ensuring the survival and vitality of the species. The way we embody and express this gift provides important insights into the nature of gay men.

To begin our exploration, let us consider the role of sensuality, or fine attunement to beauty. Beauty itself can manifest in two basic and interrelated ways: 1) that which occurs in the natural world; and 2) that which people create. Gay men have an exquisite relationship with both manifestations of beauty. As men in my groups have said, we notice beauty more quickly than other men. This more open portal to beauty makes sense, given our collective tendency to possess a more feminine energy.

Beauty itself is essentially a manifestation of the feminine. Beauty from the natural world springs from what we often refer to as Mother Earth or the goddess Gaia. Man-made beauty results from creativity, also a feminine energy. For instance, how often do we hear descriptions of artists "giving birth" to a work? Gay men possess fine attunement to the beauty in the world around us, and we create beauty disproportionate to our numbers.

As sensitive men, a large number of gay men share a fond and profound appreciation for natural beauty—a rare feminine permission that many heterosexual men also allow themselves. (This wonder for the natural world, in fact, serves as a potential bridge to form alliances between gay and heterosexual men.) Gay men with this form of attunement to beauty often take it to the realm of exquisite expression—designing and creating extensive and lush gardens and landscapes. Visit a gay man's garden on a garden tour and you'll see the characteristic flair that makes it stand out.

Gay men beautify their neighborhoods. I heard a man from Orlando, Florida, remark that in his neighborhood, residents celebrate the arrival of gay couples because of this. Here we begin to see what happens when gay men's appreciation for beauty meets the creative impulse: our fine attunement to beauty drives creative expression that benefits everyone. Given the still-large concentration of gay men in urban centers, where garden space is less accessible, we often express this appreciation in smaller forms, such as window boxes packed with colorful flowers.

On a deeper level, many gay men share a strong connection to the Earth. All people can access this connection, of course, but the way gay men do it speaks to our unique relationship with the natural world and each other. Consider all the cruising and sex that happen outdoors. Engaged in ritualistically (I explore this more in Chapter 19), this cruising is informed by a drive for ecstatic communion with nature. Engaging in sexual "hunting" and connection in natural environments taps into the primal, tribal core of the gay male experience, and tunes us into the energy of the Earth and each other. A man in one of my groups noted that, for a large segment of gay men, sex in natural settings—in the woods, particularly—holds a very strong draw.

Environments where gay men are freest to be themselves produce the clearest examples of this phenomenon. Consider, for instance, the area between Cherry Grove and the Pines on Fire Island—known affectionately as the Judy Garland Memorial Forest and, alternately, the Meat Rack. This area of dense scrub pines is famous for its cruising and sex. If the drive for privacy were the only factor, sex in the Pines and Cherry Grove would only happen indoors, not here. And even when privacy alone prompts this choice of location for sex, something deeper ends up happening.

Visit the nude beach at Provincetown's Herring Cove on any late summer afternoon, and one will observe a striking, almost meditative tableau. At this time of day, the sun has softened its sting and yields its heat to a cooling breeze. Half the men desert the beach for Tea Dance. The waves may lap gently or roar and spray. As the heat subsides, men emerge—some naked, some clothed—and stroll the dunes, searching. They gaze across the expanse of beach and the bay. They cruise the men in their path, below on the beach, and in the tidal flats behind the dunes. They look across the salt marsh, taking in the sky and the horizon. A sexual charge electrifies the air, but little sex takes place. In this mix of raw nature and often eroticism, it seems that the searching is as much about connection with the Earth as with each other.

Anyone who enjoys sex outdoors has likely experienced a stronger connection with his partner and the earth beneath him—and perhaps has even experienced something transcendent. The Orgasmic Yoga Institute, also founded by Joseph Kramer, makes this connection explicit in its video, "Earth Honoring," which invites men to commune sexually with the Earth. It is no accident that Radical Faerie sanctuaries and retreat centers such as Easton Mountain and Wildwood locate themselves in remote, unspoiled environments where men can reconnect with the energies of the Earth. In these natural settings, where we can tune into the Earth's energy more readily, we can more easily create and recreate tribe—whether or not sex is involved.

As manifestations of nature, men themselves present immense beauty, something to which gay men are powerfully drawn and which we appreciate to the extent of near worship. As visual creatures, all men are highly attuned to good looks. Gay men take this appreciation to extraordinary heights.

View any gay men's publication, website, or party advertisement, and this attunement to beauty becomes immediately apparent. Photographs of athletic, handsome men jump out. Men's bodies are so central to gay male culture that it almost needs no mention. Our pride parades celebrate the male form. We visually cruise each other as a common pastime—in person and online. Our iconic imagery, well represented by the art of Tom of Finland, worshipfully depicts exaggerated masculinity and male assets. Our prolific attention to porn speaks to our hard-wired attraction to the beauty of men and men-on-men sexuality. No doubt, gay men love male beauty.

This translates into how we tend to our appearance. We go to the gym in droves, to improve our bodies and maintain them. Gay men tend to pay fastidious attention to clothing, hair, and other aspects of physical appearance—both to accentuate our bodies, but also as a form of created beauty. The old-fashioned word "dandy" carries with it homosexual implications, or at least possibilities. The popularized term "metrosexual" acknowledges the permission gay men have given heterosexual men to attend to the details of their physical body, dress, fashion, and manner of presentation. It affirms gay men's place as cultural trendsetters.

As gay men in my groups have noted, gay men tend to be stylish, tidy, and neat. We pay attention to etiquette. Esthetics matter to gay men. We care about fashion and trends. We are not afraid to invoke the feminine in our appearance and to use it to call attention to ourselves. We value good taste and set the trends that define it. We gave the term "fabulous" a new gay meaning. We appreciate beauty wherever it lives, and we teach others how to see that beauty.

For as finely attuned to natural beauty as gay men are, we are equally adept at creating works of beauty. The open portal that we have to beauty results in gay men being over-represented in all of the creative arts. Men in my groups continually note gay men's propensity for creativity and imaginativeness, and the fact that we create much of the world's beauty. We are the artists, the performers, the entertainers, and the creative men. We renovate neighborhoods and cultures, just as we renovate people. As with appreciation for natural beauty, we don't have a monopoly on this trait, but how we manifest this leaves clues as to who we are.

Gay scholars have informed our now common understanding that men-who-loved-men fill the honor roll of art and cultural history. Often reading between the lines, and looking for subtle clues in times and places that were hostile to overt acknowledgements of same-sex attraction, we know that Leonardo da Vinci, Michelangelo Buonarroti, Christopher Marlowe, Herman Melville, Peter Tchaikovsky, and Walt Whitman, among many others shared this characteristic. (Oscar Wilde, of course, is as famous for his writings as his tragic trials, in which he was persecuted for his homosexuality.) Because this knowledge is so well documented, I won't spend much time here and will instead refer readers to books such as A.L. Rowse's *Homosexuals in History*. A quick Google search unearths a treasure trove of information about men-who-loved-

men in the arts. One good resource: http://www.lgbthistorymonth.org.
uk.

Even the awareness of the considerable contributions that men-who-love-men have made to human culture throughout the centuries has not made much of a dent in our collective narrative and self-understanding. These were, of course, exceptional men of great talent and genius. Not everyone can be a Michelangelo, and one does not have to achieve status as genius to create beauty in the world. In fact, our capacity to create much of the world's culture extends beyond fine art into nearly every type of creative endeavor. While an exhaustive list is impractical, I will name a few representative groups.

The world of live theater would collapse without gay men's contributions—play writing, acting, costume design, set design, direction. As men in my groups have pointed out, gay men have a gift for storytelling. This makes us supremely adept in the realm of theater, movies, and television. Andrew Ramer, in his channeled book *Two Flutes Playing*, suggests that this harkens back to gay men's roles as priests before the Ice Age. As gay men were driven underground by formal religions, he suggests, we took up secular forms of drama and storytelling. If we compare theater to religious services such as the Catholic Mass, this idea seems quite plausible.

In every imaginable creative field, from fashion design to dance to, yes, flower arranging and hairdressing; from movies to television to writing and music; poetry, graphic design, interior design, and architecture; window dressing and makeup artistry; opera and ballet; gay men contribute to the creation of culture disproportionately to our numbers. Engaging our masculine-feminine intelligence, gay men draw from the creative energy of the feminine and the action-oriented energy of the masculine to bring new works, trends, ideas, and movements to life. Gay men set the cultural trends that the world follows.

In keeping with our more open portal, gay men notice, value, and preserve the often-overlooked created beauty that originated in earlier eras. Will Fellows devotes a book to the subject: *A Passion to Preserve: Gay Men as Keepers of Culture*. Through personal stories of gay men who have been drawn to historic preservation, this book recounts how, beginning at very young ages, gay boys with this attunement to beauty became the keepers of their families' stories, often through close ties with their grandmothers. They treasured and collected antiques—both family heirlooms and those they found elsewhere. As these boys grew, their interest broadened into preserving old, decrepit, decaying houses. Seeing the beauty obscured by decay, they brought houses and other buildings back to life.

This gift has resulted in wholesale revitalization of decaying neighborhoods in cities across the United States—such as Greenwich Village in New York and Boston's South End. Gay men, noticing the potential that most others overlooked, lovingly restored brownstone after brownstone, until the neighborhoods became so attractive that straight people moved in, drove up rents, and turned these into the hottest areas. More than a lesson in real estate, gay men, when left free to follow their attunement to beauty, re-birth nearly-dead neighborhoods, taking risks that few others are willing to assume. As men featured in Fellows' book describe, there is something about the decay that draws them—challenging them to use their talents to restore beauty and give new life.

Why does this matter? What difference does it make if we "make things pretty," restore decrepit neighborhoods, and tell good stories?

Culture creates the ideal conditions for a society to thrive. The Oxford Dictionary defines culture as "the arts and other manifestations of human intellectual achievement regarded collectively."[104] It is perhaps impossible to imagine any society without it. Even the most repressive regimes and societies create forms of culture—however inauthentic and dissatisfying they may be.

When free of censorship, culture brings fulfillment, excitement, stimulation, and meaning to what would otherwise be workaday lives. It is the glue that holds together our collective stories and shared history. The enjoyment we experience from reading a book, listening to music, seeing a show or movie, and watching an exquisite performance of dance is profoundly sensual, as Bronski points out. Being human comes with a sensual imperative—we must have sensuality to survive. If we could imagine a society without culture, life would become drudgery. Creativity and curiosity would atrophy. Innovation would fizzle. That society would stagnate, weaken, and die.

In our focus on biological reproduction of the species, we forget that a thriving society requires contributions from all those who constitute it. While child-rearing mainly falls within the province of heterosexuals, gay men play an equally important, yet overlooked, supporting role. As humanity becomes more conscious of this essential contribution that gay men make, it will become clear how a thriving gay male community gives a society an evolutionary advantage. And conversely, as I point out in Chapter 8, it will become clear that societies that oppress and kill their gay men rob themselves of the innovation, creativity, and ideas that they need to thrive. When gay men and our lesbian, bisexual, and transgender allies around the globe understand the ways we contribute to the health and vitality of the human species, we can make an entirely new case for equality and open a new chapter in our movement.

Chapter 15
A "Gay" Spirit

"Gay men know how to celebrate life."
—Brother Lomi, Monastic of the *Amaraji Maha*
Marai (The People of Love and the Great Promise)
Society of the Compassionate Heart Sacred
Mountain Monastery, Boise, Idaho,
Participant in Gay Men of Wisdom Groups

Before teenagers and young adults began using the word "gay" to mean "lame" or "worthless," before "queer" entered the lexicon as an alternative to "gay," and before the word came to be synonymous with homosexuality, "gay" expressed an essence about who we are that remains just as descriptive, accurate, and relevant today. Our movement claimed this word because it expressed the essential energy and spirit of homosexual men—that flourishing vitality that manifests through characteristic joy, exuberance, fun, celebration, ecstasy, and a persistent youthfulness, even into old age. We would serve ourselves well to remember and reclaim this original meaning, for we carry this energy within us without being fully aware of it. Being gay is much more than mere homosexuality. Our gay spirit, in fact, has the potential to change the world.

In New York City's Greenwich Village, a small street named "Gay Street" juts off Christopher Street. The Greenwich Village Society for Historic Preservation posted a thoughtful essay on its blog exploring both the evolution of the street and the word "gay" itself. It turns out that the street was named "Gay" long before the word's current usage and was likely a family name for someone who lived in the area, but the essay sheds light on the word's meaning before the term became associated with homosexuality:

> In modern parlance, "gay" has come to mean attracted to the same sex. But this was not always so, and the word's evolution, interestingly, mirrors that of Gay Street and its environs as well. Gay originally meant happy, carefree, exuberant. However, by the late nineteenth century and especially the early twentieth century, the connotations of the word gay came to be increasingly associated with a lifestyle unfettered by the conventions of the day; as time went on, this especially came to mean the sexual conventions of the day. The term 'gay' was associated with both men and women, many of whom lived in places like Greenwich Village or Paris, often habitués of the cafes and clubs of these unconventional communities, typically unmarried, frequently without traditional jobs, who did not seem to care what the rest of the world thought of them, and lived the "gay life." No doubt some of these iconoclasts were "gay" by today's definition, but many were not. It was not until the mid-twentieth century that use of the term "gay" came to more commonly mean specifically those attracted to the same sex, and not until the late twentieth century that this definition had come to eclipse other uses and associations.[105]

In its original and bohemian connotations, "gay" captures the youthful, joyful, and celebratory spirit that characterizes gay men. If we placed gay spirit on a color wheel, it would reside near sexuality and sensuality, for all three share common roots in joy and ecstasy. Gay spirit speaks to the vitality that gay men possess, which is palpable but defies easy description.

As I was preparing to write this chapter, I found myself struggling to describe this spirit. A visit to the gay section of Riis Park, a public beach in the Rockaways section of Queens, gave me my breakthrough. Riis Park sits on a stretch of beautiful beach that spans the length of the Rockaway peninsula. The public beach abuts the conservative and almost exclusively white neighborhood of Belle Harbor; until Hurricane Sandy blew through, a chain link fence separated the two areas, making the Belle Harbor beach inaccessible. As I walked with my sister Marguerite along the newly accessible Belle Harbor beach, we noticed families sedately lounging and watching their children play. Pairs of young men played paddleboard, and a group played beach bocce. One group of young people gathered around a tent with beer bottles in hand, raising the exuberance level above the rest of the crowd. Here, the children and young people seemed to be having the most fun. Among the adults, a sense of staidness and caution pervaded. It was a common scene in which little stood out or surprised.

As we walked further, we approached the gay section of the beach—a racially and ethnically mixed group—and the energy changed markedly. I first noticed the sound of dance music. Then the densely packed blankets and chairs. Then the smiles on men's and women's faces, the gregariousness of the crowd, and an infectious sense of fun. The Queen of Queens, a man who parades the beach each day in inventive drag along with his gray parrot, was holding court and posing for photos. Men cruised each other. Women went topless. People were talking and laughing. This section of the beach reverberated with joy and love—the core of gay spirit—inviting everyone around to enjoy life. The vibrational difference between the gay and straight sections of the beach could not have been more striking. My sister, who is straight, remarked, "Now *this* is where we need to be hanging out."

At its most visible and observable level, gay spirit manifests in our propensity to have fun and experience joy. The experience at Riis Park plays itself out wherever gay men gather. People love going to gay nightclubs, for instance, because they are *fun*. Gay men excel at creating outlandish and exuberant nightlife spectacles, each with its own distinct character, but all of which share exhilarating energy. The television series *Queer as Folk* captured this quintessential party atmosphere in the fictional nightclub Babylon, which formed the hub of the characters' social lives. The musically and sexually charged atmosphere Babylon conveyed speaks to the close relationship between gay men's exuberant spirit and our expression of sexuality and sensuality.

As with our leadership in fashion and the arts, gay men's flair for creating ecstatic group dance makes us the trendsetters in nightlife. We have produced such a culture around dance that it is not uncommon for men well into their middle age to attend nightclubs. While fun usually serves as the main draw, these group experiences invoke the power and spirit of the gay male tribe, and can serve a powerfully spiritual function. The ecstatic connection experienced in a good nightclub ensures the continued circulation of sexual, creative, life-force energy. By tapping into the gay male tribal energy, gay men keep themselves and humanity fresh, alive, vital, and young. I explore this potential further in Chapter 19.

Gay spirit manifests in the less visible but no less impactful tendency to excel at creating all manner of events. Gay parties, weddings planned by gay men, and even fundraising events run by gay men have a characteristic flair. In these venues, our fine attunement to beauty, our orientation toward service, and our capacity to invoke celebration all come together to create sensual experiences that invite participants to feel joy.

The Divine Child

Gay thinkers have often reflected on the applicability of Carl Jung's *puer aeternus* archetype to gay men—the man-boy who remains forever young. In popular culture, the positive side of this archetype, known as the Divine Child, is best represented by Peter Pan. As Toby Johnson describes it, "Peter Pan…is the eternal boy whose innocence and good will are infectious—and redemptive. The eternal boy saves the day."[106] Reflecting on the shadow side of this phenomenon, Mark Thompson, in his autobiographical book, *Gay Body*, explores how it can turn destructive. "We lived in a state of protracted adolescence, with all its wildness and curiosity," he writes about his experience in pre-AIDS gay culture. "Our innocence emboldened us. Invulnerability was never doubted. And, to a point, we were transformed. But then we were confronted with mortal reality, including death in the form of an unstoppable virus."[107]

Toby Johnson suggests that this archetype remains so prevalent among gay men in part because gay men remain largely childless. "Becoming a parent creates transformation at all levels of the personality. With the birth of a child, men and women change. They begin to identify with their own parents. In their children's development, they re-experience their own childhood. This transformation appears in their bodies and their faces and their ways of being. They look older."[108]

Gerald Heard, an English-born philosopher, writer, anthropologist, and BBC commentator who lived from 1890 to 1971, believed that gay people "best represented the biological concept of neoteny—prolonged youth. Our neotenous nature allows gay people to be open and growing and mobile and exploring long after our heterosexual age peers have been forced to settle down into the specialization and stability required of parenthood and so-called maturity."[109] Edward Carpenter made a similar observation in his groundbreaking 1908 book, *The Intermediate Sex*.[110]

And yet, Johnson acknowledges that gay men's youthful spirit is not eclipsed by the demands and trials of parenthood. "Gay men who do become parents often resist the tendency to drop sexual identity and refocus on fatherhood. Even though they have children, they are still not evolving into their father's life. Homosexuality retards aging."[111] This echoes Frank Love's article in *The Advocate*, where he refuses to forego the clubs—despite other gay men's disapproval—just because he is a parent.[112]

As James Broughton sees it, "We are the Peter Pans of the world, the irrepressible ones who believe in magic, folly, and romance. And, in a sense, we never do grow old. That's part of what being gay signifies: innocence of spirit, a perennial youthfulness of soul. The gay spirit is a young spirit. Which is why the world needs us."[113] Indeed. Gay spirit, or gay men's capacity for joy, love, celebration, exuberance, and ecstasy, not only keeps us young, it ensures that, well into our old age, we continue to confer an outsize benefit to the world.

Implications of Our "Gay" Spirit

If we had to reduce "gay spirit" to one word, that word would be "joy," for this essence captures gay spirit's cause and effect. Joy can be an end unto itself—a desired state that we spend much of our lives seeking to attain. Authentic joy originates from within, but it often occurs in the company of others. In this way, joy is inherently infectious and powerful. It creates a powerful channel for love to enter the human plane. You cannot hate another person when you feel joy. When you are in a state of joy, you cannot judge, make comparisons about, or resent others. Joy invites other people closer. It establishes commonality. It dissolves differences. You cannot be violent when you feel joy. Celebration engages others in a dance that affirms our common humanity. Celebrations unleash joy. Smiles, fun, and frivolity play an adaptive function, keeping our energy light and spreading infectious joy and shared love.

Joy and resentment reside on opposite ends of the same spectrum. Joy creates openings. Resentment creates closings. The most joyful people are the most open to others. The most resentful people are the most closed to others. Listen to any arch-conservative media personality or politician, and the lack of joy and presence of resentment are immediately apparent. Resentment holds a powerful negative energy, while joy holds a powerful positive energy. Each can be used to influence the masses.

A society cannot kill or launch wars from a state of joy. A joyless people is thus more easily controlled and moved toward war. This may be one reason totalitarian leaders maintain such strict control over cultural and social expression. They know that joy unleashes love, and that love diminishes division and creates wholeness. Joy opens hearts and minds. It precludes resentment. Joy invites innovation and possibility.

Gay spirit, while seemingly frivolous even to gay men, counterbalances and offers alternatives to hatred. Much in the way that gay men's free sexual expression literally creates love, so too does our joyful, celebratory nature. Just as we did during the AIDS crisis, gay men's spirit opens the human heart. It should come as no surprise that religious and cultural conservatives view joy, celebration, ecstasy, and exuberance as degenerate. For in their view, they are right: gay spirit undermines patriarchal power structures.

Men in Gay Men of Wisdom groups had this to say about gay spirit:

- Our work is our play. Our play is our work. We bring a creative spark to the world.

- We manifest a kind of attractiveness that is appealing to others. We make attractive looking men because we have more feeling in the face. People like us.

- Gay men glow. You notice gay men in a crowd. They look happy, gay in the real sense of the word. It's something I give off as a gay man.

- Men go through stages of life and change with each stage. Gay men tend to hold onto the gift of maintaining a childlike energy throughout each of these stages. This is fundamentally different.

- We are fun and spontaneous.

- We know how to hold joy.

- We are passionate and charismatic.

- We are the pioneers.

- Gay men are playful. We laugh, make jokes, and use humor.

Gay men are keepers and cultivators of the spirit of joy and celebration well into our old age. This youthful energy ensures that, despite our small numbers, we continue channeling love, possibility, and innovation into the human energy field long after most others have resigned themselves to conventionality. Gay spirit makes all of us better people.

Chapter 16
Models of Authenticity and Courage, Cleansers of Shame

"But he isn't wearing anything at all."
—The child in *The Emperor's New Clothes*

"I'm as mad as hell, and I'm not going to take this anymore."
—Howard Beale in the film *Network*

In the mid- to late twentieth century, gay men and lesbians did something remarkable and, until that point, unthinkable: we came out. No longer content to wear masks, to hide and endure treatment as second-class citizens, we risked everything so we could live our truth openly and without shame. We created communities, took political power, changed laws, endured the horrors of a plague—made worse by society's neglect and animosity—opened hearts and minds, and changed the prevailing social climate toward homosexuality in much of the Western world. This striking act of bravery, taken individually and collectively, changed the course of history.

Our movement could be viewed as a struggle by a sexual minority to attain the same legal and political rights that the majority has always enjoyed. We often characterize the movement this way, but we all know this is only half of the story. The LGBT rights movement stands out among the progressive movements of the twentieth century. For while we sought to change the external structures that confined and harassed us—laws and societal attitudes—on a deeper level, we fought for the freedom to live *authentically*. In this sense, our movement has always been, and continues to be, a drive to free the human spirit.

Authenticity means living a life on the outside that matches what characterizes us inside. It means listening to and following our inner voice. It requires having the consciousness to discern the difference between our inner voice and the panoply of external voices—those of our parents, our family, our community, our religion, our peer group, the mass marketing machine, and so on. It means telling the truth, even when doing so entails great risk. It often entails a Hero's Journey—death of the old and birth of the new. Following this path requires strength, courage, and conviction—all decidedly masculine traits. Gay men and lesbians provide some of the best examples of authenticity for all of humanity.

Authenticity is profoundly attractive. The courage it takes to live authentically commands respect. We could never have changed laws and societal attitudes so rapidly had we not been willing to live authentically. On a very basic level, humans gravitate toward those who live authentically. Authenticity makes us better people, for by fully accepting ourselves, we open our hearts to others. The self-love that authenticity requires becomes expressed as love for others. When we choose authenticity, we take more risks in all areas of our lives, leading to greater satisfaction and innovation. The ultimate act of self-empowerment, choosing authenticity means challenging limiting conventions from wherever they originate, and reclaiming for ourselves the power that we previously granted to others. What begins with accepting our sexuality and living it truthfully transmutes into a life lived fully, and from within. We return to the state of wholeness with which we entered this life. As one man in my group stated about his journey to living authentically, "I am now the child that I was. I have returned to that earlier stage, before the world said, 'No, put that aside.' This is the recovery of joy."

Authenticity is powerful and contagious. People long to live in this state. By risking our welfare and lives, gay men give permission to our fellow human beings to live according to their inner voice. And because coming out never ends, we continually demonstrate to those around us the courage that authenticity requires. Consider the ripple effects of the millions of gay men who have come out around the globe, and the many millions of actions we take daily in which we model authenticity.

Men in Gay Men of Wisdom groups had this to say about our propensity to live authentically:

- Being our authentic selves communicates to others that they can be their authentic selves.

- We encourage people to practice acceptance of self and others, and tolerance.

- Our coming out has an impact on others; it allows them to be more authentic.

- Because we accept ourselves, we accept others. We model acceptance for humans.

- Our coming out shatters assumptions. It allows people's beliefs to evolve.

- We take risks.

- We don't conform.

- The masculine shows up in how staunchly I live my values.

- We displace the expected and the ordinary. This allows others to discover the possibility of their own individuality.

- We give permission to others by requiring none.

- That such a small minority can gain such attention makes people take notice.

- The challenges we have faced make us be more in touch with ourselves. They have created stronger, more self-aware, more conscious men.

- We have shown people the humanity of gay men—that we are human.

- I remind people of their power from a mindful, heart-centered place.

- We displace expectation.

- We challenge people.

- We inspire people through our courage.

- Humanity is hard-wired to resist change. We embody change in a real-time way.

- We make it easier for people to seek changes that allow them to realize their potential. We are a profile in change.

- We bring society back into balance through our spiritual, artistic, and cultural contributions.

- Creating change is part of our nature. It's what we are here for; it is the function we serve.

- We have a different way of looking at things, as a result of our in-between nature. That in itself creates change.

Men in my groups agreed that, by coming out, we give others permission to:

- Accept who they are.

- Be courageous and authentic.

- Exercise self-compassion.

- Drop judgments of the self and others.

- Appreciate the commonalities among people instead of the differences.

- Practice acceptance.

- Be curious about those who are different from themselves.

As men in Gay Men of Wisdom groups point out, when we accept others as they are, we spread acceptance. When we view ourselves and others non-judgmentally, we change the social conversation. When we live courageously, we inspire others to do the same. Social scientists tell us that ideas spread through social networks. Gay men spread authenticity and model the courage it takes to truly live this value.

Authenticity sounds noble in concept—like a Hollywood movie in which a hero overcomes all odds and gets the girl. Living it is an entirely different experience. Authenticity exacts a high price, which gay men disproportionately pay for the human family.

Cleansing Shame

The ass is meant for one-way traffic.
Don't be a woman.
Sissy.
Faggot.
Gay men are promiscuous.
Gay sex is sinful.
Love the sinner, hate the sin.
An abomination against God.
You're less than a man.
It's unnatural.
I don't have problems with gays, as long as they keep it to themselves.
Sodomy.
AIDS carriers.
Cock sucker.
The Bible says gays should be killed.
Batty man.
Poofter.
Queer.
Real men are masculine.
Don't be a girl.

By choosing to live authentically, we have made a bargain that places us in harm's way so that we may free the human spirit for all of humanity.

For gay men, living authentically requires wrestling with patriarchy's wily and insidious tool of mass conformity: shame. We take on a disproportionate level of shame, and we process and release it in disproportionate amounts. By facing shame fearlessly, challenging it, exposing its origins, and releasing its power over us, we deflate the force that keeps so much of the world trapped in self-reinforcing, limiting, and painful cycles. By coming out and living authentically, gay men are cleansing humanity of toxic shame.

History is as much a record of people striving to live authentically as it is of some groups preventing people from achieving this state. Authenticity is personal power. This, of course, threatens patriarchy. Shame, an extraordinarily inventive and potent tool—because of how it can attach itself to almost anything and masquerade as something unrelated—ensures social conformity by seeming to be one's own voice. In reality, shame is someone else's agenda internalized. Once learned, shame perpetuates the external rules and expectations imposed by others. Shame, like guilt, is "the gift that keeps on giving."

Shame's enduring potency derives from the violence accompanied by the original message. Consider the statements that appear above. Each is its own act of emotional violence, intended to deliver harm as a means of forcing conformity to heterosexual assumptions and narrow gender norms. Each statement implies that physical violence or social sanction could follow. These statements contain the essence of patriarchy: dominance of one group over another, and the use of any means possible by the dominant group to control and subjugate the other group.

Every gay man has faced more than his share of shame. Whether or not we experienced physical violence, we have all endured emotional violence. We all must take our own individual paths to confront and cleanse ourselves from shame and the violence that delivered it. Facing shame about one's sexuality, gay men know, requires courage that most heterosexuals will never be called to summon.

Gay men and lesbians have made an extraordinary and unprecedented agreement to banish shame. After Stonewall, we collectively agreed to come out, tell the truth, and live our authenticity. No other group has formed with this specific purpose. Gay men, by virtue of the distinct and singular vitriol that we face as men who love and have sex with men, and as men who have a more feminine energy, bear the brunt of society's shame around homosexuality. By consciously committing to freely express our sexuality, we have chosen the path of the spiritual warrior. Cleansing shame requires the presence of self-love; thus, we have set ourselves on the path toward self-love. When we transform shame into self-love, we change the energy on the planet. We inspire others who are shackled by their own shame. A gay man who has resolved his shame shines a beacon of light and a clean, powerful energy that sets an example for all other humans.

When I speak of self-love to gay men, I often hear a barrage of comments about all the ways we hate ourselves. I do not intend to suggest that all gay men have cleansed themselves of their shame and reached a profound state of self-love. Many men have, but our collective journey continues. Shame retains its potency. It shows up in how we treat ourselves individually and in the abysmal ways we can still treat each other (see Chapter 18). As men in my groups have discussed, releasing sexual shame results in greater personal responsibility; without someone else's agenda running us, we must take ownership of our actions and our behavior toward others. Like the inmate released after a long stay in prison, this newfound freedom can be frightening and disorienting. And yet, by living openly, we have consciously chosen to walk a path that serves an evolutionary function.

At this time in history, the gay male role is inextricably tied to cleansing human shame and replacing it with self-love. This path contains an inherent paradox: when we embrace our authenticity and cleanse ourselves of shame, we discover that the enemy is not the other, but rather ourselves. The enemy consists of other people's ideas, which we have embraced and given life to. When we realize our power to change our thinking, we live freely. Gay men inspire people around the globe to live from within, to attune to their inner voice. By courageously engaging as spiritual warriors, gay men awaken the spiritual warrior in those around us. We show humanity the path to wholeness. And we expand the pool of love available to all people on the planet.

Chapter 17
Outsiders Driving Evolutionary Advancement

*"Humanity muft expand its experience from persons (subjects)
thinking objectively, thinking competitively—in a nutshell,
thinking opportunistically and nearly always in terms of
self-advantage—to thinking subject-to-SUBJECT, equal-
to-equal, sharer to sharer…Humanity muft expand its
experience to thinking of another…not as object—to be used,
to be manipulated, to be maftered, to be consumed—but
as subject, as another like him/her self, another self to be
respected, to be appreciated, to be cherished."*
—Harry Hay[114]

Gay men occupy an outsider's place by virtue of our innate differences, our minority status, and the perspective that these confer. Nearly every gay writer, when commenting on gay men's
place in society, has observed this phenomenon. Christian de la Huerta
describes this as the archetype of the Outsider Looking In: "As outsiders, queer people help society to more accurately perceive itself…
Having 'outsider status' is thus intrinsic to being able to see the bigger
picture, the forest from the trees." De la Huerta notes that, to serve a
reflective function for humanity, one must have a certain distance from
it. "This quality is what makes so many queer people good observers and
chroniclers of society, why we excel as writers, filmmakers, historians,
and journalists." [115] As Harry Hay noted, gay people fill this role *without*

judgment, mirroring back the essence of who people are without the sting of shame that society inflicts.[116]

Toby Johnson describes this outsider position, and the frame of reference it creates, as "gay perspective"—the title of one of his books. He proposes that the gay outsider's perspective sees commonality where others see division; we see connections where others see separateness. He explains: "Conventional thinking, dominated by the influence of straight males, asserts: 'I'm right and you're wrong.' Non-polarized thinking transforms that: 'We're both right and we're both wrong, from different perspectives.' Therefore both sides can coexist and help one another. There is no competition. This is the basis for love of neighbor and love of enemy." Johnson refers to conventional thinking as seeing "either/or" and the gay perspective as seeing "both/and." [117] In short, gay men have the innate ability to see duality and embrace paradox.

The utility of this skill cannot be overestimated. As Johnson suggests, it is the key to resolving individual and global conflict. It allows for healing to take place. It forges consensus and collaboration. It unleashes innovation and creates new pathways for humanity. Gay men are certainly not the only ones who possess this ability; indeed, the survival imperative in a shrinking and increasingly ecologically frail planet requires that consciousness evolve in this direction. Activists of many stripes have called for this new way of relations. But gay men's outsider perspective exquisitely positions us to lead humanity through The New Way Forward.

The world has yet to recognize the great untapped resource it has in its gay men and lesbians. Gay men and lesbians are humanity's default outside perspective. We are the observers, mirrors, and problem-solvers. Present in every society on the planet, we bring a way of seeing the world that humanity needs more than ever. It seems no accident that gay men and lesbians chose this time in history to come out—we might even consider the possibility that, on a higher level, humanity collectively chose to manifest LGBT consciousness at this time in our evolution. While we mostly fill this role without full awareness right now, when we come to better understand this role and own our power, we can change the direction of history. The world really is waiting for us.

Gay men's outsider perspective informs or can be observed in the 13 other Distinct Gay Male Gifts. Consider the examples below:

The Outsider Perspective and the Distinct Gay Male Gifts

Masculine-Feminine Intelligence	The wholeness and connections we see from our gay perspective echo in our masculine-feminine intelligence. From our perspective of wholeness and integration, we recognize and can help others achieve this potential within themselves.
A Gentle, Collaborative Social Orientation	Because we see commonalities and connection, we work with instead of against. Those who recognize commonality and interdependence are less inclined to act aggressively. When we see wholeness and connection, it becomes much more difficult to foment division.
An Orientation toward Service	We heal others so effectively because we invite others to fully integrate disowned parts of themselves. Our dual perspective predisposes us to be less judgmental and non-judgmental of others. (Unless it relates to poor taste, which is, of course, unforgivable.)
Reformers of Religion, Spiritual Leaders	Our rejection from the world's religions gives us the perspective to challenge and expose creeds' and hierarchies' hypocrisy. As religious exiles, we innovate spiritual paths that integrate authenticity, sexuality, and honor for the Earth.
Teachers of Compassion, Generosity, and the Authentic Masculine	Even though the majority displayed indifference at best, our non-polarized perspective enabled us to create solutions to the AIDS crisis that saved countless lives.
Models of Forgiveness	With an innate understanding of human shortcomings, gay men forgive those who have caused them some of the most grievous harm.
Friends, "Soul Mates," and Co-Revolutionaries with Straight Women	From our place outside, we poignantly recognize the ruse and harm of rigid gender norms and conspire with our friends to expand them.
Esthetic Outsiders and Gender Tricksters: The Art of Camp and Drag	From our place outside the majority, we recognize and welcome those ideas and individuals who don't fit society's norms.

The Outsider Perspective and the Distinct Gay Male Gifts
Continued

Modeling Sustainable Manhood	Our location outside heterosexuality enables us to critically evaluate and re-create manhood.
Sexual Leadership	Nowhere does our outsider status take on more prominence and visibility than in how we express "forbidden" sexuality. Our free sexual expression fuels our prodigious social and cultural contributions to humanity.
Fine Attunement to Beauty, Creators and Keepers of Culture	Our location outside the majority enables us to observe, reflect on, and contribute cultural vision, which ensures the welfare and vitality of the human race.
A "Gay" Spirit	The freedom that comes with being an outsider enables us to experience incredible joy and spread it to others. Joy promotes peace.
Models of Authenticity and Courage, Cleansers of Shame	The freedom that comes from being outside enables us to live lives based on authenticity and courage, inspiring others to do the same.

Living with Duality and Paradox: The Nature of the Gay Male Path

"It's not easy being green."
—Kermit the Frog

"She had not known the weight until she felt the freedom."
—The narrator describing Hester Prynne in Nathaniel
Hawthorne's *The Scarlet Letter*

Part of what drives gay men's ability to hold duality and paradox springs
from the lived experience of the outsider. We possess a distinct perspective because we occupy a location outside the majority of humanity.

This experience also creates poignant and often painful dualities and paradoxes. Thus, the outsider's perspective and our lived experiences reinforce each other. This makes gay men a laboratory for this evolutionarily advanced skill. Paradox seems less scary to us because we live it. Consider how dualities and paradoxes color the gay male experience:

The Dualities and Paradoxes of the Gay Male Experience

Being gay gives us great freedom	Being gay exacts great pain and requires strength of spirit
Gay men affirm and validate others	We challenge others and the larger culture
We soothe and heal	We provoke
We are integral to human family	We reside outside the majority, and we are "other" even in own families
We are men	We don't always feel like men
We make outsize cultural contributions	We express our sexuality in an outsize manner
We serve as the bridge between men and women	We are not women, and we have significant differences from most men
We comfort others	We instigate reforms
We make and preserve culture	We challenge the dominant culture
We are uniquely gifted	We are uniquely wounded
We have an exuberant, joyful spirit	We know great suffering
We reinvent manhood	We fear violence from men
We teach compassion	We struggle to have compassion for ourselves and each other
We free the human spirit	We pay a price for freeing the human spirit. We struggle to free ourselves.
We model courage and authenticity	We know great doubt and uncertainty
We model forgiveness	We expose hypocrisy
Society thrives on the cultural contributions we make	Society scorns the sexual energy that drives these contributions
We create what's new	We hasten death of the old

Most people who live in the majority never experience this level of duality and paradox. Being part of the dominant culture thus confers a distinct advantage, enabling individuals to move through life without having to question basic societal assumptions. Our religions and politicians preach a black-and-white version of right and wrong, but the lived experience teaches us infinite nuance. To many people in the majority, economic and racial injustice live in the heads of those who are less fortunate—or reflect some essential character defect. Anyone on the other side of these experiences knows better.

Personal and regional conflicts persist when both sides cling to their identity as victims but fail to recognize their own responsibility. The solution to peaceful human relations lies in the ability to grasp duality and tolerate paradox. Gay men live this every day, so it should come as no surprise that we gift this perspective to humanity. And it should come as no shock that, as outsize love-makers, gay men are preeminent peacemakers. Another duality?

Part III
A Call to Action

Chapter 18
Owning and Managing the Shadow

"We exist in a society that...denies its shadow and therefore projects it onto others. Society is still so powerfully a hateful place, a dysfunctional place, that it's almost suicide to speak out about its shadow... What's missing from gay life is first of all a naming of all these issues, much less what you do about them."
—Mitch Walker[118]

Gay men's distinct gifts exhibit the remarkable generosity that we bring to the world. We heal, nurture, challenge, serve, teach, and forgive humanity. We are engaged in a revolution of evolutionary proportions. Gay men are what the world has been waiting for.

For as much generosity as we bestow upon the bulk of humanity, and for as much mutual support as we give each other in many instances, gay men can be remarkably hurtful toward each other. I have heard this sentiment expressed in every group I have run. The most resistance I have encountered in my Gay Men of Wisdom work has come on two occasions, when I led discussions premised on the idea that gay men share a common set of values. Both times, just minutes into the session, I began to receive heated and angry challenges from the men. Their comments shared a common tenor that expressed: "How can you say that we share common values when gay men have been so cruel to me?" In fact, throughout the Gay Men of Wisdom work, I have heard near consensus that gay men feel more wounded by other gay men than by heterosexuals.

What's going on here? A group of men that has the capacity to help humanity discover The New Way Forward finds itself more wounded by its own members than by those who oppressed them? Of course, that is not the whole story. An emotional response does not mean that gay men *actually* victimize each other more than the larger world oppresses us. It might just *feel* that way. We would not have the friendships and romantic partnerships that bring us together; nor our social groups, community centers, and advocacy and social service organizations if we victimized each other more than we expressed care. Still, the double standard—that we give our gifts generously to heterosexuals and often withhold them from each other—warrants attention and action.

Our poor treatment of each other, which occurs frequently enough to inflict deep pain, should come as no surprise: we are human. To some extent, this behavior reflects internalized homophobia, which we project onto each other without conscious understanding that we are doing so. It reflects the pain of growing up as outsiders. Some psychologists liken the effects of growing up in a homophobic environment to post-traumatic stress disorder—the state of trauma persists long after the actual events have passed. Indeed, every time homophobic events occur in one's life or the world, this trauma can become reactivated. These scars complicate our relationships with other gay men. Some of our poor treatment of each other results from our choice to sexually objectify each other, as I discuss below. And some of the wounds we inflict on each other result from carelessness and even cultivated callousness.

These hurts keep us disempowered. Through them, we enforce the dominant culture's values, even as we proudly claim to shed those values. They prevent full liberation, keep us divided, and they stop us from achieving our full potential as forces for positive change. And more than anything, they make us miserable and cause us great pain. We deserve better than that.

This dark side of gay men reflects what the Swiss psychiatrist Carl Jung called the shadow. According to Jung, the shadow consists of those (mostly negative) aspects of our personality that we deny the existence of or remain unconscious about. Because we refuse to acknowledge these traits and deem them unacceptable to us, we project them onto others.

Thus, the traits that we dislike the most in others are often the hidden and disowned parts of ourselves—our personal shadow.[119] For gay men, in many cases, the shadow represents the dark side of our gifts; in others it simply reflects our human flaws. Acknowledging and managing one's shadow requires a willingness to confront oneself. As Jung describes it:

> The shadow is a moral problem that challenges the whole ego-personality, for no one can become conscious of the shadow without considerable moral effort. To become conscious of it involves recognizing the dark aspects of the personality as present and real. This act is the essential condition for any kind of self-knowledge, and it therefore, as a rule, meets with considerable resistance.[120]

It is easy to point fingers, to become enraged, and to reenact the drama of being the victim within our own group. It is much more difficult to accept our own responsibility for victimizing others. Few people truly see themselves as perpetrators of harm. Most want to believe that they are fundamentally good, and that they act nobly—or at least they "do the right thing." The fact is that we are all perpetrators. Every gay man has, at some point—and sometimes at many points—cast judgment upon, belittled, dismissed, ignored, insulted, derided, demeaned, jabbed at, avoided, recoiled from, expressed disgust for, or otherwise hurt another gay man. Each of us has perpetrated these acts of violence on each other.

Interrupting this cycle requires a measure of wisdom: that we acknowledge, own, and manage our shadow. It necessitates accepting radical responsibility for our part in creating our experiences with other men—and relinquishing our cherished sense of victimhood. It also requires forgiveness—for those gay men who have hurt us, and for ourselves. When we recognize the harm we have caused other gay men, and forgive ourselves for doing so, we can begin to create stronger, more honest, and more loving relationships with each other. The healer accepts that he is also the perpetrator.

A Gay Network, Not a Community

I hear the constant refrain among gay men that they do not feel part of the gay community—a sense that it belongs to others, those on the inside. In fact, I have never heard a gay man express that he feels *part* of the gay community. I see two related factors driving this sense of exclusion. First, gay men live such disempowered lives as children and even as adults that we feel like perpetual outsiders. *And we are, Blanche, we are.* It is our role in and gift to the human family. Being on the outside remains with and defines the interior life of gay men. And so we bring a sense of feeling excluded even in relation to our own group. It makes me wonder, though, if most gay even know what "insiderness" feels like. Would we recognize it if it walked up to us and gave us a hug?

At the same time, the language we use contributes to the problem. The word "community" creates expectations that ultimately lead to disappointment. The word implies several inaccuracies:

• That a center exists within the gay world comprised of a cluster of individuals, groups, and institutions

• That a physical center such as a city or a neighborhood exists

• That leadership, authority, and "insiderness" emanate from those centers

The way we invoke this concept, "the gay community" does not consist of a Faerie circle where we make decisions by consensus. Rather, our shared idea reflects hierarchical expectations—that a central authority represents and leads gay men. The "community" turns members into "followers." It allows us to project our expectations onto the places, groups, institutions, and individuals that we believe constitute that authority. If we are outsiders and followers, we can—from our safe remove—cast judgment on those who are "inside." We can nurse our wounds and perpetuate the belief that we are victims who will never belong. When those places and institutions fail to live up to our expectations, we experience disappointments large and small, which we had expected anyway.

Visually depicted, "the gay community" might look as follows:

Gay "Community"

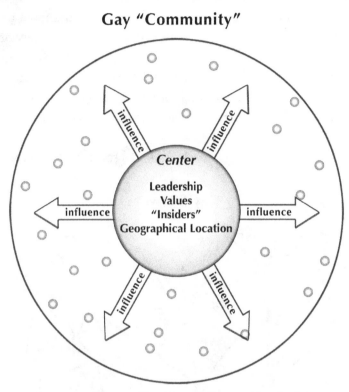

In this view of the gay world, authority and leadership emanate from the center, and members become followers. A sense of exclusion and resentment develops on the part of "members" based on their perception of being outsiders.

The term "gay community," however, does not factually describe how we organize ourselves. No institution or place holds the central authority for gay men: we are not the Catholic Church with a pope who dictates worldwide policy from the Vatican. A more accurate term would be a "gay male network." This network, which consists of individuals, groups, and institutions, has no single center. Each individual, group, and institution is a single point. Some points serve as hubs, exerting greater influence than others and offering gathering spaces. Each point or hub is connected, representing relationships and two-way influence. Given gay men's cruising rituals and propensity to connect sexually, this network is tightly woven. As such, our actions have great potential to influence—for good or harm—other gay men.

When we understand that gay men form an international network, we can fathom the paradox: each of us is the center of this network, and yet it contains no center. With no authority onto which we can project responsibility or assign blame, we become responsible for our own experience and accountable to each other. We come to understand that a more loving gay male network begins with our own choices, actions, beliefs, and perceptions.

Visually depicted, the gay network looks something like this:

Gay Network

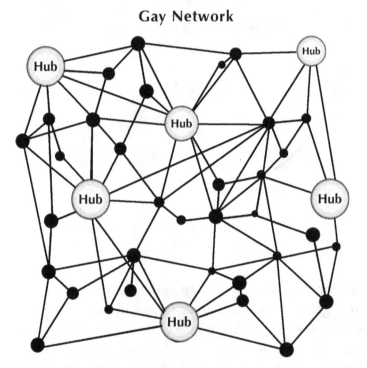

In this understanding, gay men are tightly connected, whether through friendships, affiliations, or sex. Hubs represent meeting spaces and influencers, but influence travels in two directions. Ideas, feelings, beliefs, attitudes, and trends spread quickly from point to point, reverberating throughout the network.

To become conscious of our actions, we must first name them. When we name them, we can make clearer choices in the future. When we recognize our part in the re-wounding of gay men, we can begin to better understand the implications of our actions. When we continue to harm our fellow gay men, we cannot effectively serve the world. To reconcile within ourselves, and among each other, we must acknowledge and own our wrongs. In this vein, and for this purpose, I include a catalogue of the hurts that gay men have expressed to me, and others that I have observed. To create a stronger, more loving gay male network, we must understand where we need to do better.

Sexual Objectification

In the shadows of our cruising rituals, gay men turn each other into objects to be obtained and discarded. Our electronic applications enable us to quickly assess the desirability of a potential partner, and the sheer volume of available men and the anonymity that these media offer allow us to casually dismiss and cruelly reject each other. It becomes all too easy to ignore advances from undesired men, and many of us choose to forgo even simple consideration or a brief "no thanks." Some lash out with cruelty at undesired men who approach us—or those who do not return our advances. We cannot ascribe all of this to electronic overload, however. We do this in person too—in bars, clubs, bathhouses, and anywhere else men search for sex.

This dynamic comes entirely at our own hands, for as we choose continual cruising as a primary means of connection, we expose ourselves to the continual possibility of rejection. From our place of wounding, rejection stings deeply. We take it very personally and sometimes lash out at our rejecters, forgetting that we too possess the inviolable right to choose with whom we do and do not have sex.

Our habit of cruising each other becomes so ingrained that we forget to turn it off when we are not actively searching for sex. In fact, it can become our primary way of relating to one another. Our propensity to dismiss undesired partners translates into rendering invisible those men we do not wish to have sex with. This creates sexual stratification in social, non-sexual settings, leading to a high-school-style separation of men based on gradations of desirability. Men who are less attractive ultimately feel excluded and dismissed. Older men, who could serve as friends, mentors, and sources of wisdom, report feeling discarded by younger gay men. The environment of continuous sexual tension trains those who feel less desirable to actually believe they have less worth. Moreover, younger gay men report feeling objectified by older gay men and fear that any interaction will result in a sexual pass.

Men in Gay Men of Wisdom Groups had this to say about our sexual objectification of each other:

- Everything becomes sexual; we become obsessed with sex.

- We lack sensitivity for others.

- We objectify each other.

- We can depersonalize sex.

- We engage in sex as danger seeking.

- We have a huge drug culture around sex.

- We display a lack of concern for each other when it comes to sex.

- We demonstrate lack of fidelity [when it comes to honoring our commitments to our partners].

- We take risks when it comes to sex.

- We can engage in sex to fill an emotional hole in our lives.

- We can reject each other in ways that are far more cruel than those outside our community.

- We have to be conscious about how social media feeds into this. Many gay men meet online. They make quick surface judgments. This is toxic.

- I have dismissed men who are older than me for fear they wanted sex.

Enforcing Narrow Male Gender Norms

It should come as no surprise that gay men wrestle with society's expectations of men's gender expression. As the men who are closest to the feminine, we endure the greatest harassment and hatred for it. On subtle and overt levels, however, we often enforce society's narrow gender norms within the gay male network and pass it off as desirability. In the shadow of our gift for attunement to beauty, we fetishize and worship masculinity. We insist that our sexual partners be "masculine," proclaim our own masculinity, and devote inordinate energy to sculpting our bodies into a narrow definition of desirability. We learn that, to become noticed and valued, even in non-sexual settings, we must appear masculine in our physique, in the way we carry ourselves, and in our voice. We immediately dismiss those who do not hold to that standard, and cast judgment upon feminine gay men. Thus, we perpetuate a narrow vision of manhood and attractiveness.

Nowhere does gay men's fear of the feminine emerge as clearly as when it comes to Gay Pride. Around nearly every parade, disputes break out, with some men deriding the "flamboyant" gays—the queens, those in drag and costume—as "freaks" who mar (or reinforce) the public image of gay men. Rather than confront society's limited notions of masculinity and manhood and honor those men who take the heat for all gay men—because they cannot hide—we shame and devalue them. Some gay men would rather "act straight" than acknowledge and honor the feminine within themselves.

Men in Gay Men of Wisdom groups shared this about our shame around the feminine:

- We reject the feminine in other gay men.

- "Straight acting" is valued; it tears us apart. We are not in our wisdom when we are "acting."

- We want "straight acting," not "gay acting": this is a measure of our internalized homophobia.

- If I hate the feminine side of myself, I hate the feminine and the female around me.

- We don't accept femininity in other men. We value "straight acting" men.

- Gay men can use the masculine as a shield.

- We borrow intolerance from the larger world when it comes to gender expression and roles.

- When I would walk into a bar, I would judge those who are too gay and I would distance myself from them. I was disowning and pushing away parts of myself that I judged. It was too scary to face, so I pushed these men away.

The Isms

Gay men may model some of the best instincts for all of humanity, but we can also embody some of the worst. Surprisingly, in the shadow of our close friendship with women, and not surprisingly, in the shadow of our camp sensibilities, gay men can exhibit some of the harshest misogyny. Behind women's backs, we can minimize, devalue, insult, and degrade women. Based on our patterns of continual cruising, which creep into our non-sexual social experiences, we can overlook women just as we do men for whom we have no sexual interest. In our desire to connect with other gay men, we can render lesbians invisible and create environments that do not welcome them. We can be shockingly insensitive to women and unaware of their presence.

As men living in a patriarchy, we too can manifest racism. We see this propensity in the segregated nature of many of our gathering places and even institutions—though LGBT people often make greater efforts toward inclusion and understanding than the larger world. Many gay men of color maintain that the gay rights movement lacks sensitivity to or fails to address the distinct challenges that they face. Of course, the further away one falls from the top of patriarchy's hierarchy of social value, the more layers of wounding. If a gay man embodies a second devalued identity, such as being African-American, he must contend with the negative messages about, and the challenges posed by, both of these identities. This often makes the road longer and harder for gay men of color.

We also see segregation reflected in many gay men's choices for sexual partners—undeniably a complex area to wade into. For instance, it is common to see white men express preference for white men only, and for black men to express preference for black men or men of color only. Some gay men, of course, prefer men of other races and ethnicities than their own. While there is no right or wrong to attraction—it simply is— segregation in this arena, and in other social settings, raises questions about our openness to each other.

One could argue that gay men cannot be blamed for the segregation of the races, or the economic injustice that prevents people of color from accessing the same opportunities. But one could also argue that our outsider position should lead us to question segregation and economic injustice just as we do homophobia. When we fail to question, we perpetuate the problem—because we allow our unexamined assumptions to govern our behavior. When we question ourselves and face our shadow, we discover how each of us has the propensity to perpetuate the status quo. In many ways, the groups in the LGBT umbrella serve as an example to the larger world about how to value difference. When we commit to examining our own assumptions, we can do even better.

In the shadow of our fine attunement to beauty, gay men can display heartbreaking dismissal of and scorn for men who are overweight. The quickest way to render oneself invisible among gay men is to gain too much weight. With diminished sexual desirability comes diminished social currency. Fat men's experiences mirror those of other men who fall outside of the narrow range of accepted desirability: if we are not a potential sex partner, we do not exist. The emergence of bear identity and appreciation is a promising and hopeful trend.

Men in the Gay Men of Wisdom groups shared these ideas about our "isms":

- We can display a vicious misogyny when no one else is listening.

• The easiest way to not be a sissy is to degrade women. The way to do that is to distinguish myself from women.

• There is a shadow side of our humor. While it can poke fun, it can be a slippery slope. Camp makes fun of the dominant culture's stereotype of women, but it can easily descend into bitchiness.

• We don't always treat each other with the openness and tolerance that we expect from the larger world.

• We judge people who are overweight very harshly.

• We judge others based on how they look.

Bitchiness

The biting humor and wit of camp can easily slip into the shadow feminine. This shows up in the bitchy, passive-aggressive, and cruel way gay men can insult and dismiss each other. Because camp contains within it exquisite esthetic sensibilities, its shadow can swiftly slice open someone or something that offends this esthetic sensibility. Gay men can be critical, judgmental, and mean when channeling this dark energy. It can manifest as standoffishness, nearly always a defensive mechanism, but one that can inflict as much damage as a sharp insult. A quick stroll into most gay bars will reveal physically defensive postures among patrons that communicate exclusion, mild bitchiness, and cliqueishness.

Gay Men of Wisdom groups shared these insights about this trait:

• We can be divas, primadonnas, narcissists, and bitchy queens.

• We can have no filter.

• Bitchiness: the shadow side of camp. A feminine form of aggression.

Overly Harsh Judgment, Eating Our Own

On the shadow side of our tremendous gift for empathy, understanding, and non-judgmental mirroring, gay men have a singular propensity to shred each other with venom and judgment. Much of this comes from our place of wounding—by the larger world, and sometimes by each other—where we project onto each other our hurts, expectations, and disappointments. While we might give heterosexuals more latitude and understanding, we can hold each other to such high standards as to render those standards impossible to meet. This happens most visibly in political organizations, where we make enemies of each other simply for holding different opinions. The vitriol that gay men hurl at each other is often informed by a sense of betrayal—as if we had expected betrayal all along. We project our anger, our hurt, and our marginalization onto each other, which we express with swift and harsh judgment. Gay leaders beware: We eat our own.

On a personal level, gay men can deploy this swift judgment and condemnation against those who are considered to be "transgressing." Harsh judgment awaits for those deemed "promiscuous," celibate, "too gay," "flamboyant," taking pre-exposure prophylaxis ("Truvada whores"), choosing safe sex ("condom queens"), those who have open relationships ("cheaters"), those who have monogamous relationships ("repressed"), and so on. In many cases, this judgment serves to enforce the dominant culture's values and reflects our own discomfort with ourselves. In other cases, it reflects a cultivated callousness and sense of permission that it is okay to slice each other to bits. And in still others, we can be quick to condemn based on perceived slights about which we would give others the benefit of the doubt. In too many cases, we re-enact the wounding we experienced at the hands of our biological families.

Men in my groups expressed these insights about this phenomenon:

- I've been mean and horrible to other gay men. I didn't have peace within myself, so I wasn't taking responsibility for myself.

- We need to understand the distinction between consciousness and unconsciousness: we must recognize and confront our phobias rather than projecting them and/or judging them in others.

- I have criticized and dismissed other gay men because I could not understand their experience. And I too have been dismissed.

- I have seen gay men undermine each other because of jealousy and insecurity.

- I fear the wounding from my gay peers. It's why I'm driven to feel safer with straight people.

- Being wounded by your own is the hardest slash.

Shame

If we believe that shame ends when we come out, we fool ourselves. In some ways, we just begin to confront shame at that point. Shame takes many forms, reflecting society's messages that we have internalized. Shame can manifest as any of the shadow traits mentioned above. It can become so buried in our psyche that we do not even realize we are acting from shame. The presence of judgment or condescension, however, provides a strong indication that shame is at work. As a group, gay men would do well to always challenge judgment when it surfaces among us, because it always attempts to enforce society's rules on us.

Shame can lead us to act in illogical and hurtful ways. When it comes to sex, it can propel us to treat other men as objects, and to discard each other quickly to avoid confronting our shame. Sexual shame can run the show, keeping us from honestly connecting with each other, and from expressing our true desires. As men in my groups pointed out, when we release sexual shame, it becomes easier to connect with the essence of another person. Without sexual shame, there is greater freedom but also greater adult responsibility. We have to take responsibility for ourselves, our actions, and our conduct in relationship to the person we are having sex with.

Domestic Violence

While most gay men exhibit a gentler, collaborative social orientation, there is no denying that some gay men abuse and batter their partners.

Despite our best hopes for a tribe of entirely gentle men, some gay men have violent and sociopathic tendencies. As with heterosexual men who commit abuse, some gay male abusers were themselves abused as children and suffer from mental illnesses as a result.[121] A recent review of research, published in the *Journal of Sex and Marital Therapy*, found that domestic violence occurs as much and possibly more among same-sex couples than among opposite-sex couples.[122] In his autobiography, *All Grown Up Now*, Kenneth King gives a harrowing account of a long-term friend's abuses at the hands of his boyfriend—including rape using a loaded gun—and his friend's eventual escape.[123] Gay men who suffer from domestic violence—the victims as well as the perpetrators—warrant our understanding and attention. We have long left them in the shadows due to our collective disbelief that gay men could perpetrate such horrors. It's time to bring this shadow element into the light of day.

Excessive Idealism

On the shadow side of gay men's drive for excellence lies our propensity to be excessively idealistic. Gay men have a tendency to want things and people to be "perfect." This serves an incredibly important function when we apply it to achievement; the world is a better place for this gift of ours. When we apply it to each other, however, it leads to disappointment. Too often we search for a mate who is "perfect" and end up overlooking the good man in front of us.

In 1957, Helen Branson published a unique book, *Gay Bar*, in which she shares her observations of gay men from the time she ran a gay bar in Los Angeles in the 1950s. Branson was a pioneering advocate for gay men, an early straight ally. It was illegal to operate a gay bar at the time she ran hers, yet she kept the police from ever raiding it. The cover of the original book—author Will Fellows re-published it in 2010—features a mother hen protecting her chicks: Helen protecting her "boys." One of Helen's most poignant observations rings true even today: she often noticed an excessive idealism among her "boys," a search for perfection that left many of them single, often lonely, and sometimes depressed. She writes:

The excessive idealism, which is their most common trait, spurs them to seek a love that is perfect. And there is no such thing. I know one who is musical, paints, writes and who has been hunting for years for a companion who is artistic. He has never found his ideal. He strives for perfection in his artistic fields but now he is a complete cynic about love. He cannot accept anything short of perfection in love.[124]

As Helen observed so insightfully more than fifty years ago, in our drive to seek Mr. Perfect, gay men often fail to recognize that humans come in imperfect packages.

Owning Our Shadow

On one level, every gay man is the young boy seeking love, understanding, and acceptance from his family. Then the world wounds us—deeply. When we enter the gay world, we expect to be greeted with open arms. But we don't always realize that we carry with us the shadow from our core wounding. When we meet other men who have been wounded similarly and differently from us, our wounds can emerge and our affinities recede.

In our popular understanding, the Gay Hero's Journey ends when we come out. But we know better. The process of coming out and healing from homophobia can last a lifetime. Our shared narrative tells a story of overcoming injustice and winning the rights and protections that all other people enjoy. We should concurrently move against a more insidious foe: our internalized self-hatred. To a great extent, we allow our wounds to identify us. We hold onto the pain of being victimized because we have known it for so long. It becomes, in a way, comfortable. We cast judgment upon other gay men when we have not fully accepted ourselves. In some ways, we can become harsher enforcers of the dominant culture's values than those outside the gay network.

The path to wisdom requires that each of us face our shadow head on. It requires that we question judgment when it comes up for us. It necessitates that we ask ourselves whether the injustice we feel in the moment is happening now, or whether that event is touching on something that happened long ago and with which we have not yet made peace. It means challenging our fear of the feminine in all of its manifestations—even down to our sexual preference for classic masculine male beauty. Wisdom recognizes our own triggers. It acknowledges when we are re-enacting old, limiting patterns. Wisdom means embracing our shadow, and forgiving ourselves for its trespasses.

Where there is negativity, anger, judgment, and harshness, the shadow is often running the show. We can become seduced into perceiving that these things come from outside of ourselves—but most often our deepest pain originates from our old wound. Too often, we project our history of pain onto others.

In his book *Gay Body*, Mark Thompson emphatically states, "To be wounded is not enough. We can claim our shame, count off each infraction against the Self as we would list souvenirs from a once-in-a-lifetime trip around the world…. But it is not enough only to see and say what happened. There comes a time in every man's life when he must ask: What is to be done about it?"[125]

Men in Gay Men of Wisdom groups echo Thompson's insights:

- The key is discovering the teacher in our pain: Where do I have to go within myself for my woundedness to become a resource for others? We need to get to the point that says, "This is my pain, but pain is part of being alive." If something can happen within me to see it as my share of human pain, and to turn it into compassion, it allows me to relate to another's woundedness. I can say, "This is my share of human pain. I know what it is like."

- If pain is to be a teacher, we need to learn from it [and not transmit it].

Dealing with the shadow means taking complete responsibility for ourselves and our current state of being. It means doing our inner healing work and not expecting someone else—a lover, a friend, the straight world—to do it for us. It means being honest about our addictions. It means recognizing the patterns that keep us stuck in the past. It means getting help when we need it—to overcome addictions, inner demons, unhealthy patterns of behavior, our anger, our abusiveness, etc. It means honestly assessing our inner bitch. It means becoming aware of our judgments of other gay men—and ourselves. It means acting with love whenever possible, and becoming aware of our triggers.

The gay male shadow is our individual responsibility to understand and manage. It takes awareness, commitment, and hard work. No one ever claimed that the gay male path would be easy.

How does your shadow manifest?

Take the Gay/Straight Differential Test

Awareness is the point of choice. Start to become aware of how you act toward heterosexuals, and how you behave toward other gay men. Notice any differences. Become aware of your thoughts, and especially your feelings:

What expectations
do you hold
of heterosexuals?
_____
_____
_____
_____

What expectations
do you hold of
other gay men?
_____
_____
_____
_____

What would you say
to other gay men
that you would never
say to a heterosexual
man or woman?
_____
_____
_____
_____

When you see gay men or
couples in mainstream
settings, what goes
through your mind?
How does your
comfort level change
in these instances?
_____
_____
_____
_____

Chapter 19
The New Way Forward

Gay men possess the gifts, skills, and talents to lead humanity out of patriarchy and find The New Way Forward. The emergence of a global network of gay men—along with our lesbian, bisexual, and transgender allies—comes at a time of great crisis. Humanity needs new ways of solving its problems and relating to each other. Gay men possess the innate consciousness and capacity to lead this transition. But we have only begun to tap into our potential. When we fully recognize our gifts—and know at the core of our being what roles we play in the human family—we can truly serve as enlightened, evolutionary leaders. Right now, we are just halfway there.

At this time in history, gay men play the profoundly challenging role of processing humanity's deep wounds. We are releasing the shame that traps all men. We have already proven our ability to transform hatred into love, and fear of the feminine into balance. We can and will teach all kinds of men to master and honor the feminine and masculine within them, particularly men's relationship to the feminine. When we do this, we will heal ourselves.

The New Way Forward requires new ways of being—and that means for gay men too. If we are to lead humanity, we must model more loving, aware ways of being. The New Way Forward will recognize and value interconnectedness. It will empower individual authenticity—a life lived from our inner knowingness, not external authority—and yet it will balance that drive with awareness of how our actions affect others. The New Way Forward will foster balance between people and the Earth, and it will profoundly respect the masculine and feminine. On a deep level, gay men know we can lead humanity in this direction. We see this potential reflected in our gifts. Gay men will unleash our individual and collective power when we recognize the shining gifts that we are—and when we allow ourselves to give these gifts to each other.

If we wish to help humanity discover The New Way Forward, we must radically love ourselves for *all* of who we are. We must fall in love with each other. We must be able to recognize how we fit into the human family and serve an integral purpose. We possess immense joy. We have within us deep spiritual capacity. We must create new ways to consciously connect with other gay men in ways that respect and honor each other, and which celebrate our collective joy, spirit, and contributions. Great rewards await the gay man who deeply loves himself, and great rewards await our network of gay men when we embody more conscious, loving ways of interacting. When we live in love and joy, we will lead humanity toward love and joy. This will not happen if we maintain the status quo. We must make deliberate and conscious change both individually and collectively.

I propose the following steps to launch us on this journey.

Steps on the Path to Human Leadership

Individual Action

Doing our work. Processing pain and shame is hard work. It requires courage, commitment, and a willingness to face ourselves. We cannot serve as leaders when wounds run our lives. We cannot model the best instincts when we behave unconsciously toward each other. Radical self-love requires a commitment to peeling back the layers of messages and shame that bind us, until we are truly free. It means becoming aware of when a current situation triggers an old wound, and having the awareness to respond to what is happening now rather than what happened in the past. It means becoming aware of what we project onto others. It means understanding how we disempower ourselves, create separation from others, and repeat old patterns.

In Gay Men of Wisdom groups, I have led men through journeys to discover their "otherness myth"—that mechanism we developed as children, adolescents, and young adults to cope with the pain, and sometimes the danger, of being gay in a straight world. We often carry this response with us into adulthood and our interactions with other gay men, and we inadvertently recreate the experience of not belonging or connecting. Consider how this old defense mechanism plays out for men in Gay Men of Wisdom groups:

• I hid so well, I still can't come out.

• I knew I would have to go it alone. I didn't have a word for it.

• I suppressed my emotional responses, because it was not safe to be unfettered, free, or joyful.

• I needed to be the best little boy in the world. I adopted perfectionism as a way to compensate.

• I am in the habit of not socializing, because I have been in the habit of being alone for so long.

• My hiding during childhood caused me to be so guarded that I still choose to isolate myself. My guardedness has made it difficult for me to connect with gay men. I want to be accepted by gay men, but I fear them, and I feel wounded by them.

• I became invisible. I made sure I was always looking out, scanning for what was dangerous. I did not have friends in high school. I became guarded around gay men. I would have my walls up, and so I would feel invisible in gay bars.

• I have the tendency to sit back, watch, and observe without commitment. Or I tend to take charge of a given situation. This way I don't have to be too emotionally involved.

• I developed such a comfort being alone and self-sufficient that I became blind to the needs of others. I am so used to doing things by myself.

- I became extremely introverted, and it is very difficult to stop. It has interfered with my career.

- It's very easy to start thinking of other gay men as either special and superior to me, or as lacking interest and inferior to me.

- You get so stuck in the experience that happened in the past that you don't realize there can be another way, that patterns can be overwritten.

- My otherness myth? Other people need to do their work, not me. I'm not the problem. If they do their work, I'll be okay.

- My otherness myth? I am beyond love—even self-love. It's a default system that kicks in.

- Being gay is a setup for post-traumatic stress disorder.

- I fear that gay men will project my own pain into my heart.

- I'm not odd or damaged. I reacted and learned to behave because of being gay. I am perfectly normal and behaved normally under the circumstances.

- I'm reminded how much pain gay men carry. You don't always see it. I am reminded to have more compassion.

I asked one group of men: "What habits and patterns have you developed in response to being "other"? Here are some of their answers:

- I have built impenetrable walls.

- I told lies, which has led to a lifetime of lies.

- I hid my sexuality—and everything about myself.

- I never feel a part of, even among other gay men.

- I don't identify with other gay men.

- I became numb.

- I feel shame.

- I became judgmental of others.

- I overcompensated.

- I acted "straight."

- I acted mechanically.

- I feel inferior.

This exploration alone reveals the depth of the wounds that we carry with us into our relationships with other gay men. Awareness and support from caring others—whether that be a therapist or another healing professional—can aid us on our journey to wholeness and leadership. If we do not engage in introspection and personal growth work, we remain stuck in our journey. The path to enlightened, evolutionary leadership requires that we do our personal work. We must, as Mark Thompson prescribes, grow from our wound.

Honestly assessing the masculine and feminine within. The core challenge for gay men is also the core challenge for all men: accepting and embracing the feminine within. Because we tend to have more of the feminine, and because society associates our sexuality with the feminine, we carry a heavier burden for all men. Fear of the feminine is at once a deeply personal issue and a global issue. Humans' toxic beliefs about the feminine translate into interpersonal violence and planetary destruction. Gay men's personal choice to honor the feminine within themselves will tip the scales on a global level. We already see evidence of this impact. But large numbers of gay men continuing to live in shame over their feminine—and imitating men's masculine "act"—impedes further progress.

Fear of the feminine lives within nearly every gay man. When we choose to honor our feminine, we will give all men permission to honor the feminine within them. This will mean challenging each other and ourselves around our preferences for "masculine only" and "straight-acting men," and even rethinking how we have fetishized the classic male figure. It will mean creating new standards of beauty that reflect balance. It will mean honoring the queens among us.

At the same time, gay men have significant work to do regarding the masculine. The shadow masculine—aggression, domination, and violence—has characterized manhood for so long, most men associate manhood with those traits. Gay men tend to choose one of two paths in response: either wholeheartedly adopting the heterosexual model of manhood—imitating its act—or embracing the feminine to such an extent that we deny, devalue, or simply fail to appreciate the masculine that lives within us.[126] As gay men, we need to create a shared concept of balanced, integrated gay manhood. We need to identify what manhood is and is not, and to embrace our embodiment of manhood. When we publicly acknowledge and respect our manhood, we will lead the way for all men to discover what manhood truly means to them. When we can easily recognize the masculine in the nelliest queen, and the feminine in the butchest lumberjack, we will know that we have achieved and embraced balance.

Collective Action

Consciously invoking the gay male tribe. Gay men share an innate attraction to each other. Despite our commonly accepted belief, this includes more than just sexuality. When gay men gather in the spirit of love and support—when we truly see each other—we invoke the spirit of the gay male tribe. Magic happens. This spirit exists whether we tap into it or not, and it is always available, like a river that continually flows. We need only visit it and dip our cup into its water.

Gay men subconsciously seek connection with this tribalism on a continual basis. It manifests in our propensity to attend night clubs and parties, where we can experience ecstatic group connection. Gay men understand how to create these group rituals; indeed, we could consider ourselves the high priests of ecstatic dance. The not infrequent use of drugs at these events represents an attempt to heighten that ecstasy and connection. We see this drive in gay men's group-sex-seeking, which can at times take on a tribal, ritualistic element. It also manifests in our cruising. On a deep level, gay men long for and are wired to seek the communal, ritualistic, and transcendent experience of connecting with each other.

Without consciously appreciating this need for tribal connections, however, we leave its fulfillment to chance. Because we don't have the language for this need—or even the conscious awareness that it exists—we can't always meet it. When we bring consciousness to this need, however, we can create opportunities to invoke the power of the tribe in any group setting. In fact, we need to expand our repertoire of tribal connection-seeking beyond the dance floor and the bathhouse. Other settings, in fact, can create more deeply meaningful and satisfying connections—exposing us to gifted men whom we might never have met had we considered them only as potential sex partners or mates.

Gay spirituality, and places such as Easton Mountain, provide an established model for invoking the experience of the tribe beyond sexual settings. From my experience and observation, the deep connection of tribe requires several conditions:

- A welcoming, safe, and inclusive setting. This can be established with or without words. Often, actions and body language suffice, though working agreements can help.

- A spoken or unspoken agreement to see each other beyond just our physical bodies—to look within. Again, behavior models this agreement best, but words can help too.

- A commitment to suspending negative judgments.

- An intention of gathering in love.

- A specific reason for gathering—a clear focus.

When we invoke the gay male tribe using this model, we invite men to share their gay gifts with each other. All of those brilliant and beautiful traits that we freely bestow upon the outside world—and that we too often withhold from each other—unleash our gay spirit. We soar. We feel that—*finally*—other gay men see and value us. Within these settings, we can grow, heal, find joy, celebrate, and even find sexual connection if we choose. We revel in the love and companionship of our gay brothers. We have come home.

Gay men need this invocation of tribe. We must create new and more opportunities within our vast network for gay men to connect on this level. When we leave the competition, isolation, and alienation of the bars and online meeting places behind, we reconnect with the traditional roles that gay men have played in indigenous cultures throughout history. These connections, in fact, help us discover how we serve as modern-day shamans—leaders in The New Way Forward.

Modeling a collective mindset. The New Way Forward for humanity rests on collaboration, something for which gay men have a natural predisposition. As we adopt a greater awareness that we inhabit a gay network, versus a hierarchical gay community, our thinking and actions will shift. Instead of only bestowing this gift on the larger world, we will begin working *with each other* more collaboratively. This means applying all of our gifts in service to each other. When we experiment with and refine collective ways of relating to each other in our cultural laboratory, we become better teachers of these approaches. The Radical Faerie model has shown up in the Occupy Wall Street movement; what could a truly collaborative gay male network contribute to human relations?

Adopting an Ethic of Human Service. The New Way Forward requires gay men who consciously choose to serve humanity to use their gifts. This could mean everything from simply adopting an understanding of our leadership capacity to inventing entirely new ways to serve our fellow humans. When we understand our potential, and what we really do in the world, we automatically go about our lives differently. Those gay men who become inspired to serve humanity at a greater level might create new spiritual paths and religions that integrate and honor sex and personal authenticity, and new healing modalities. We might establish new businesses and organizations dedicated to advancing peace, and helping all men integrate the feminine and masculine within themselves. I imagine a new generation of gay male teachers introducing new ways of thinking and being, serving needs that currently go unmet.

This requires a shift in consciousness from victimhood to enlightened service and leadership. We need only imagine, come together as a tribe, and turn our vision into reality.

Adopting a set of ethics and agreements. For further evidence that our network is not a hierarchical community, consider the fact that no central body has emerged to define or attempt to enforce a set of ethics among gay men. Not that we would want such an authority. Still, we have not developed a shared agreement about how we behave toward each other. Far too many of us take permission to treat each other as open targets. We can do better than that.

The next chapter, Share the Love: The Seven Agreements, proposes a set of ethics. Commit to embracing them. Let's spread the norm throughout our network that gay men treat each other with love, kindness, and consideration. When we do, we will truly model the best instincts for humanity.

Leaving an intergenerational legacy. AIDS robbed us of much of the wisdom of an entire generation—men who would have mentored us, taught us what it meant to be gay, and helped us to discover what it means for *our* generation to be gay. We have some elders with us. These men have information for all of us. We must create the kind of tribe in which younger and older gay men interact with, appreciate, and teach and learn from each other. In this way, we will allow for wisdom to be transferred—from elder to younger, and younger to elder—while easing the burden on each young gay man to discover himself alone. When we consider the needs of the younger generation, we will maintain a sense of continuity, despite the ever-changing nature of our identity and the world.

Some deliberate efforts to leave an intergenerational legacy have begun. In Los Angeles, Donald Kilhefner, co-founder of the Los Angeles Gay and Lesbian Center, led the creation of the Gay Elder Circle, which officially launched as a nonprofit organization in 2011. The circle describes its primary purpose as "being useful to younger gay men and of service to the gay and larger community." It recognizes that, "Throughout history and across cultures...life usually consists of four stages—

youth, adult, elder, and ancestor. The Gay Elder Circle is designed to assist gay men and others to make the transition from adult to elder, in the process consciously assuming a new role in the community—a life of continuing usefulness to others within the context of group support, encouragement, and genuine brotherhood."[127]

At Easton Mountain, program director Harry Faddis has sparked personal conversations and led group discussions about what it means to be a gay elder. In 2014, he led several Death Cafes based on the model that originated in the United Kingdom— group discussions of thoughts and feelings about death. Faddis has begun important conversations that can lead to new endeavors as more gay men reach elderhood.

We need to germinate these seeds and foster their growth. Greater intergenerational connections will strengthen our entire tribe and create the sense of purpose and belonging we crave. As the Gay Elder Circle wisely observes, each generation—youth, adult, and elder—relies on and needs the others.

Because the role of the gay man changes in each generation, we must create ways for younger men to discover who they are today, and to learn where we as a tribe came from. Just as we invented a rite of passage that each of us adopts when we come out, we can create rituals that invite and welcome new men into the tribe, recognizing their courage and communicating that there is a place for them.

When elders, adults, and young people teach and learn from each other; when we demonstrate true respect for one another; when we ask how we can be of service to each other; and when we commit to helping one another at each stage of our lives, we will leave a lasting legacy of intergenerational connection, love, support, and guidance.

Chapter 20
Share the Love:
The Seven Agreements

We will strengthen our connections with each other when we commit to a higher standard of behavior toward one another. These agreements provide suggested principles for ethical and loving behavior. They will hold sway when we choose to adopt them freely, and when our actions inspire others. I hereby invite you to adopt these, and to invite other gay men to adopt them as well.

Share them on your social media and dating profiles. Talk about them with your friends. Let's share the love.

My Seven Agreements

I choose to do my part to create a stronger, more loving brotherhood of gay men. As such, I commit to:

Mindful Kindness. I choose to see the humanity in each gay man I encounter, whether I find him physically attractive or not, and to greet him with kindness.

Responsibility. I take full responsibility for my actions and for my part in creating my life experience. In any conflict with another gay man, I seek to understand my own responsibility first.

Self-Love. I give myself permission to fall in love with myself and release all aspects of shame. I encourage other gay men to fall in love with themselves.

Owning My Shadow. I continually seek to understand my darker motivations and tendencies, and my projections; to manage these; and to take responsibility when I express them.

Brotherhood. I belong to a brotherhood of gay men globally. I commit to sustaining the vitality of this brotherhood by contributing positively to it.

Accountability. When another gay man manifests bad behavior toward me, I constructively name it and work to resolve the conflict with him. I invite other gay men to do the same with me.

Forgiveness. I choose to forgive gay men for how they have hurt me, understanding that it has often come from their own place of wounding. I request forgiveness when I have hurt another gay man.

Chapter 21

A Self-Assessment for the
14 Distinct Gay Male Gifts

Now that you have read how gay men serve as evolutionary leaders for humanity, where do you fit in? Take this two-part assessment to gain a sense of the Distinct Gay Male Gifts you possess, and to what extent you embody them.

Part One of the assessment helps you gauge the masculine and feminine within you. It contains three components, representing the three dimensions of the masculine and feminine:

1. Personality traits

2. External (visible/audible) traits

3. Energy

Because masculine-feminine intelligence represents fluidity and responsiveness to different circumstances, this assessment will not capture that gift per se, but it will give you a sense of your overall masculine and feminine.

Part Two of the assessment will help you glean the extent to which you possess the 12 remaining gifts. I leave one gift out of this assessment—teachers of compassion, generosity, and the authentic masculine—because it references gay men's early response to the AIDS epidemic, a historic event, and because these elements appear within the other gifts.

Note: a downloadable version of this assessment is available on the Gay Men of Wisdom website, **www.gaymenofwisdom.com**.

Part One: Masculine and Feminine Personality Traits

The following is a list of masculine and feminine personality traits, as generally understood in the United States. *These traits are culturally determined. They* are not scientific, nor are they fixed in stone. Different societies may assign these traits differently. To complete this component, consider whether each of the 20 masculine and 20 feminine traits applies to you. For each trait, ask yourself: Do you tend to exhibit this trait in your daily life? Is it the way you usually act or behave? If you answer "Yes," place a check next to it. When you finish, add up the total number of your masculine and feminine traits. You will see a ratio of masculine to feminine traits when you are done.

Masculine Traits	Check if Applies	Feminine Traits	Check if Applies
Acts as leader		Affectionate	
Aggressive		Cheerful	
Ambitious		Childlike	
Analytical		Compassionate	
Assertive		Does not use harsh language	
Athletic		Eager to soothe hurt feelings	
Competitive		Feminine	
Defends own beliefs		Flatterable	
Dominant		Gentle	
Forceful		Gullible	
Has leadership abilities		Loves children	
Independent		Loyal	
Individualistic		Sensitive to needs of others	
Makes decisions easily		Shy	
Masculine		Soft spoken	
Self-reliant		Sympathetic	
Self-sufficient		Tender	
Strong personality		Understanding	
Willing to take a stand		Warm	
Willing to take risks		Yielding	
Totals:			

Part One: External Masculine and Feminine Traits

Circle as many traits as apply to your voice/speech, the way you *most often* carry your body, and your typical style of dress. Bring the total number of circled traits from each column to the bottom.

My Voice/Speech		My Body Movements/Posture		My Style of Dress	
Masculine	Feminine	Masculine	Feminine	Masculine	Feminine
Deeper	Higher	Hands at one's sides	Hand on hip	Fewer colors, more muted tones	Multi – colored, colorful
More dominant	Gentler	Legs crossed: ankle over knee	Legs crossed: knee over knee	Looser fit	Fitted
Less talkative / use fewer words	More talkative / use more words	Straight wrist	Bent wrist	Narrower range of attire	Wider range of attire
Fewer adjectives	More adjectives / flowery language	Sitting: legs open	Sitting: legs closed	Showing little skin	Showing more skin
Limited emotional vocabulary	Greater range of vocabulary	Stride/walk	Sashay	Long / baggy shorts	Shorter / fitted shorts
Less expressive	More expressive	Closed arms	Open arms / body posture	Looser style	A more planned, considered style
Clear diction	Lisp	Hold one's body rigidly	Greater range of body movements. More flowing.	More conservative / traditional	More stylish
Total #:	Total #:	Total #:	Total #:	Total #:	Total #:

Part One: Your Energy

Think about your energy. It is both intangible and palpable to most people. How would the people around you describe your energy? Do you tend to be dominant, collaborative, or passive? Would people describe you as aggressive, gentle, or somewhere in between? Is your energy sharper or softer? If you have trouble answering these questions, ask someone you know well.

Note your answers in your head for the moment.

Your Three-Dimensional Masculine-Feminine Profile

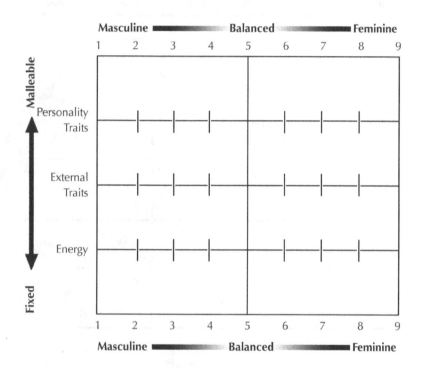

The Three-Dimensional Masculine-Feminine Model

For each dimension (Personality Traits, External Traits, and Energy), place yourself on a scale of 1 to 9, with 1 being the most masculine and 9 being the most feminine, marking an "X" on the applicable number on the three scales below. Follow these instructions:

Personality Traits: Consider the number of masculine to feminine traits you selected. If you selected an equal number of masculine and feminine traits, place yourself at 5 on this scale, representing balance. If you manifest more masculine than feminine traits, place yourself ac-

cordingly to the left of the center. If you have more feminine than masculine traits, place yourself accordingly to the right of the center.

External Traits: Consider the number of masculine and feminine
traits you selected for Voice/Speech, Body Movement/Posture, and Style
of Dress. As with Personality Traits, the closer the number of masculine
and feminine traits, the closer you would place yourself at the center of
the scale. The more masculine traits, the more you would place yourself
left of center; the more feminine, the more you would place yourself
right of center.

Energy: Use your gut on this one.

What do your three dimensions of masculine/feminine tell you?

Assessment Part Two: Your Distinct Gay Gifts

Of the remaining 12 Distinct Gay Male Gifts, consider the extent to
which these apply to you. Where do you see yourself represented within
the gay male tribe? Which gifts do you most embody? Which gifts manifest less through you?

To help see where you fit, a list of traits for each gift appears below.
Place a check mark beside each trait that applies to you, even if it manifests just sometimes. Use this list of checkmarks to help you identify
the extent to which you embody each gift on a scale of 1 to 10, with 1
being the least and 10 being the most. In the wheel that appears at the
end of this chapter, draw a curved line in each section along the dotted
line that corresponds to your self-rating. Because the gifts overlap, you
will see some of the same traits in different gifts.

Your wheel may look "balanced" or "unbalanced." There is no single
way that the completed wheel "should" look. This assessment will give
you a visual representation of your gay gifts. Everyone's wheel will look
different.

Top Traits for Each Gift

Serving and Healing

A Gentle, Collaborative Social Orientation Check If It Applies	
Ability to see multiple perspectives versus black and white	
Accommodating	
Collaborative	
Communicative	
Cooperative	
Confidante for others	
Consensus builder	
Considerate	
Consultative / collaborative versus an authoritarian style of leadership	
Empathetic	
Egalitarian	
Emotionally intelligent	
Gentle	
Good listener	
Intuitive	
Kind	
Less competitive/compete differently	
Less inclined to control others	
Non-aggressive	
Non-violent	
Open to difference and diversity	
Peaceful	
Propensity to empower others	
See vulnerability as a strength	
Sensitive	
My Self-Rating (1-10)	

An Orientation toward Service	*Check If It Applies* ⬇
Able to appreciate and understand multiple and even competing perspectives	
Able to organize, bring order, direct processes	
Able to sense and anticipate people's needs	
Able to understand and "speak the language" of emotions	
Accountability: able to hold yourself and others accountable, to deliver on promises	
Assertive	
Attuned to people's feelings	
Best-little-boy-in-the-world approach to excellence	
Bridge between men and women—understand both perspectives, no need for a translator	
Capacity to understand and validate people's emotions	
Collaborative	
Caregiver	
Decisive	
Desire to excel	
Desire to help others, make things better, do good	
Desire to respond to people's needs	
Empathy	
Good organizer	
Healer for others	
Intuitive	
Mastery of competencies of a given service profession or field	
Nurturing	
Provide a non-judgmental mirror for others / see people for who they are	
Sensitive to injustices	
Sensitive	
My Self-Rating (1-10)	

Religious Reformers and Spiritual Leaders	Check If It Applies
Actively consider the meaning and purpose of being gay	
Actively question religious dogma about gays and lesbians, whether from within a religious tradition as a member, or from outside	
Advocate for greater LGBT inclusion in a religious tradition	
Discovered your own authentic spiritual path after being excluded from religion	
Embrace awareness of and/or appreciation for the Earth as integral to your spirituality	
Engage in explorations that seek transcendent experiences through sexuality, the body, and/or the Earth	
Engage in a religious tradition as openly gay man	
Engage in some form of spirituality: a search for meaning; the desire to experience some form of transcendence; a practice, or some form of expression	
Integrate indigenous and/or pagan ideas into spiritual beliefs	
Left a religious tradition at least in part because it treats gays and lesbians poorly	
Participate in group explorations and/or rituals to explore the deeper meaning and purpose of being gay	
Seek and/or embrace a spirituality that includes more than it excludes, sees connection more than division, invokes wholeness more than separation	
Take a leadership role within a religious tradition as an openly gay man	
My Self-Rating (1-10)	

Models of Forgiveness	Check If It Applies
Felt the desire to forgive as something you need to do	
Forgiven someone for having held homophobic beliefs	
Forgiven someone whose homophobia has deeply hurt you	
Achieved peace with those whom you have forgiven	
Forgiven more people for homophobic beliefs than those you remain angry at for holding those beliefs	
Name those you have forgiven:	
My Self-Rating (1-10)	

Reinventing Manhood

Friends, "Soul Mates," and Co-Revolutionaries with Straight Women	Check If It Applies
Admire female icons and role models	
Are/were close with your mother and/or grandmother	
Count straight women among your closest and best friends	
Embrace a range of gender expression wider than that which most men allow themselves	
Engage or have engaged in activities that other men might sneer at because they consider them "for women" or "not manly"	
Gravitated toward playing with girls as a child	
Have always felt inherently comfortable around girls and women	
Have commiserated with straight women about men	
Have stood up for a woman who was being mistreated by a man	
Relate to feminism	
Serve as a sounding board for your women friends	
Share sensibilities and interests with women	
Treat women inherently as equals	
Understand how women think	
Understand straight women's gripes about straight men	
Understand women's emotions	
My Self-Rating (1-10)	

Esthetic Outsiders and Gender Tricksters	Check If It Applies
Appreciate outlandish, over-the-top, or "excessive" forms of creative expression	
Appreciate the social / cultural commentary of drag	
Appreciate female sensibilities in popular culture	
Engage in drag	
Enjoy blurring gender lines	
Enjoy drag as a spectator	
Have a favorite drag character or characters	
Have your own drag character	
Recognize beauty that others overlook	
Understand the value of and enjoy creative expression that falls outside the norm	
Use drag to express your creativity	
Use drag as a vehicle to express or get in touch with the feminine within	
Use and/or appreciate humor that defuses, thwarts, or inverts painful situations	
Value ideas that fall outside the norm	
Value people who are clearly outsiders, even when they appear within the mainstream	
My Self-Rating (1-10)	

Modeling Sustainable Manhood	Check If It Applies
Challenge narrow definitions of manhood and masculinity, wherever they appear	
Embrace those traits that define a gentler, more collaborative social orientation	
Embody the masculine and feminine in balance, and possess the ability to move in and out of each as the situation requires	
Express affection with other men	
Express traits other men might consider "feminine"	
Give yourself permission to express both masculine and feminine	
Not afraid to have and show feelings	
Not worried about appearing "manly"	
Value and honor the feminine within yourself	
Value and honor the masculine within yourself	
Value and honor the feminine within other gay men, and other men	
Value and honor the masculine within other gay men, and other men	
Understand and embrace the distinction between the authentic masculine and shadow masculine	
My Self-Rating (1-10)	

Freeing and Enriching the Human Spirit

Sexual Leadership	Check If It Applies
Approach sex honestly	
Approach your sexual partner(s) as equals	
Bring consciousness to sexual expression, without lingering baggage from society and religion	
Bring erotic energy into your life	
Communicate and ask for what you want	
Engage in sexuality and relationships based on what authentically works for you and your partner(s) versus adhering to what others think or an external set of rules	
Engage in, explore, or have experienced the spiritual aspects of sexuality	
Engage in sexuality consciously, not to fill another unmet need or addiction	
Feel free of shame	
Invite sexual exploration	
Model freedom and responsibility	
Model inner-motivated sexuality based on the embrace of pleasure, personal freedom, choice, and authenticity	
Reject external control over your sexuality, including shame	
My Self-Rating (1-10)	

Fine Attunement to Beauty, Creators and Keepers of Culture	Check If It Applies
Attuned to the beauty of the human body; appreciate physical beauty in others	
Attuned to beauty that humans create; appreciate creative expression in its many forms	
Attend to beauty in one's physical appearance; maintain one's body	
Attend to beauty and style in one's clothing and other manner of presentation	
Attuned to beauty in the natural world; appreciate nature, have strong connection to the Earth	
Attuned to trends in fashion and style	
Bring sensuality, attunement to beauty, and/or creativity into your home's presentation	
Create beauty through hobbies such as gardening in the ground, pots, or window boxes, designing your home's landscape	
Creatively express yourself through any one or more of the arts, including but not limited to the fine arts, music, dance, performance, writing, theater; the design professions, such as graphic, interior, and landscape design, architecture; and personal services such as hair styling, flower arranging, and so on	
Employ a personal style that sets and/or adopts the cutting edge of fashion and style	
Have a strong appreciation for and/or collect antiques	
Possess a keen understanding of and/or are drawn to the esthetics of earlier eras	
See/recognize the beauty in that which is old, decaying, neglected, or abandoned	
Serve as the keeper of your family's stories/history	
My Self-Rating (1-10)	

A "Gay" Spirit	Check If It Applies
(If you have difficulty with this part of the assessment, ask someone you know well to complete this for you; these traits may be difficult to spot in oneself.)	
Charismatic	
Enjoy parties, dance clubs, and other forms of group fun	
Have an outsize capacity for joy, love, celebration, exuberance, and ecstasy	
Know how to have fun	
Notice that people your own age seem "older" than you	
Open-hearted	
Passionate	
People describe you as having a sense of joy	
Playful	
Possess and embody a youthful spirit	
Quick to smile or laugh	
Quick to use humor	
Retain a sense of innocence	
Spontaneous	
Tend to see commonalities with others versus differences	
My Self-Rating (1-10)	

Models of Authenticity and Courage, Cleansers of Shame	Check If It Applies
Accept yourself for who you are	
Actively confront the shame taught by society, family, religion, etc.	
Actively work to release those layers of sl...me, even if not all shame has been resolved	
Feel you have resolved much of your shame	
Live openly as a gay man	
Live a life on the outside that matches what characterizes you inside	
Listen to and follow your inner voice around sexuality	
Listen to and follow your inner voice in all other areas of life	
Live your truth	
Live with consciousness and awareness	
On a path to self-love	
Understand the difference between your inner voice and external voices—those of parents, family, community, religion, peer group, mass marketing, etc.	
My Self-Rating (1-10)	

Outsiders Driving Evolutionary Advancement	Check If It Applies
Ability to embrace paradox, different perspectives at the same time	
Ability to see what many people in the majority cannot see	
Ability to solve problems because of one's outsider perspective	
A feeling, as a gay man, of residing outside the majority, outside the norm	
Observe the larger culture, and those in it	
Possess an outsider's perspective	
Provide a non-judgmental mirror for others	
Recognize patterns that keep many people in the majority trapped or stifled	
See wholeness and connection instead of division and separation	
My Self-Rating (1-10)	

Now that you have identified those traits that apply to you within the 12 remaining Distinct Gay Male Gifts, place your 1 to 10 rating for each gift (1 being the least applicable to you, 10 being the most) on the wheel below.

What does this assessment tell you about your role as an evolutionary leader for humanity?

The Distinct Gay Gifts Wheel

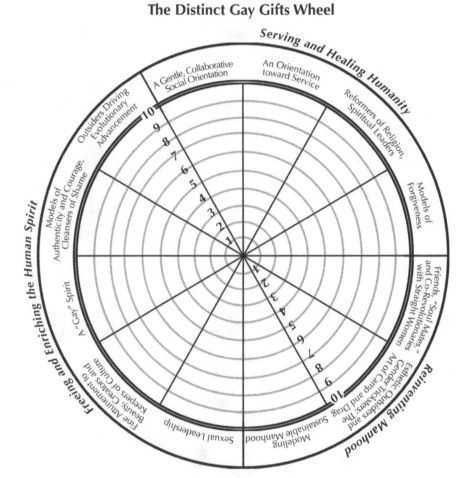

Epilogue

A Vision for the Future

In the future, parents will greet the arrival of a son with the awareness that they hold responsibility for helping their boy discover whether he belongs to a majority or a minority of men. They will identify and nurture his social orientation, and they will support him in activities that best allow him to express it. They will use language that invites their boy to express his emotional preference for boys or girls. When adolescence arrives, they will invite their boy to participate in a rite of passage that helps him discover and clarify his sexual orientation. When they have a gay boy in their midst—which they will suspect long before they receive confirmation—they will help their boy find other boys who are like him, so he can learn who he is. They will recognize that this boy lives as one of them, and yet has a special mission requiring that he explore life outside his family of origin. The parents will be elated to see this boy blossom into his social role and will know they have a special being among them.

The society in which this boy develops will have come to appreciate its special men. It will welcome their contributions, understanding that it is enriched by them. It will seek to support this vibrant community of men, knowing that its vitality contributes to the health and welfare of all of its residents. In this society, these men will be valued and known for their social contributions.

No Easy Path for Evolutionary Leaders

In the future, when the human family finally honors gay men in every culture on the globe, when lesbian and gay people have achieved full equality under all societal laws, and when the paths for gay boys to develop into well-adjusted adults have become well-trodden, we will still be a minority living in the midst of a majority. Gay boys will be born mostly into heterosexual families. We will look to our families and not see critical parts of ourselves. We will need to look within ourselves to know who we are, and we will need to radically trust in our own vision. We will need to find each other to see our essence mirrored. We will still need to travel the Gay Hero's Journey that requires the death of one identity in order to come into our own.

The gay male path will always inflict a wound. Societal acceptance and understanding may significantly diminish this pain, but it can never entirely remove it. As a minority even in our families of origin—apart from the few who have gay or lesbian siblings or parents—we enter this life destined to live with one foot outside.

We may want to believe that a future scenario of full equality will remove the pain of being gay, but that seems unlikely. Being gay is hard work, and on some level it will always be. The content of the dualities we experience may change with the times, but the pattern will remain the same. Gay men do essential cleansing work required for human consciousness to expand. By embodying paradoxes, we resolve them—for ourselves and humanity. The gay male experience comes with outsize reward, and daunting challenge. We won't ever escape this life with an easy ride. It is simply the nature of the gay male path.

Index

Notes

Chapter 1: The Coming Out Continuum and the Gay Hero's Journey

1   Will Roscoe, *Queer Spirits: A Gay Men's Myth Book* (Boston: Beacon Press, 1995), xiii.

Chapter 2: The Limitations of Our Current Identity

2   National Coalition for Health Professional Education in Genetics, "Race & Genetics FAQ," http://www.nchpeg.org/index.php?option=com_content&view=article&id=142&Itemid=64, accessed November 12, 2014.

3   Paul Vitagliano, *Born This Way: Real Stories of Growing Up Gay* (Philadelphia: Quirk Books, 2012).

4   "Maslow's Hierarchy of Needs," Wikipedia, last modified December 8, 2012, accessed October 22, 2014, http://en.wikipedia.org/wiki/File:Maslow's_Hierarchy_of_Needs.svg.

Chapter 3: An Invitation to Explore

5   Mark Thompson, *Gay Soul: Finding the Heart of Gay Spirit and Nature with Sixteen Writers, Healers, Teachers, and Visionaries* (Harper San Francisco, 1994), 68.

Chapter 4: Masculine-Feminine Intelligence: The Foundational Gift

6   Christian de la Huerta, *Coming Out Spiritually: The Next Step* (New York: Tarcher/Penguin, 1999), 42.

7   Mark Thompson, *Gay Spirit: Myth and Meaning* (New York: St. Martin's Press, 1987), 284.

8   Mark Thompson, *Gay Soul: Finding the Heart of Gay Spirit and Nature with Sixteen Writers, Healers, Teachers, and Visionaries* (Harper San Francisco, 1995), 56.

9   Multiple Intelligences Oasis, http://multipleintelligencesoasis.org, accessed December 1, 2014.

10   Howard Gardener, *Multiple Intelligences: New Horizons in Theory and Practice* (Basic Books, 2006), 6.

11   Cheryl Holt and Jon Ellis, "Assessing the Current Validity of the Bem Sex-Role Inventory," *Sex Roles* 39, nos. 11/12 (1998): 929-941, accessed October 22, 2014, http://www.ekgp.ugent.be/pages/nl/vragenlijsten/Validity_BEM.pdf. And Patricia Oswald, "An Examination of the Current Usefulness of the Bem Sex-Role Inventory," *Psychological Reports* 94, no. 3c (2004): 1331-1336, accessed October 22, 2014, http://www.amsciepub.com/doi/abs/10.2466/pr0.94.3c.1331-1336?journalCode=pr0.

12   David Thorpe's insightful and open-hearted film, *Do I Sound Gay?*, which explores the nature and implications of "gay voice," premiered at the 2014 Toronto Film Festival.

13   Malcolm McLaren and the Bootzilla Orchestra, "Deep in Vogue," *Waltz Darling*, CBS, 1989.

14   John Gerzema and Michael D'Antonio, *The Athena Doctrine: How Women (And Men Who Think Like Them) Will Rule the Future* (San Francisco: Jossey-Bass), 255-6.

Chapter 5: A Gentle, Collaborative "Social Orientation"

15   Harry Hay, *Radically Gay: Gay Liberation in the Words of Its Founder*, ed. Will Roscoe (Boston: Beacon Press, 1996), 144.

16   Will Fellows, *A Passion to Preserve: Gay Men as Keepers of Culture* (Madison: The University of Wisconsin Press, 2004), 25.

17   David Halperin, *How to Be Gay* (Cambridge: The Belknap Press of Harvard University Press, 2012), 93.

18   Joe Drape, Steve Eder, and Billy Witz, "Before Coming Out, a Hard Time Grow-
      ing Up: Michael Sam's Troubled Upbringing in Texas," *New York Times*, Febru-
      ary 11, 2014, accessed July 15, 2014, http://www.nytimes.com/2014/02/12/
      sports/football/for-nfl-prospect-michael-sam-upbringing-was-bigger-challenge-
      than-coming-out-as-gay.html?_r=0.

19   Tyler Conway, "Who Is Michael Sam?", *Bleacher Report*, February 9, 2014, ac-
      cessed July 15, 2014, http://bleacherreport.com/articles/1954016-who-is-mi-
      chael-sam.

20   Catherine Tuerk, Edgardo Menvielle, and James de Jesus, *If You Are Concerned
      about Your Child's Gender Behaviors: A Guide for Parents* (Washington: Children's
      National Medical Center, Outreach Program for Gender-Variant Behaviors and
      their Families, 2003), 4. Also available at http://childrensnational.org/depart-
      ments/gender-and-sexuality-development-program.

21   Harry Hay, 181-216, and Stuart Timmons, *The Trouble with Harry Hay* (White
      Crane Institute, 2012, Centenary Edition), 284-285.

22   Kirk Snyder, "Why Gay Men Are Outperforming the Good-Old-Boys in Busi-
      ness," *The Huffington Post*, May 25, 2011, accessed May 1, 2014, http://www.
      huffingtonpost.com/kirk-snyder/why-gay-men-are-outperfor_b_21899.html.

23   Kirk Snyder, *The G Quotient: Why Gay Executives Are Excelling as Leaders…and
      What Every Manager Needs to Know,* (San Francisco: Jossey-Bass, 2006).

Chapter 6: An Orientation toward Service

24   Mark Thompson, *Gay Soul: Finding the Heart of Gay Spirit and Nature with
      Sixteen Writers, Healers, Teachers, and Visionaries* (Harper San Francisco, 1994),
      244.

25   Christian de la Huerta, *Coming Out Spiritually: The Next Step* (New York: Tarch-
      er Putnam, 1999), 10.

26   Harry Hay, *Radically Gay: Gay Liberation in the Words of Its Founder*, ed. Will
      Roscoe (Boston: Beacon Press, 1996), 296.

27   Frank Love, "You Can Have It All — Unless You're Gay," *The Advocate*, July 17,
      2014, accessed July 25, 2014, http://www.advocate.com/parenting/2014/07/17/
      you-can-have-it-all-—-unless-youre-gay.

28   Partially drawn from de la Huerta, *Coming Out Spiritually,* 25.

29   Denise L. Carmody and John Tully Carmody, *Ways to the Center: An Introduction to World Religions* (Belmont, California: Wadsworth, 1989), 33, as cited in http://www.cabrillo.edu/~crsmith/shaman.html, accessed July 15, 2014.

30   Will Roscoe, *Jesus and the Shamanic Tradition of Same-Sex Love* (San Francisco: Suspect Thoughts Press, 2004), 131.

31   Will Roscoe, *Jesus and the Shamanic Tradition of Same-Sex Love*, 132-133.

32   Randy Conner, *Blossom of Bone: Reclaiming the Connections between Homoeroticism and the Sacred* (Harper San Francisco, 1993).

33   Mark Thompson, *Gay Spirit: Myth and Meaning* (New York: St. Martin's Press, 1987), 78.

34   Mark Thompson, *Gay Spirit*, 80-81.

Chapter 7: Religious Reformers and Spiritual Leaders

35   Toby Johnson, *Gay Perspective: Things Our [Homo]sexuality Tells Us about the Nature of God and the Universe* (Maple Shade, New Jersey: Lethe Press, 2008, Revised Edition), 12.

36   Derrick Sherwin Bailey, *Homosexuality and the Western Christian Tradition* (London: Longmans Green, 1955), cited in Rollan McCleary, *A Special Illumination: Authority, Inspiration, and Heresy in Gay Spirituality* (London: Equinox Publishing, 2004), 44.

37   Robert Wood, *Christ and the Homosexual* (New York: Vantage Press, 1960) as cited in Rollan McLeary, 44.

38   Rollan McCleary, *A Special Illumination*, 45.

39   Rollan McCleary, *A Special Illumination*, 75.

40   Rollan McCleary, *A Special Illumination*, 45-46.

41   Metropolitan Community Church, accessed September 15, 2014, http://mccchurch.org/overview/ourchurches/.

42   DignityUSA, accessed September 15, 2014, http://www.dignityusa.org/content/what-dignity.

43   John Gehring, "The Year of Pope Francis, Top Ten Papal Quotes," *The Huffington Post*, December 23, 2013, accessed September 15, 2014, http://www.huffingtonpost.com/john-gehring/the-year-of-pope-francis-_b_4482650.html.

44   The Episcopal Church, "LGBT in the Church," accessed September 20, 2014, http://www.episcopalchurch.org/page/lgbt-church.

45   Unitarian Universalist Association, "Unitarian Universalist LGBTQ History & Facts," accessed September 20, 2014, http://www.uua.org/lgbtq/history/185789.shtml.

46   Robert P. Jones, Daniel Cox, and Juhem Navarro-Rivera, *A Shifting Landscape: A Decade of Change in American Attitudes about Same-sex Marriage and LGBT Issues* (Washington: Public Religion Research Institute, February 26, 2014), 3-4, accessed September 20, 2014, http://publicreligion.org/site/wp-content/uploads/2014/02/2014.LGBT_REPORT.pdf.

47   Gallup, "Religion," accessed September 20, 2014, http://www.gallup.com/poll/1690/religion.aspx#1.

48   "Europe's Irreligious: In Which European Countries Are People Least Likely to Attend Religious Services?" *The Economist*, August 9, 2010, accessed September 23, 2014, http://www.economist.com/node/16767758.

49   Margaret Burkhardt, "Spirituality: An Analysis of the Concept," *Holistic Nursing Practice* 3, no. 3 (May 1989), 60-77, cited in Neil Greenberg, "Can Spirituality Be Defined?" (University of Tennessee: October 8, 2008), accessed September 25, 2014, http://notes.utk.edu/bio/unistudy.nsf/935c0d855156f9e08525738a006f2417/bdc83cd10e58d14a852573b-00072525d?OpenDocument.

50   Stuart Timmons, *The Trouble with Harry Hay* (New York: White Crane Institute, 2012, Centenary Edition), 295-298; Rollan McCleary, *A Special Illumination: Authority, Inspiration, and Heresy in Gay Spirituality* (London: Equinox Publishing, 2004), 127, 139.

51   Rollan McCleary, *A Special Illumination*, 146-147.

52   Christian de la Huerta, *Coming Out Spiritually: The Next Step* (New York: Tarcher Putnam, 1999), 207.

53   Bill Rodgers, *Gay Sex and Spirit* 1, no. 15, 1997, 7-16, as cited in Rollan McCleary, 141.

54   Sisters of Perpetual Indulgence, "Who Are the Sisters?" accessed September 25, 2014, http://www.thesisters.org.

Chapter 8: Teachers of Compassion, Generosity, and the Authentic Masculine

55   Martin Duberman, *The Martin Duberman Reader: The Essential Historical, Biographical, and Autobiographical Writings* (New York: The New Press, 2013), 10.

56   Lest I paint too rosy a portrait of GMHC, I should note the intense and biting politics that took place on staff and leadership levels. This led to a union drive— which ultimately failed—and which simultaneously cropped up at AIDS service organizations around the country. My dismay over this trend led me to write an article, which appeared in *Gay Community News* in 1994, entitled "AIDS Goes Union." To my knowledge, this acrimony never translated into diminished service to clients.

57   H. Turner, J. Catania, and J. Gagnon, "The Prevalence of Informal Caregiving to Persons with AIDS in the United States: Caregiver Characteristics and Their Implications," *Social Science and Medicine* 38, no. 11 (1994): 1543-1552, cited in David Nimmons, *The Soul Beneath the Skin: The Unseen Hearts and Habits of Gay Men* (New York: St. Martin's Press, 1994), 42.

58   Swarthmore College, "U.S. AIDS Coalition to Unleash Power (ACT-UP) Demands Access to Drugs, 1987-89," Global Nonviolent Action Database, accessed August 1, 2014, http://nvdatabase.swarthmore.edu/content/us-aids-coalition-unleash-power-act-demands-access-drugs-1987-89.

59   Wikipedia, "Gran Fury," http://en.wikipedia.org/wiki/Gran_Fury, last modified July 16, 2014, accessed November 13, 2014.

60   David Halperin, *How to Be Gay* (Cambridge: The Belknap Press of Harvard University Press, 2012).

Chapter 9: Models of Forgiveness

61   Lewis B. Smedes, *The Art of Forgiving: When You Need to Forgive and Don't Know How* (Nashville: Moorings, 1996), 178.

Chapter 10: Friends, "Soul Mates," and Co-Revolutionaries with Straight Women

62   Robert Hopcke and Laura Rafaty, *A Couple of Friends: The Remarkable Friendship between Straight Women and Gay Men* (Berkeley: Wildcat Canyon Press, 1999), 3.

63   Available on YouTube, accessed August 2014, https://www.youtube.com/watch?v=jA4DR4vEgrs.

64   Michael LaSala, "Gay Men and Their Mothers: Is There a Special Closeness?" *Psychology Today*, August 23, 2011, http://www.psychologytoday.com/blog/gay-and-lesbian-well-being/201108/gay-men-and-their-mothers-is-there-special-closeness.

65   Will Fellows, *A Passion to Preserve: Gay Men as Keepers of Culture* (Madison: The University of Wisconsin Press, 2004), 26.

66   Will Fellows, *A Passion to Preserve*, 26.

67   Mankind Project, "What Does It Mean to Be a Modern, Mature Man?", accessed September 2014, http://mankindproject.org.

68   College Humor, "Gay Men Will Marry Your Girlfriends," published November 20, 2012, accessed August 2014, https://www.youtube.com/watch?v=X-YC-dcnf_P8.

69   Thomas DiPrete and Claudia Buchman, *The Rise of Women: The Growing Gender Gap in Education and What It Means for American Schools* (New York: The Russell Sage Foundation, March 2013), as cited in the executive summary, available at https://www.russellsage.org/publications/rise-women, accessed August 2014.

Chapter 11: Esthetic Outsiders and Gender Tricksters: The Art of Camp and Drag

70   Susan Sontag, *Against Interpretation and Other Essays* (New York: Picador USA, 2001), 275, (originally published in 1966). *Notes on Camp* first appeared in the *Partisan Review* in 1964. Text available at http://faculty.georgetown.edu/irvinem/theory/Sontag-NotesOnCamp-1964.html.

71   Richard Dyer, *Heavenly Bodies: Film Stars and Society* (London: Routledge, 1986, Second Edition), 176.

72   Richard Dyer, *Heavenly Bodies*, 1986.

73   David Halperin, *How to Be Gay* (Cambridge: The Belknap Press of Harvard University Press, 2012), 149-185.

Chapter 12: Modeling Sustainable Manhood

74   Brainy Quote, accessed August 2014, http://www.brainyquote.com/quotes/quotes/a/alberteins121993.html.

75   Michael Kimmel, "Masculinity as Homophobia: Fear, Shame, and Silence in the Construction of Gender Identity," in Harry Brod and Michael Kaufman (eds.), *Research on Men and Masculinities Series: Theorizing Masculinities* (Thousand Oaks, California: SAGE Publications, Inc., 1994), 119-142, available at http://faculty.ucc.edu/psysoc-stokes/Masculinity.pdf.

76   Nathan Palmer, "Masculinity as Homophobia," Sociology Source, last updated May 24, 2010, accessed August 2014, http://www.sociologysource.org/home/2010/5/24/masculinity-as-homophobia.html.

77   World Health Organization, *Global and Regional Estimates of Violence against Women: Prevalence and Health Effects of Intimate Partner Violence and Non-partner Sexual Violence* (Geneva, 2013), accessed August 2014, http://apps.who.int/iris/bitstream/10665/85239/1/9789241564625_eng.pdf.

78   American Foundation for Suicide Prevention, "Facts and Figures," accessed August 2014, https://www.afsp.org/understanding-suicide/facts-and-figures.

Chapter 13: Sexual Leadership

79   Michael Shernoff, *Without Condoms: Unprotected Sex, Gay Men & Barebacking* (New York: Routledge, 2006), 237.

80   Mark Thompson, *Gay Body: A Journey through Shadow to Self* (New York: St. Martin's Press, 1997), 258.

81   Christian de la Huerta, *Coming Out Spiritually: The Next Step* (New York: Tarcher Putnam, 1999), 13.

82   Leslie-Lohman Museum of Gay and Lesbian Art, "The Piers: Art and Sex along the New York Waterfront," curated by Jonathan Weinberg with Darren Jones, April 4 – May 10, 2012, available at http://leslielohman.org/exhibitions/2012/piers/Leslie-Lohman-Museum_The-Piers_Exhibition-Brochure.pdf. (The exhibit was extended due to popular demand.)

83   Lisa Cohen, "Does Sexuality Differ for Men and Women?" *Psychology Today*, February 14, 2011, accessed August 2014, http://www.psychologytoday.com/blog/handy-psychology-answers/201102/does-sexuality-differ-men-and-women.

84   Michael Bronski, *The Pleasure Principle: Sex, Backlash, and the Struggle for Gay Freedom* (New York: St. Martin's Press, 1998), 9.

85   *Sex and the City*, Season 2, Episode 14, "The Fuck Buddy," directed by Alan Taylor, release date September 5, 1999, HBO, via IMDb, accessed August 2014, http://www.imdb.com/title/tt0698681/.

86   Justin Garcia, Chris Reiber, Sean Massey, and Ann Merriwether, "Sexual Hookup Culture: A Review," *Review of General Psychology* 16, no. 2 (June 1, 2012): 161–176.

87   Cathy Crimmins, *How the Homosexuals Saved Civilization: The True and Heroic Story of How Gay Men Shaped the Modern World* (New York: Tarcher Penguin, 2004), 101-102.

88   David Nimmons, *The Soul Beneath the Skin: The Unseen Hearts and Habits of Gay Men* (New York: St. Martin's Press, 2002), 84-85.

89   Tara Parker-Pope, "Love, Sex and the Changing Landscape of Infidelity," *New York Times*, October 27, 2008, accessed July 2014, http://www.nytimes.com/2008/10/28/health/28well.html.

90   Scott James, "Many Successful Gay Marriages Share an Open Secret," *New York Times*, January 28, 2010, accessed June 2014, http://www.nytimes.com/2010/01/29/us/29sfmetro.html.

91   Blake Spears and Lanz Lowen, *Beyond Monogamy: Lessons from Long-Term Male Couples in Non-Monogamous Relationships*, February 10, 2010, accessed June 2014, http://thecouplesstudy.com/wp-content/uploads/BeyondMonogamy_1_01.pdf.

92   Michael Shernoff, "Negotiated Non-Monogamy and Male Couples," *Family Process* 45, no. 4, December 2006: 407–418.

93   David McWhirter and Andrew Mattison, *The Male Couple: How Relationships Develop* (Englewood Cliffs, New Jersey: Prentice-Hall, 1984).

94   David Nimmons, *The Soul Beneath the Skin*, 84.

95   W. Burdon, "Deception in Intimate Relationships: A Comparison of Hetero-sexuals and Homosexuals/Bisexuals," *Journal of Homosexuality* 32, no. 1, 1996: 77-91, as cited in David Nimmons, 89.

96   Cited in Scott James, January 28, 2010 (se note 90).

97   Benoit Denizet-Lewis, "The Scientific Case to Prove Bisexuality Exists," *New York Times*, March 20, 2014, accessed June 2014, http://www.nytimes.com/2014/03/23/magazine/the-scientific-quest-to-prove-bisexuality-exists.html?_r=0.

98   Benoit Denizet-Lewis, March 20, 2014. The survey reviewed by the Williams Institute was published in 2009 in *The Journal of Sexual Medicine*.

99   Toby Johnson, *Gay Spirituality: The Role of Gay Identity in the Transformation of Human Consciousness* (Maple Shade, New Jersey: Lethe Press, 2004), 36.

100   Erotic Engineering, www.eroticengineering.com. For the video trailer, see https://www.youtube.com/watch?v=jVENRkvczxA.

101   Flesh & Spirit Community, http://www.fleshandspirit.org, accessed November 7, 2014.

Chapter 14: Fine Attunement to Beauty, Creators and Keepers of Culture

102   Michael Bronski, *Culture Clash: The Making of Gay Sensibility* (Boston: South End Press, 1984), 213.

103   Christian de la Huerta, *Coming Out Spiritually: The Next Step* (New York: Tarcher/Putnam, 1999), 21.

104   The Oxford Dictionary, www.oxforddictionaries.com

Chapter 15: A "Gay" Spirit

105   Andrew Berman, "Is Gay Street Really Gay?" *The Blog of the Greenwich Village Society for Historic Preservation*, October 10, 2012, accessed July 15, 2014, http://gvshp.org/blog/2012/10/10/is-gay-street-really-gay/.

106   Toby Johnson, *Gay Spirituality: The Role of Gay Identity in the Transformation of Human Consciousness* (Maple Shade, New Jersey: Lethe Press), 144.

107   Mark Thompson, *Gay Body: A Journey through Shadow to Self* (New York: St. Martin's Press, 1997), 141.

108   Toby Johnson, *Gay Spirituality,* 143.

109   Mark Thompson, *Gay Spirit: Myth and Meaning* (New York: St. Martin's Press, 1987), 127-128.

110   Cited in Toby Johnson, http://tobyjohnson.com/CarpenterPreface.html, accessed November 7, 2014.

111   Toby Johnson, *Gay Spirituality,* 144.

112   Frank Love, "You Can Have It All — Unless You're Gay," *The Advocate*, July 17, 2014,   http://www.advocate.com/parenting/2014/07/17/you-can-have-it-all- —-unless-youre-gay.

113   Mark Thompson, *Gay Spirit*, 206.

Chapter 17: Outsiders Driving Evolutionary Advancement

114   Harry Hay, *Radically Gay: Gay Liberation in the Words of Its Founder*, ed. Will Roscoe (Boston: Beacon Press, 1996), 208.

115   Christian de la Huerta, *Coming Out Spiritually: The Next Step* (New York: Tarcher Putnam, 1999), 10.

116   Harry Hay, *Radically Gay,* 296.

117   Toby Johnson, *Gay Perspective: Things Our [Homo]sexuality Tells Us about the Nature of God and the Universe* (Maple Shade, New Jersey: Lethe Press, Revised Edition, 2008), 71.

Chapter 18: Owning and Managing the Shadow

118   Mark Thompson, *Gay Soul: Finding the Heart and Soul of Gay Spirit and Nature with Sixteen Writers, Teachers, Healers, and Visionaries* (Harper San Francisco 1994), 255-256.

119   Wikipedia, *Shadow (psychology)*, http://en.wikipedia.org/wiki/Shadow_(psychology), accessed November 7, 2014.

120   Carl G. Jung, *The Portable Jung*, ed. Joseph Campbell (New York: Viking Penguin, 1971), cited in Practical Philosophy, http://www.practicalphilosophy. net/?page_id=952, accessed November 7, 2014.

121   Center for American Progress, "Domestic Violence in the LGBT Community: A Fact Sheet," accessed September 15, 2014, http://www.americanprogress.org/ issues/lgbt/news/2011/06/14/9850/domestic-violence-in-the-lgbt-community/.

122   Colleen Stiles-Shields and Richard A. Carroll, "Same-Sex Domestic Violence: Prevalence, Unique Aspects, and Clinical Implications," *Journal of Sex & Marital Therapy*, accessed September 15, 2014, posted online September 4, 2014, http:// www.tandfonline.com/doi/abs/10.1080/0092623X.2014.958792#preview.

123   Kenneth King, *All Grown Up Now: A Friendship in Three Acts*, 2012.

124   Will Fellows and Helen P. Branson, *Gay Bar: The Fabulous, True Story of a Daring Woman and Her Boys in the 1950s* (Madison: The University of Wisconsin Press, 2010), 115.

125   Mark Thompson, *Gay Body: A Journey through Shadow to Self* (New York: St. Martin's Press, 1997), 237.

Chapter 19: The New Way Forward

126   To put "straight acting" in context, it is important to note that this concept has some of its roots in post-Stonewall liberation. Prior to the Stonewall Riots, gay men formed partnerships that followed heterosexual models, with one partner assuming the top/manly role, and other the bottom/womanly role. Liberated homosexuality of the 1970s advanced equality and rejected hetero-imitation. Gay men began wanting other men who appeared just like them—or at least how they hoped they appeared.

127   Gay Elder Circle, http://www.gayeldercircle.net/index.html, accessed November 7, 2014.

About the Author

Raymond L. Rigoglioso is the founder of Gay Men of Wisdom (**www.gaymenofwisdom.com**) and is certified as a life coach through the International Coach Federation. His professional background includes more than two decades as a writer and editor for nonprofit organizations in New York City and Boston.

In 1989, two months after Ray came out, he and a friend co-founded the Danbury [Connecticut] Area Gay and Lesbian Youth Group. He facilitated this group for a year before moving to New York City. After receiving his bachelor of arts degree from The New School in 1991, Ray landed a job at the only place he wanted to work at the time: Gay Men's Health Crisis. In 1993, while living in Provincetown, Massachusetts, for the summer, he met his partner, Keith D. Pettey. Ray and Keith live in White Plains, New York, with their dog, Baxter.

CPSIA information can be obtained
at www.ICGtesting.com
Printed in the USA
BVHW032306160422
634503BV00005B/108